Godot 4 Game Development Cookbook

Over 50 solid recipes for building high-quality 2D and 3D games with improved performance

Jeff Johnson

BIRMINGHAM—MUMBAI

Godot 4 Game Development Cookbook

Group Product Manager: Rohit Rajkumar

Publishing Product Manager: Nitin Nainani

Content Development Editor: Abhishek Jadhav

Technical Editor: Simran Ali

Copy Editor: Safis Editing

Project Coordinator: Aishwarya Mohan

Proofreader: Safis Editing

Indexer: Manju Arasan

Production Designer: Nilesh Mohite

Marketing Coordinator: Nivedita Pandey

First published: June 2023

Production reference: 1100523

Published by Packt Publishing Ltd.

Livery Place

35 Livery Street

Birmingham

B3 2PB, UK.

ISBN 978-1-83882-607-9

www.packtpub.com

To Juan Linietsky and Ariel Manzur for creating Godot.

Contributors

About the author

Jeff Johnson is a game developer who started using Unity 4.0 in 2014 and released a couple of games on itch.io. In 2018, he created 999 Dev Studio. Toward the end of developing *Escape from 51*, he changed engines to Godot 3.0.2. He ported over almost the whole game to Godot from Unity. He released *Escape from 51* on itch.io, as well as some mobile games on Google Play, all made with Godot.

About the reviewers

Yogendra Manawat is a bachelor's student in computer science. He is an indie game developer and a product designer. Though he primarily learned development skills, he has acquired knowledge in programming languages such as C++, Python, C#, and GDScript.

Yogendra's interest in games and movies led him to start making 3D animation with Blender, and he continues to work on game development projects while also contributing to the Godot Engine community.

With over three years of experience in game development, Yogendra has developed multiple small games and is currently focused on creating his original RPG game, *TALKAD*, using the Godot Engine. He continuously learns about new technologies and experiments with different game development techniques to create unique and engaging games. Yogendra is also an active participant in game development forums and communities, where he exchanges ideas and collaborates with other game developers.

Simon Dalvai is a free and open source game developer from Italy. You can find the source code for his games, such as *Ball2Box* and *Pocket Broomball*, on GitHub under the username `dulvui`. As a solo developer, Simon enjoys automating repetitive tasks, including taking screenshots and exporting and uploading games to publishing platforms with scripts and CI/CD tools such as GitHub Actions.

He learned to program in school and is currently working full-time as a software architect. Simon taught himself game development and has created games in his free time since 2018. He follows a strict policy of not including ads or user tracking in his games.

Initially, he used libGDX to develop his first games but switched to the Godot Engine in 2019.

Daniel Fulton has been a professional programmer since 2011. He has worked on a wide variety of iOS apps and games.

He has given tech talks on augmented reality, 3D game programming in SceneKit, software architecture, image performance, test-driven development, and readable code.

His hobbies include building games in Godot, Unity, and Unreal Engine, tinkering with electronics, rock climbing, and natural farming. In the past, he received a bachelor's degree in photography and worked as a freelance photographer.

Table of Contents

5

Playing with Shaders in Godot 4   97

6

Importing 3D Assets into Godot 4   129

7

Adding Sound and Music to Your Game   141

8

Making 2D Games Easier with TileSet and TileMap   157

9

Achieving Better Animations Using the New Animation Editor   185

10

Exploring New Multiplayer Features in Godot 4   215

Index   231

Other Books You May Enjoy   236

Preface

Want to transition from Godot 3 to 4? Look no further than the Godot 4 Game Development Cookbook. This comprehensive guide covers everything you need to become proficient with the latest GUI, GDscript 2.0, Vulkan 2D/3D rendering, shaders, audio, physics, TileSet/TileMap, importing, sound/music, animation, and multiplayer workflows. With its detailed recipes, the book leaves no stone unturned.

The Godot 4 Cookbook begins by exploring the updated graphical user interface and helps you familiarize yourself with the new features of GDscript 2.0. Next, it delves into the efficient rendering of 2D and 3D graphics using the Vulkan renderer. As it guides you in navigating the new Godot 4 platform, the book offers an in-depth understanding of shaders, including the latest enhancements to the shader language. Moreover, it covers a range of other topics, including importing from Blender, working with audio, and demystifying the new Vulkan Renderer and the physics additions for 2D and 3D. The book also shows you how the new changes to TileSet and TileMap make 2D game development easy. Advanced topics such as importing in Godot 4, adding sound and music to games, making changes in the Animation editor, and including workflows for multiplayer in Godot 4 are covered in detail.

By the end of this game development book, you'll have gained a better understanding of Godot 4 and will be equipped with various powerful techniques to enhance your Godot game development efficiency.

Who this book is for

The Godot 4 Game Development Cookbook is for seasoned game developers who want to acquire skills in creating games using a contemporary game engine. It is an invaluable resource for indie game developers and Godot developers who are familiar with Godot 3 and have some level of expertise in maneuvering the interface.

What this book covers

Chapter 1, *Exploring the Godot 4 Editor*, covers the changes to the Godot Editor from Godot 3.x to Godot 4.0, and the new features in the Project settings and Editor settings.

Chapter 2, *Transitioning to GDScript 2.0*, teaches you about annotations, properties, the await keyword and coroutines, the super keyword, typed arrays, lambda functions, and using callables with signals.

Chapter 3, *2D and 3D Rendering with Vulkan*, helps you understand SDF Global Illumination, volumetric fog, the FogVolume node, and particle nodes, using decals.

Chapter 4, *Practicing Physics and Handling Navigation in Godot 4*, teaches you how to use the Heightmap for 3D terrain, set up and move a CharacterBody2D/3D body, use NavigationServer3D/2D, and use SoftBody for 3D games.

Chapter 5, *Playing with Shaders in Godot 4*, helps you to create shaders with the Shader Creation dialog, and covers uniform arrays in the shader language, global and instance uniforms, the Visual Shader context menu, Integer and Comment nodes, creating nodes using Texture3D and CurveTexture, and using the Billboard and UVFunc nodes, Sky Shader, and Fog Shader mode.

Chapter 6, *Importing 3D Assets in Godot 4*, teaches you how to import Blender blend files, FBX files, and glTF files, and use the Import dialog.

Chapter 7, *Adding Sound and Music to Your Game*, helps you to understand how to use the polyphonic support in the AudioStreamPlayer and directional sound with 2D and 3D.

Chapter 8, *Making 2D Games Easier with TileSet and TileMap*, helps you understand the new TileSet editor, TileMap layers, TileMap tools, Tile Atlas Editing, TileSet physics, and navigation, creating custom data layers with TileSet, painting and transitioning terrain in TileMap, and organizing isometric tiles with TileSet.

Chapter 9, *Achieving Better Animations Using the New Animation Editor*, teaches you about the changes with transform tracks, the new Bezier Curve workflow, 3D rotation animations, bone posses, triggering a transition, and the new Movie Maker mode.

Chapter 10, *Exploring New Multiplayer Features in Godot 4*, helps you understand the new multiplayer spawner, multiplayer synchronizer, and how to use Headless mode and port forwarding on a peer-to-peer network using the UPNP class.

To get the most out of this book

You will need the latest version of Godot 4. All code examples have been tested using Godot 4.0.2 on the Windows OS. However, they should work with future version releases.

Software/hardware covered in the book	Operating system requirements
Godot 4.0.2	Windows, macOS, Linux, Android, or Web Editor

If you are using the digital version of this book, we advise you to type the code yourself or access the code from the book's GitHub repository (a link is available in the next section). Doing so will help you avoid any potential errors related to the copying and pasting of code.

Download the example code files

You can download the example code files for this book from GitHub at `https://github.com/PacktPublishing/Godot-4-Game-Development-Cookbook`. If there's an update to the code, it will be updated in the GitHub repository.

We also have other code bundles from our rich catalog of books and videos available at `https://github.com/PacktPublishing/`. Check them out!

Download the color images

We also provide a PDF file that has color images of the screenshots and diagrams used in this book. You can download it here: `https://packt.link/5fnG6`.

Conventions used

There are a number of text conventions used throughout this book.

`Code in text`: Indicates code words in text, database table names, folder names, filenames, file extensions, pathnames, dummy URLs, user input, and Twitter handles. Here is an example: "The `super` keyword refers to the parent class object and makes it easier to call the parent class methods."

A block of code is set as follows:

```
5      var value: int = 10: set = set_value, get = get_value
6
7    func set_value(new_value: int) -> void:
8        value = new_value
9        print('setter', str(value))
```

Bold: Indicates a new term, an important word, or words that you see onscreen. For instance, words in menus or dialog boxes appear in **bold**. Here is an example: "Click the **Add Environment to Scene** tab at the bottom right of the dropdown."

> **Tips or important notes**
> Appear like this.

Get in touch

Feedback from our readers is always welcome.

General feedback: If you have questions about any aspect of this book, email us at customercare@packtpub.com and mention the book title in the subject of your message.

Errata: Although we have taken every care to ensure the accuracy of our content, mistakes do happen. If you have found a mistake in this book, we would be grateful if you would report this to us. Please visit www.packtpub.com/support/errata and fill in the form.

Piracy: If you come across any illegal copies of our works in any form on the internet, we would be grateful if you would provide us with the location address or website name. Please contact us at copyright@packt.com with a link to the material.

If you are interested in becoming an author: If there is a topic that you have expertise in and you are interested in either writing or contributing to a book, please visit authors.packtpub.com.

Share Your Thoughts

Once you've read *Godot 4 Game Development Cookbook*, we'd love to hear your thoughts! Scan the QR code below to go straight to the Amazon review page for this book and share your feedback.

```
https://www.amazon.in/review/create-review/error?asin=1838826076
```

Your review is important to us and the tech community and will help us make sure we're delivering excellent quality content.

Download a free PDF copy of this book

Thanks for purchasing this book!

Do you like to read on the go but are unable to carry your print books everywhere?

Is your eBook purchase not compatible with the device of your choice?

Don't worry, now with every Packt book you get a DRM-free PDF version of that book at no cost.

Read anywhere, any place, on any device. Search, copy, and paste code from your favorite technical books directly into your application.

The perks don't stop there, you can get exclusive access to discounts, newsletters, and great free content in your inbox daily

Follow these simple steps to get the benefits:

1. Scan the QR code or visit the link below

https://packt.link/free-ebook/9781838826079

2. Submit your proof of purchase

3. That's it! We'll send your free PDF and other benefits to your email directly

Exploring the Godot 4 Editor

Godot is a free open source game engine that was created by Juan Linietsky and Ariel Manzur in 2007. It was released under the MIT License in 2014. You can download Godot from `https://godotengine.org/`. The following is from the Press Kit on the website:

> *The name Godot Engine should always be written in Title Case. Also, Godot should be written with only one capital letter – it's not "GoDot". Godot is named after the play Waiting for Godot, and is usually pronounced like in the play... For native English speakers, we recommend "GOD-oh"; the "t" is silent like in the French original.*

Godot uses a tree of nodes inside a scene. A scene can be instanced in many different scenes. Godot's integrated language, GDScript, is a Python-like language that is very easy to learn.

Godot is written in C++, which you can use to edit the Godot Engine or contribute to the engine itself. Godot also officially supports C#; to use C# with Godot 4, you need to download Godot Engine - .NET. There are community-supported languages, such as Rust, Nim, Haskell, Clojure, Swift, and D, that you can use: `https://godotengine.org/`.

Godot 4 is the newest version of the Godot Engine. It uses the Vulkan renderer, which is more powerful for 3D and 2D games than OpenGL, which was used in Godot 3.x. In this book, we will learn what was changed or added to Godot 4 and how to use these features to create games whether to sell or just for fun.

In this chapter, we'll look at the changes between Godot 4 and Godot 3.x in the **Inspector** tab under **Node | Process | Mode**. We will also look at the new preview **Sun** and **Environment** dialog. In the **Project Settings** dialog in Godot 4, we'll look at the **Advanced Settings** button, and in the **Input Map** tab, we'll look at the **Show Built-in Actions** button as well as the **Shader Globals** tab. In the **Editor Settings** dialog, we'll look at the differences between the **Interface | Editor** tab and the **Interface | Text Editor** tab.

This chapter is a little different in that we are looking at the differences between Godot 3.x and Godot 4, so there is not much to do except to show the differences. The reason we've included this chapter is that some things have changed, and you might find it difficult to find what you are looking for; for example, now you need to click a button to show you the **Input Map** options.

In this chapter, we will cover the following recipes:

- Navigating in the new Godot 4 Editor
- Exploring new features in the **Project Settings** dialog
- What's new in the **Editor Settings** dialog

Technical requirements

For this chapter, you need the standard version of Godot 4.0 or later running on one of the following:

- Windows 64-bit or 32-bit
- macOS
- Linux 64-bit or 32-bit
- Android
- Web Editor

Navigating in the new Godot 4 Editor

For this recipe, open up Godot 4 and follow along. To have a look at the **process_mode** property, select the new preview **Sun** and **Environment** dialogs and then select **Inspector | Node | process_mode**. We'll then look at the three renderer options in Godot 4.

How to do it...

Let's execute the following steps:

1. Open a new project in Godot 4.
2. In the **Scene** tab, click on **3D Scene**.
3. Click the three vertical dots on the viewport toolbar to the left of **Transform**. You can see them highlighted in a blue box in *Figure 1.1*.
4. Click the **Add Environment to Scene** tab on the bottom right of the dropdown.

   You can preview the **Sun** or **Environment** nodes when you import models, or you can add them to the scene.

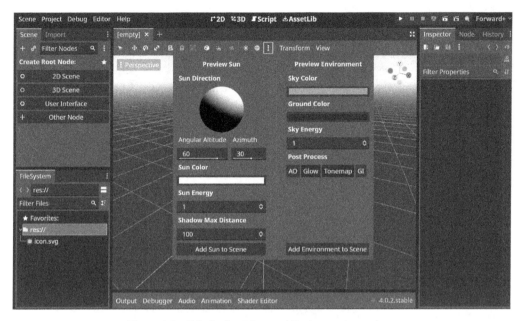

Figure 1.1 – Edit Godot 4 Sun and Environment settings

5.   Click on **World Environment** under **Node3d** in the **Scene** tab.

6.   In **Inspector**, click on the **Environment** type and then click on **Sky**. The two resources are now highlighted in different colors.

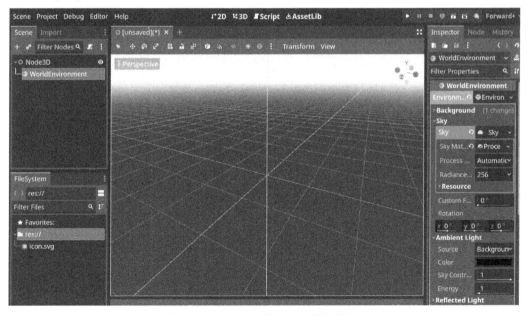

Figure 1.2 – Godot 4 Inspector highlights

The following screenshot shows what it looked like in Godot 3.x.

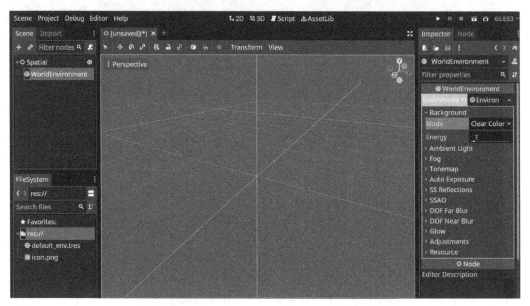

Figure 1.3 – Godot 3.x Inspector highlights

7. Click on the **Node3d** node in the **Scene** tab and hit the *Delete* key, or right-click and select **Delete**.

8. In the **Scene** tab, click **2D Scene**.

9. In **Inspector**, under **Node**, you will see **Process**. Open it by clicking on it and notice **Mode** with **Inherit** to the right with a drop-down arrow.

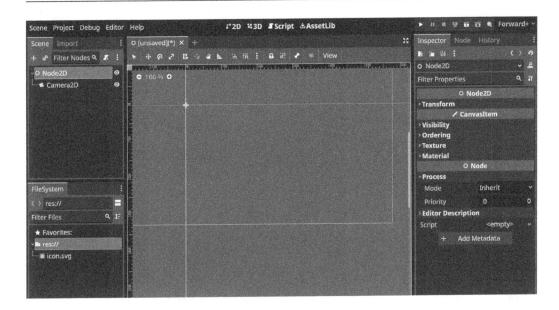

Figure 1.4 – Godot 4 Inspector with Process opened, showing the default values

10. Click on the down arrow on the far right or on **Inherit** to open the options.

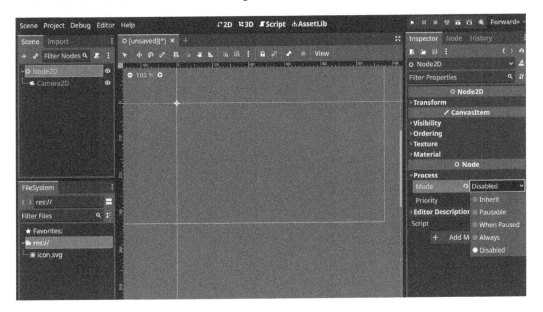

Figure 1.5 – Godot 4 Inspector with Process and Mode opened

> **Note**
>
> **Pause Mode | Process** in Godot 3.x is now **Process | Mode**, and you can now disable a node. If you do, the node will be grayed out on the SceneTree.

The Godot 3.x **Pause Mode** option can be seen in the following figure.

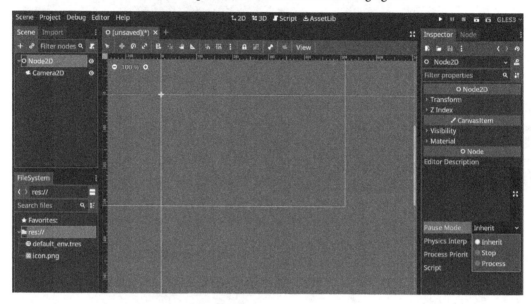

Figure 1.6 – Godot 3.x Pause Mode

In the top right-hand corner of the Godot Editor is a green **Forward+** button. If we click on this, we will see **Forward+**, **Mobile**, and **Compatibility**.

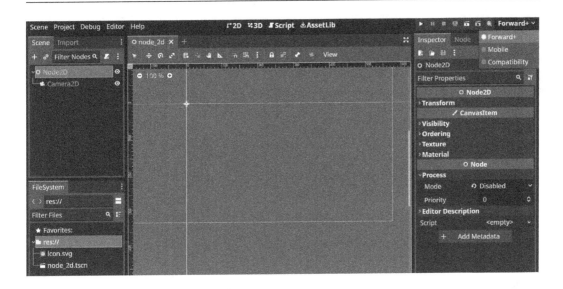

Figure 1.7 – Change the renderer

How it works...

We opened the new **Sun** and **Environment** dialogs, which can be used to preview imported assets or when editing 3D scenes to see how they look when lighting is added. You can also add the Sun and/ or the environment to the game easily from the **Sun** and **Environment** dialogs.

We looked at how resources and sub-resources are highlighted in **Inspector** and how they stand out because of the different colors, which makes it easier to see a sub-resource over a resource. In Godot 3.x, it was all one color, so sometimes, you didn't know where a sub-resource stopped and another began.

Then, we saw how the process and pause settings are now in a single menu and you can disable a node as well. Once disabled, the node is grayed out on the SceneTree. The node and any children of the node will not be processed at all.

We clicked on **Forward+** in the top right-hand corner of the Editor and a drop-down list with **Forward+**, **Mobile**, and **Compatibility** appeared. These are the renderers that we can use in a project. **Forward+** is a high-end renderer that scales well with complex scenes for desktop devices. **Mobile** is for mobile devices that do not scale as well to large scenes with many elements like **Forward+** does. **Compatibility** is for older devices that need to use a low-end renderer.

Exploring the new features in the Project Settings dialog

In this recipe, we will look at the **Advanced Settings** button in **Project Settings**, which opens all of the options available for all of the project settings listed. The **Input Map Show Built-in Actions** button opens all of the available user input actions that can be set for your game. The **Shader Globals** tab in **Project Settings** is for global uniforms.

How to do it...

To find the **Project Settings Advanced Settings** button, the **Input Map Show Built-in Actions** button, and the **Shader Globals** tab, execute the following steps:

1. Open a new or any existing project in Godot 4.

2. In the top-left menu, click **Project**, and then click **Project Settings**.

    The default settings now only show the basic settings.

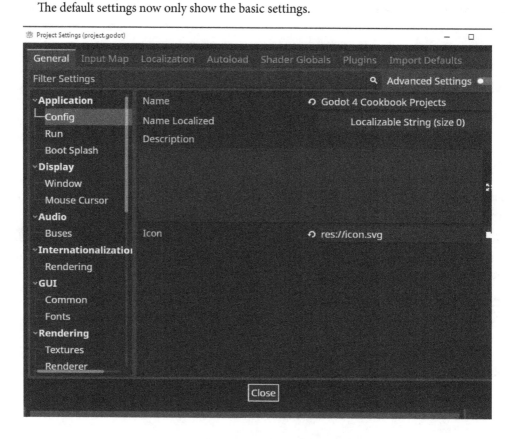

Figure 1.8 – Godot 4 Project Settings default settings

3. On the right of the **Search** box, click the **Advanced Settings** button.

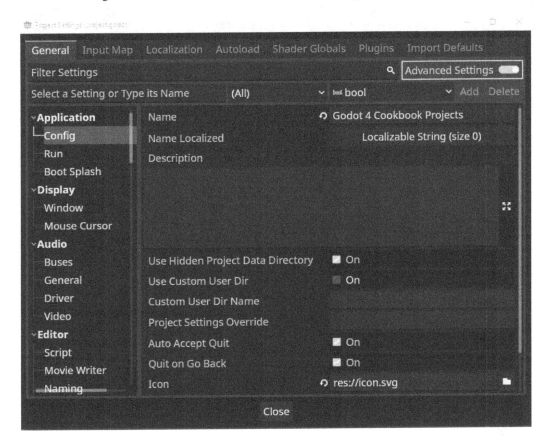

Figure 1.9 – Godot 4 Project Settings Advanced Settings button clicked

Now all of the settings options are viewable like in Godot 3.x.

4. Click the **Input Map** tab to the right of the **General** tab. Notice that there is nothing shown.

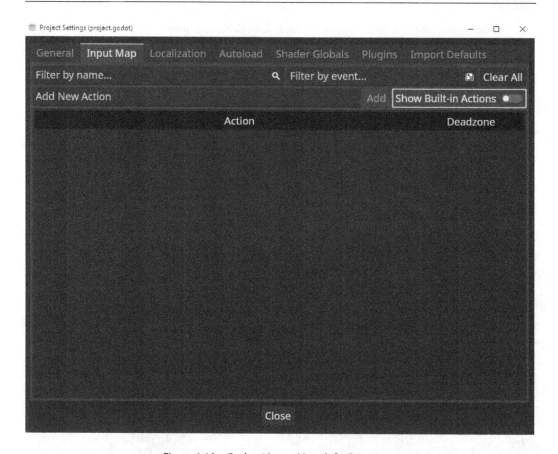

Figure 1.10 – Godot 4 Input Map default settings

5. Click the **Show Built-in Actions** button to the right of the search field. Notice that it now has many more options than Godot 3.x. Scroll down to see all of the options.

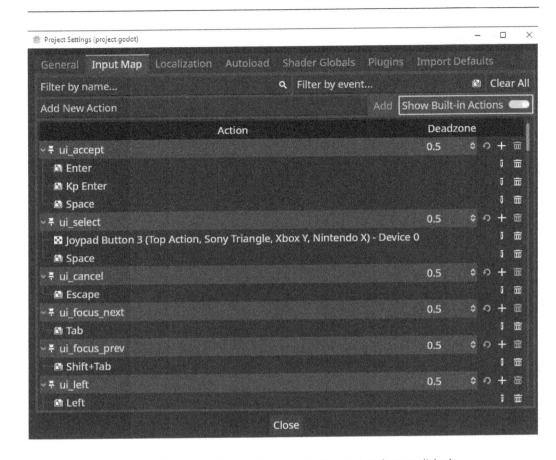

Figure 1.11 – Godot 4 Input Map Show Built-in Actions button clicked

6. Click the **Shader Globals** tab, which is the third tab to the right of **Input Map**. This is a new addition in Godot 4 to use with global uniforms.

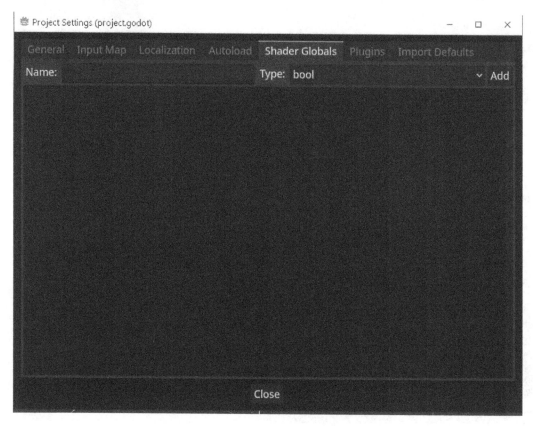

Figure 1.12 – Shader Globals tab in Project Settings

How it works...

We opened the **Project Settings** dialog and noticed that there was not much showing like in Godot 3.x. We saw that a new **Advanced Settings** button was added that showed everything.

Next, we opened the **Input Map** tab and found there was nothing showing by default. We learned that a new **Show Built-in Actions** button was added and when pressed, all of the user input options of Godot 3.x and more are shown.

We opened the new **Shader Globals** tab, which is used for global uniforms and allows you to change many shader behaviors at the same time.

What's new in the Editor Settings dialog

In this recipe, we will look at the differences in the Editors and Text Editors in **Editor Settings** between Godot 3.x and Godot 4.

How to do it...

To find the Editors and Text Editors in **Editor Settings**, execute the following steps:

1. Open a new or any existing project in Godot 4.

2. In the top-left menu, click **Editor**, and then click **Editor Settings**.

3. On the left, where you see **Interface**, scroll down to **Text Editor**.

4. Click **Theme** under **Text Editor**.

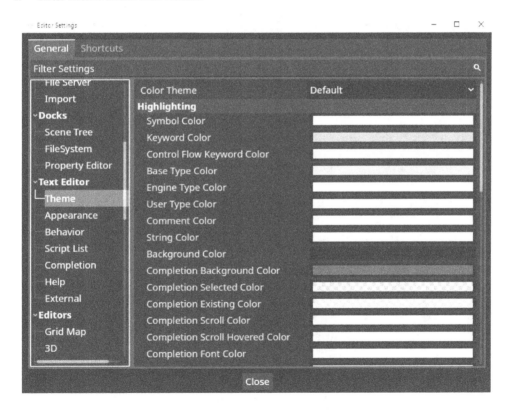

Figure 1.13 – Godot 4 Text Editor – Theme

The following screenshot shows what it looked like in Godot 3.x.

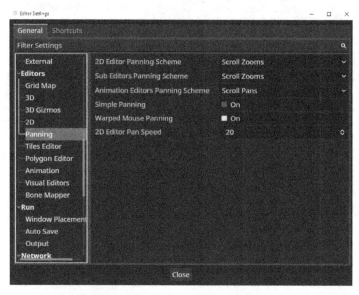

Figure 1.14 – Godot 3.x Text Editor – Highlighting

Notice that the **Highlighting** settings in Godot 3.x are now under **Theme** in Godot 4.

5.   Scroll down to the next section, called **Editors**, and click on **Panning**, which is new to Godot 4.

Figure 1.15 – Godot 4 Editor – Panning

The following screenshot shows what it looked like in Godot 3.x.

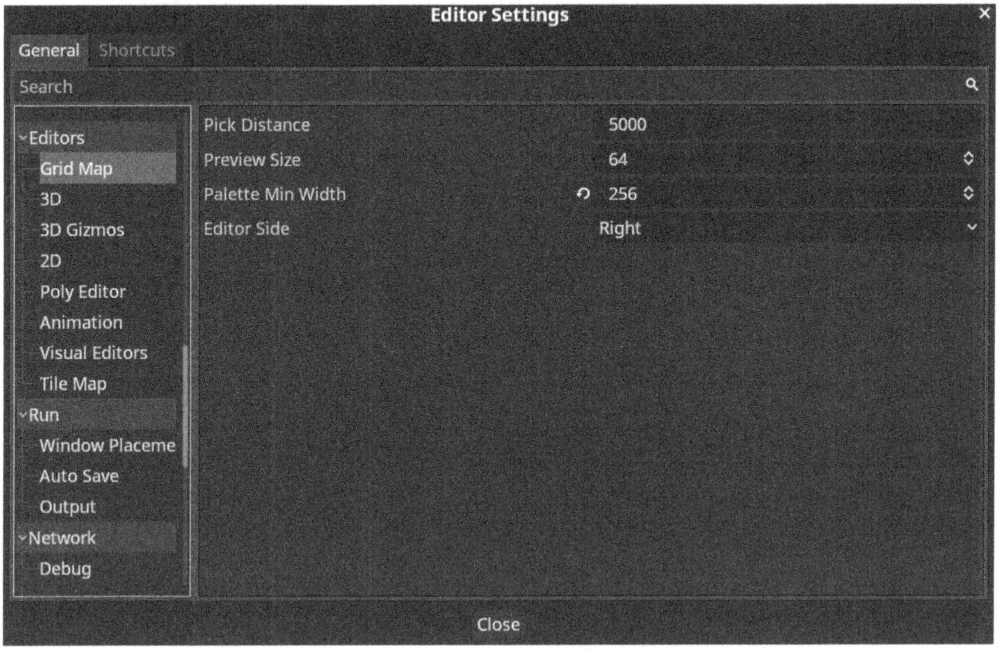

Figure 1.16 – Godot 3.x Editor – no panning

Notice the new **Panning** and **Bone Mapper** settings.

How it works...

In this recipe, we looked at **Theme** in the **Text Editor** settings in *steps 2-4* and noticed that there are fewer settings compared to Godot 3.x. The **Highlighting** settings can now be found under **Theme**.

We looked at the new **Panning** settings, where we can change the 2D Editor's, Sub Editors', and Animation Editors' Panning Schemes to make the mouse scroll wheel pan or zoom in those editors. We saw that **Bone Model** was also added to the Godot 4 Editor settings. Go through all of the **Project Settings** and **Editor Settings** tabs to see what has changed.

2
Transitioning to GDScript 2.0

In Godot 4, the GDScript language backend was rewritten, allowing the runtime to be faster and more stable than it was in Godot 3.x. Some additions to the language were also implemented, which we will look at in this chapter: annotations that replace some keywords, such as `export`; the `set` and `get` properties, which replace `setget`; the `await` keyword, which replaces `yield`; and the `super` keyword, which refers to the parent class object and makes it easier to call the parent class methods.

Typed arrays now allow us to create arrays of a specific type such as all strings, which helps to cut down on errors. We will look at two ways to write a lambda function with a button signal along with other examples using lambda functions. We will also look at two callable static methods and how to use callables with signals.

In this chapter, we will cover the following recipes:

- Investigating annotations in Godot 4
- Using properties with getters and setters
- Using the new `await` keyword and coroutines
- Using the `super` keyword to call a function
- Working with typed arrays
- Working with lambda functions
- Using callables with signals

Technical requirements

For this chapter, you need the standard version of Godot 4.0 or later running on one of the following:

- Windows 64-bit or 32-bit
- macOS
- Linux 64-bit or 32-bit

- Android

- Web Editor

You can find the code and the project files for the projects in this chapter on GitHub: `https://github.com/PacktPublishing/Godot-4-Game-Development-Cookbook/tree/main/Chapter%202`.

Investigating annotations in Godot 4

In this recipe, we will first look at `@export` and some of the variations associated with that annotation and then show how to use `@onready`.

Getting ready

For this recipe, open Godot 4 and start a new project called `Chapter 2`.

How to do it...

To investigate annotations, we will use each in a script by doing the following:

1. Open a new project in Godot.

2. In the **Scene** tab, click **2D Scene**.

3. Click on the paper icon above **Node2D** and to the right of the filter **Search** box or in the **Inspector** tab under **Node | Script**. Click **<empty>**, then select **New Script**, and name the script `Annotations`.

4. Click on **Script** at the top of the editor to look at the new script we added.

5. `@export` is the same as `export` in Godot 3.x, so we will add a score to the node so we can see it in the **Inspector** tab:

```
1   extends Node2D
2
3   @export var score = 0
```

6. As you saw from the auto-completion, there are new `@export` options available now. Let's add `@export_range()` to *line 4*:

```
4   @export_range(0, 100, .1) var input_range
```

> **Note**
> This gives a range from 0 to 100 in increments of .1 to the `input_range` variable, which you can change in the **Inspector** tab.

7. We can show named `enum` values in the **Inspector** tab by adding the following to *lines 5 and 6*:

```
5       enum WeatherEnum {Sunny, Rainy, Cloudy = -1}

6       @export var weather: WeatherEnum
```

8. On *line 7*, let's add a file to show up on the **Inspector** tab using `@export_file`:

```
7       @export_file("*.txt") var file
```

9. Click on **Node2D** in the **Scene** tab. Then, click on + under **Scene** in the **Scene** tab to bring up the **Create New Node** window.

10. Then, type `camer2d` in the **Search** box. Select and add **Camera2D** to **Node2D**.

11. The `onready` keyword is now `@onready`. We will add a **Camera2D** node and use `@onready` with the camera on *line 7*:

```
8       @onready var camera = $Camera2d
```

12. Click on **Node2D** at the top of the tree in the **Scene** tab to see everything we used with @ export in the **Inspector** tab.

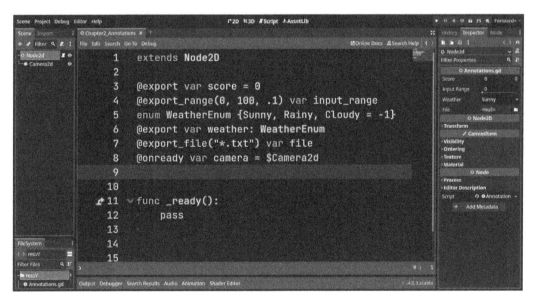

Figure 2.1 – Annotations.gd

How it works...

We added a `score` variable so we can could see it in the **Inspector** tab using `@export` instead of the `export` keyword.

We added `@export_range(0, 100, .1) var input_range` to show a range of 0 to 100 that snapped the value in `.10` increments. You could also just use `@export_range (0, 100) var input_range` or `@export_range (0, 100) var input_range:   float`.

We created an `enum` and then we used `@export var weather:   WeatherEnum` to put the `enum` into the `weather` variable so we could see it in the **Inspector** tab. You could also do `@export_enum(Sunny, Rainy, Cloudy) var weather`.

We used the `@export_file("*.txt") var file` to show how a file is seen in the **Inspector** tab.

We added a **Camera2D** node to **Node2D** so we could use `@onready` with it. First, we just used `@onready var camera = $Camera2d` to add the **Camera2D** node to the `camera` variable.

Using properties with getters and setters

In Godot 4, the `setget` keyword is gone and has been replaced by using properties, so you don't have to use dedicated functions. We will go through some examples of how to use getters and setters.

Getting ready

For this recipe, create a new scene by clicking + to the right of the current **Scene** tab and add **Node2D**. Click on the word **Scene** in the top menu next to **Project**, then select **Save Scene As**, and name it `Properties`.

How to do it...

There are two ways we can use getters and setters. The first is like Godot 3.x, where we assign `get` and `set` to functions. The second way is to define `get` and `set` after we declare the variable. First, let's create a button:

1. In the new scene named **Properties** that you created, add a **Button** node and make it big enough to see.

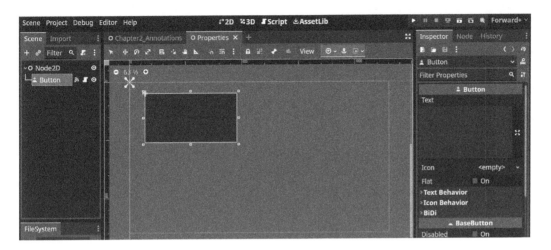

Figure 2.2 – Creating a Button node

2. Add a script named `Properties.gd` to the **Button** node and delete everything except for *line 1*.

3. At the top center of the editor, left-click on **2D** in the **Workspace** section. Add a signal to the **Button** node by going to the **Node** tab to the right of the **Inspector** tab located under **BaseButton** and selecting **pressed()**:

```
1   extends Button
2
3
```

4. The `setget` keyword used in Godot 3.x is now gone. We will assign `get` and `set` to functions as was done in Godot 3.x:

```
5   var value: int = 10: set = set_value, get = get_value
6
7   func set_value(new_value: int) -> void:
8       value = new_value
9       print('setter', str(value))
10
11  func get_value() -> int:
12      print('getter', str(value))
13      return value
14
15  func _on_pressed():
16      value -= 1
```

5. Now click the **Run the current scene** button or hit the *F6* key. Look at the **Output** section in the bottom panel.

6. Highlight *lines 5–13* and hit *Ctrl + K* to comment out these lines.

7. Now we will try using a variable declaration and no functions. Let's start on *line 15*. *Lines 23 and 24* should still be there from *step 4*. They were *lines 15 and 16*:

```
15 var value: int = 10:
16     set(new_value):
17         value = new_value
18         print('setter', str(value))
19     get:
20         print('getter', str(value))
21         return value
22
23 func _on_pressed():
24     value -= 1
```

8. Now click the **Run the current scene** button or hit the *F6* key.

How it works...

We added a button and connected the `pressed()` signal so we could see that the getters and setters were working.

In *lines 7–9*, we created the `set_value` setter function with an integer parameter called `new_value`. This function does not return a value so we used `-> void:`. We then made `value` equal to `new_value`, and finally, we printed `setter` with `value`.

In *lines 11–13*, we created the `get_value` getter function, which returns an integer, so we used `-> int:`. We printed `getter` with `value` and then we returned `value`. In *line 16*, we added `value = value - 1` to the `_on_pressed()` function that was created when we hooked up the signal in *step 3*.

We entered the code to call the `get` and `set` functions as was done using the `getset` keyword in Godot 3.x. In *line 5*, we created a variable called `value`, which is an `int` value equal to `10`. We then assigned `set` to the `set_value` function and `get` to the `get_value` function.

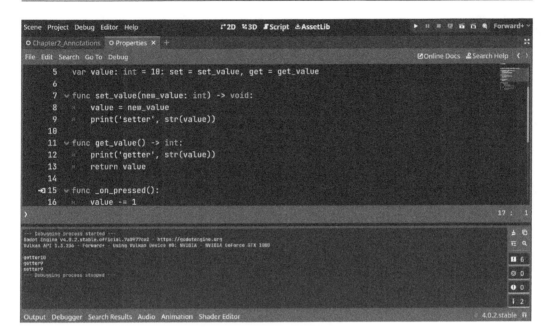

Figure 2.3 – The GDScript and console output results

When the button was clicked, the value variable in the setter was decreased by one and then printed on the console, as well as the value getter variable before and after the button was pushed, to show that the getter and setter were working.

We commented out *lines 5–13* so we could use the get and set properties with the variable declaration.

On *line 15*, we created an integer variable called value and assigned it to equal 10. Then, on *line 16*, we used the set property with new_value as the parameter. On *lines 17–18*, we made value equal to new_value and printed setter with value. On *line 19*, we saw the get property. On *lines 20–21*, inside of the get property, we printed getter with value.

Figure 2.4 – The GDScript and console output results

We select **Run the current scene** and notice that we get the same output on the console as we did when we used functions. The `value` variable in the setter is decreased by one and then printed on the console, as well as the `value` getter variable before and after the button was pushed.

Using the new await keyword and coroutines

The `yield` keyword has been removed and replaced by the `await` keyword. You can use `await` with coroutines or signals. It pauses the function it is in and waits for a signal to be emitted, or if a called coroutine is finished, it then resumes the function where it was originally called.

Getting ready

For this recipe, create a new scene by clicking + to the right of the current **Scene** tab and adding **Node2D**. Select **Save Scene As** and name it `Await`.

How to do it...

We will go through a very simple example of how `await` works with a coroutine using a button as a character dialogue box. When the button is clicked, it skips to the next character dialogue box:

1.   In the new scene named `Await` that you have created, add a **Button** node and make it big enough to see the text that we are going to place in it with code.

2. Add a script named `Await` to **Node2D** and delete all of the default lines except *line 1*.

3. Let's use `@onready` and create a variable called `button` to reference our **Button** node:

```
1   extends Node2D
2
3   @onready var button = $Button
```

4. On *line 5*, we will create a new function called `game_dialogue()` and call it in the `_ready()` function:

```
4
5   func _ready():
6       game_dialogue()
7
8   func game_dialogue():
9       button.text = "Dialogue text."
10      print("In the game_dialogue function.")
11      var next_dialogue = await skip_dialogue()
12      if next_dialogue:
13          print("At the end of game_dialogue function.")
```

5. On *line 15*, we created a new function called `skip_dialogue()`:

```
15  func skip_dialogue():
16      print("Now in the skip_dialogue() function.")
17      await button.button_up
18      button.text = "New dialogue text."
19      print("At the end of skip_dialogue function."
20      return true
```

6. Now click the **Run the current scene** button or hit the *F6* key.

Figure 2.5 – GDScript for steps 3 to 5 (the code for Await.gd)

How it works...

We added a **Button** node and made it big enough for us to read the text on the button that we will code in later. Then we added a script called `Await` to **Node2D** and deleted all of the default lines except *line 1*.

We used `@onready` with the `button` variable so we could load the reference when the `_ready()` function was called.

We created a function called `game_dialogue()`. In *line 9*, we added text to the button. In *line 10*, we printed that we were in this function so we could see it in the console to see how the `await` keyword works. In *line 11*, we declared a variable called `next_dialogue` equal to the `skip_dialogue()` function written in *step 5*.

This is where the program will pause and go to the coroutine of the `skip_dialogue()` function. In *lines 12–13*, we have an `if` statement that checks that `next_dialogue` is `true`, and if so, then prints that we are back in the `game_dialogue()` function. For it to be `true`, the `skip_dialogue()` function has to run and return `true`.

We created the function called `skip_dialogue()`. In *line 16*, we printed to the console that we were now in this function. In *line 17*, we waited for the user to click the button. In *line 18*, we changed the text on the button. In *line 19*, we printed to the console that we were at the end of the `skip_dialogue()` function. In *line 20*, we return `true` so that when we go back to the `game_dialogue()` function, we can print the last `print` statement.

We selected **Run the current scene**.

You see In the game_dialogue function. and Now in the skip_dialogue() function. on the console before you click the button. The default text on the button is Dialogue text.. After you click the button, you see At the end of skip_dialogue function. and At the end of game_dialogue function. on the console and the text on the button is New dialogue text..

Using the super keyword to call a function

In Godot 3.x, we used to call a function of the parent class from a subclass by using the .function of the parent class. Now we use the super keyword. In the example, we will use in this recipe, we have SniperEnemyClass, which is inherited from DefaultEnemyClass. If we wanted to call the rifle function in DefaultEnemyClass from SniperEnemyClass, we would use the super keyword, but in Godot 3.x, we use .rifle().

Getting ready

For this recipe, create a new scene by clicking + to the right of the current **Scene** tab and clicking **Node2D**. Select **Save Scene As** and name it Super.

How to do it...

We will create two classes called SniperEnemyClass, which is inherited from DefaultEnemyClass. The DefaultEnemyClass class has two functions called rifle and orders. We will use the super keyword from SniperEnemyClass to call the two functions:

1. Add a script named Super to **Node2D** and delete all of the default lines except *line 1*.

2. Let's start on *line 11* and create DefaultEnemyClass:

```
11 class DefaultEnemyClass extends Node2D:
12     func rifie():
13         print("Basic rifle")
14     func orders():
15         print("Guard the front gate.")
```

3. Now let's create SniperEnemyClass starting on *line 17*:

```
17 class SniperEnemyClass extends DefaultEnemyClass:
18     func rifle():
19         print("Sniper rifle")
20         super.orders()
21         super()
```

4. We need to add a couple of variables to the `_ready()` function so we can see the output of the `print` statement on the console. Let's start on *line 3*:

```
3   func _ready():
4       var enemy = DefaultEnemyClass.new()
5       var sniper = SniperEnemyClass.new()
6
7       enemy.rifle()
8       enemy.orders()
9       sniper.rifle()
```

5. Now click the **Run the current scene** button or hit the *F6* key.

Figure 2.6 – super keyword code (GDScript for steps 2–4)

How it works...

We added a script to **Node2D** and named it `Super`. Then we deleted all of the lines in the script except *line 1*.

We made a class called `DefaultEnemyClass`, which extends Node2D so, later, we can see the output on the console. In *lines 12–13*, we made a function called `rifle` to print out a rifle. In *lines 14–15*, we made a function called `orders` to print out the orders.

We made a class called `SniperEnemyClass`, which extends `DefaultEnemyClass`. In *lines 18–19*, we created a `rifle` function, which prints out a sniper rifle. In *line 20*, we called the `orders` function in the DefaultEnemyClass class using the super keyword. In *line 21*, we called the rifle function in DefaultEnemyClass from SniperEnemyClass using the super() keyword. As long as you are in a function that is in both parent and child classes, you can use super(). If you want to call a different function in DefaultEnemyClass, then you have to use super.function.

In *lines 4–5*, we created enemy and sniper instances for the two classes. In *line 7*, we called the rifle() function in DefaultEnemyClass to see which rifle was set as the default. In *line 8*, we called the orders() function in DefaultEnemyClass to see the enemy orders. In *line 9*, we called the rifle() function in SniperEnemyClass.

We ran the current scene. We saw **Basic rifle**, **Guard the front gate.**, **Sniper rifle**, **Guard the front gate.**, and **Basic rife** on the console.

We get the following console output when we run the current scene:

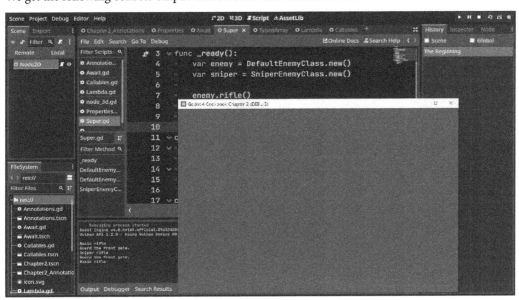

Figure 2.7 – super keyword console output

Working with typed arrays

In Godot 4, we can use typed arrays so if you are only going to use an array of strings, you can set the element type to **String** and Godot will throw an error if you try to put anything other than a string in that array. Types are validated at runtime and not when compiling, which causes slightly faster performance.

Getting ready

For this recipe, create a new scene by clicking + to the right of the current **Scene** tab and adding **Node2D**. Select **Save Scene As** and name it TypedArray.

How to do it...

In this recipe, we are going to set up three arrays. The first is not a typed array, the second is a typed array, and the third infers the type of the array:

1. Add a script named TypedArray to **Node2D** and delete all the default lines except *line 1* and the _ready() function.

2. On *line 3*, let's create a regular array:

```
1   extends Node2D
2
3   var regular_array = [4, "hello",434]
```

3. On *line 4*, we will create a typed array of int. Try adding a string to this array:

```
4   var typed_array: Array[int] = [16, 32, 64]
```

4. On *line 5*, we will create an inferred array of string. Try adding an integer to this array:

```
5   var inferred_array := ["hi", "hello"]
```

5. On *lines 7–10*, in the _ready() function, we print out all the arrays to the console:

```
7   func ready():
8        print(regular_array)
9        print(typed_array)
10       print(inferred_array)
```

6. Now click the **Run the current scene** button or hit the *F6* key.

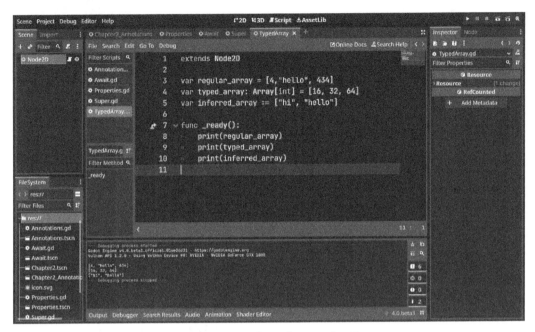

Figure 2.8 – GDScript for steps 2 to 5

How it works...

We added a script to **Node2D** and named it `TypedArray`. Then we deleted all of the lines in the script except *line 1* and the `_ready()` function. We created a regular array with two integers and one string value. We can put anything in this array.

We created a typed array of `int` and tried to enter a string in the array to see the resulting error. In *step 4*, we created an inferred array of **String** and tried to enter an integer into the array to see the resulting error.

We printed out all of the arrays to the console. We ran the current scene. We saw `[4, "hello", 434]`, `[16, 32, 64]`, and `["hi", "hello"]` printed on the console.

Working with lambda functions

In this recipe, we are going to go through some examples of how to use lambdas in Godot 4. First, we create a lambda that takes a *greeting* parameter, then we will call the lambda and pass in `"hello"` to the parameter. In the next example, we declare a variable called `health` outside of the `player_health` lambda and call the variable inside of the lambda. We will learn two ways to write a lambda function with a button signal. Finally, we use a lambda function, moving the button across the screen with a tween.

Getting ready

For this recipe, create a new scene by clicking + to the right of the current **Scene** tab and adding **Node2D**. Select **Save Scene As** and name it Lambda.

How to do it...

Let's start by creating a Button node and referencing it to the button variable:

1. Add a script named Lambda to **Node2D** and delete all of the default lines except *line 1* and the _ready() function.

2. In the new scene named Lambda that you created, add a Button node and make it big enough to see.

3. Let's use @onready and create a variable called button to reference our Button node:

```
1    extends Node2D
2
3    @onready var button = $Button
```

4. On *line 5*, in the _ready() function, we create a lambda that will pass in "hello" to the lambda parameter greeting:

```
5    func _ready():
6        var lambda = func(greeting):
7            print(greeting)
8        lambda.call("hello")
```

5. On *line 10*, we declare a variable called health:

```
10        var health = 100
```

6. On *line 11*, we create a lambda function called player_health:

```
11        var player_health = func(): print("Current health ",
health)
```

7. On *line 12*, we call the player_health lambda function:

```
12        player_health.call()
```

8. On *line 14*, we create a lambda function to run when the button is pressed:

```
14        button.pressed.connect(func(): print("button was
pressed"))
```

9. On *lines 16–18*, we create a lambda to run when the button is released:

```
16      var button_released = func():
17          print("Button released")
18      button.button_up.connect(button_released)
```

10. On *lines 20–21*, we create a `tween` to move the button across the screen:

```
20      var tween = create_tween()
21      tween.tween_method(func(pos): button.position.x = pos, 0,
    500, 1)
```

11. Now click the **Run the current scene** button or hit the *F6* key.

Figure 2.9 – Lambda code (GDScript for steps 3–10)

How it works...

We added a script called `Lambda` to **Node2D** and deleted everything in the script except *line 1* and the `_ready()` function. Then, we created a `Button` node in the **Scene** tab. In the `Lambda` script, we used `@onready` to declare a variable called `button` to the **Button** node.

We created a variable called `lambda` equal to the lambda function with the `greeting` parameter, which prints the greeting. Since lambdas are a type of **callable**, we call the `lambda` variable with the `"hello"` string to be used as the greeting.

We declared a variable called `health` and gave it a value of `100` in *line 10*. You can use variables from the outer class or outer function inside the lambda. In *line 11*, we created a lambda called player_health, which prints out **Current health** and the value of the health variable. In *line 12*, we call the player_health lambda to print out ("Current health ", health) to the console.

We pass the lambda as a function argument. When the pressed() button signal is emitted, **Button was pressed** will be printed to the console.

We essentially do the same thing we did last in the step except we use more than one line. When the button_up() signal is emitted, **Button released** is printed to the console.

On *line 20*, we create a tween. On *line 21*, we use a lambda in tween_method() to move the Button node from position (0) to position (500) with a duration of (1). If we wanted the button to go slower, we would increase the duration number.

We run the current scene. It shows the button move across the screen and on the console, you will see "hello" and "Current health 100". After you click the button, you will see **Button was pressed** and **Button released**.

Figure 2.10 – Button and console output

Using callables with signals

In this recipe, we will see how callables can be used with signals. We will also look at the call and bind callable methods. Callables can be held in variables and passed into functions. As such, you can use them in arrays and in dictionaries as the key or the value.

Getting ready

For this recipe, create a new scene by clicking + to the right of the current **Scene** tab and adding **Node2D**. Select **Save Scene As** and name it Callables.

How to do it...

Let's start by creating a Button node and referencing it to the button variable:

1. Add a script named Callables to **Node2D** and delete all of the default lines except *line 1* and the _ready() function.

2. In the new scene named **Callables** that you created, add a Button node and make it big enough to see.

3. Let's use @onready and create a variable called button to reference our **Button** node:

    ```
    1   extends Node2D
    2
    3   @onready var button = $Button
    ```

4. On *line 8*, we create a function called signal_callable():

    ```
    8   func signal_callable():
    9       print("This method was called by the button pressed
    signal.")
    ```

5. On *line 5*, in the _ready() function, we connect a callable signal to the signal_callable() function:

    ```
    5   func _ready():
    6       button.pressed.connect(signal_callable)
    ```

6. Now click the **Run the current scene** button or hit the *F6* key.

7. Let's use the .bind method when we connect the signal. On *line 6*, add .bind after signal_callable:

    ```
    6       button.pressed.connect(signal_callable.bind("binding_"))
    ```

8. We need to add a parameter to the signal_callable function:

    ```
    8   func signal_callable(param):
    9       print(param, "This method was called by the button
    pressed signal.")
    ```

9. Now click the **Run the current scene** button or hit the *F6* key.

10. Let's add a new function on *line 11* called `player_text`:

```
10 func player_text(param: String):
11     print(param)
```

11. Go to *line 7*, hit the *Tab* key, and add more code to the `ready` function.

12. Let's create a variable called `pt` equal to `player_text`:

```
7      var pt = player_text
8      pt.call("Hello, NPC!")
```

13. Now click the **Run the current scene** button or hit the *F6* key.

How it works...

We added a script called `Callables` to **Node2D** and deleted everything in the script except *line 1* and the `_ready()` function. Then we created a `Button` node in the **Scene** tab. In the `Callables` script, we used `@onready` to declare a variable called `button` to the `Button` node.

We created a function that we want to run when the `button pressed` signal is `true`. Notice that we don't have to connect the signal in the editor. We can use any method that we want.

In the `_ready()` function, we used the button reference to connect the `signal_callable` function when the signal pressed is `true`, which happens when the button is pressed.

We ran the current scene. In the console, we saw **This method was called by the button pressed signal.** after we clicked the button.

Figure 2.11 – Using callables with signals (code for steps 4–6)

We used the callable `bind` method. In *line 6*, we added `.bind` like this:

```
button.pressed.connect(signal_callable.bind("binding_")).
```

We needed to add a parameter to the function and inside of the `print` statement to see what we added with `bind`.

We ran the current scene. In the console, we saw **binding_This method was called by the button pressed signal.** printed after we clicked the button.

Figure 2.12 – Using callable with the bind method (code for steps 7–9)

We added a function called `player_text`, which takes a parameter called `param` that only accepts strings. It prints out the parameter that will be passed in when we use `.call`.

We created a variable for the `player_text()` function When you enter `var pt = player_text`, autocomplete wants to add the `()` at the end – make sure you delete it. We converted the function into a variable, so now we can use the function in arrays, dictionaries, or in any other way you can use a variable.

We ran it to see **Hello, NPC!** printed in the console.

Figure 2.13 – Using .call() with a variable of the function (code for steps 10–13)

3

2D and 3D Rendering with Vulkan

In this chapter, we'll take a look at the new Vulkan renderer for 2D and 3D. We'll start by looking at the new global illumination systems. **Signed distance field global illumination (SDFGI)** can be used in 3D open-world games; we'll look at how we can use it in this chapter. Then, we'll look at Volumetric Fog in 3D games, as well as how to use the **FogVolume** node to make our games look realistic. After, we'll look at the GPU-based particles node, attractors, collision, trails, and 2D particles. Decals can be used to project a texture onto a mesh, which we will look at in the last recipe.

In this chapter, we will cover the following recipes:

- Showing off SDFGI
- Using Volumetric Fog to enhance your games
- Understanding the **FogVolume** node
- Working with particle nodes in Godot 4
- Using decals in your game

Technical requirements

For this chapter, you need the standard version of Godot 4.0 or later running on one of the following systems:

- Windows 64-bit or 32-bit
- macOS
- Linux 64-bit or 32-bit
- Android
- Web Editor

You can find the code and the project files for the projects in this chapter on GitHub at `https://github.com/PacktPublishing/Godot-4-Game-Development-Cookbook/tree/main/Chapter%203`.

Showing off SDFGI

In this recipe, we will download a 3D asset so that we can see how **signed distance field global illumination** (SDFGI) looks and go through all of the settings to see what they do. SDFGI is a real-time global illumination method that uses **Signed Distance Fields** (SDFs) to create lighting in real time.

We will also look at **Screen-Space Indirect Lighting** (SSIL), which works with SDFGI or VoxelGI and is indirect lighting that allows diffuse light to bounce off of nearby objects.

Getting ready

For this recipe, open Godot 4 and start a new project called `Chapter 3`. Go to the `https://polyhaven.com/a/ship_pinnace` website and download the free `glTF 2.0` file using the drop-down arrow. Double-click the ZIP file and extract the file to a new folder called `Ship Pinnace` or whatever you want to call it:

Figure 3.1 – glTF file download

You can also download the project from this book's GitHub repository.

Make sure the renderer is set to **Forward+**. In the top-right corner of the **Editor** area, you should see a green **Forward+** button. If you don't, then click on **Mobile or Compatibility** and select **Forward+** from the drop-down list.

How to do it...

In this recipe, we will set up a 3D environment and add a free 3D asset. We will then add a camera to put into the model and go through the SDFGI settings to see how they look:

1. In the new project, click on **3D Scene** and rename **Node3D** to World. Then, save the scene as SDFGI.

2. As we saw in *Chapter 1*, *Exploring the Godot 4 Editor*, click on the three vertical dots to the left of the **Transform** view on **Viewport Toolbar** to edit the **Sun and Environment** settings.

3. Add **Sun and Environment** to the scene by left-clicking the **Add Sun to Scene** button at the bottom while holding down the *Shift* key.

4. Click on **DirectionalLight3D** in the **Scene** tab. In the **Inspector** tab, under **Transform |
Position**, enter 210 for **x**, 650 for **y**, and –265 for **z**:

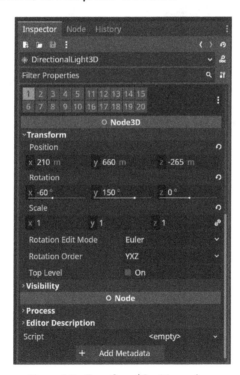

Figure 3.2 – Transform | Position values

5. Take the folder you saved the ship in and drag it into the **FileSytem** tab.

6. Open the folder and drag the ship_pinnace_4k.gltf file onto the **World** node in the **Scene** tab.

7. Add a **Camer3D** and place it in the boat. I put it by the stairs:

Figure 3.3 – Camera3D position by the left stairs

8. Click on the **AssetLib** tab to the right of **Script** to go to the **Godot Asset Library** area.

9. In the **Search** box, type camera and look for **Free Look Camera**; download it.

10. Add the free_look_camera.gd script to **Camera3D**.

11. Add a **MeshInstance3D** and rename it Orb.

12. Click on <**empty**> to the right of the mesh in the inspector. A drop-down list will appear. Now, click **New SphereMesh**.

13. To the right of the mesh, where we just clicked <**empty**>, click on **SphereMesh**.

14. Click on <**empty**> to the right of **Material** in the **Inspector** area. A drop-down list will appear. Now, click **New StandardMaterial3D**.

15. In the **Inspector** area, click on **Material** to open the options. Click on **Metallic**, then change the value of **Metallic** from 0 to 1.

16. In the **Inspector** area, click on **Roughness** to open the options. Change the value of **Roughness** from 1 to 0.

17. Bring the **Editor** camera somewhere behind **Camera3D**, which we placed earlier.

18. Click **View**, which is to the right of **Transform**, to make a drop-down list appear. Click on **2 Viewports (Alt)**:

Figure 3.4 – All viewport options

19. Click **WorldEnvironment** in the **Scene** tab. Then, at the top of the **Inspector** area, to the right of **Environment**, click **Environment** to see the available options.

20. In the **Inspector** area in **WorldEnvironment**, click on **SDFGI** to open the options menu. Click on **Enabled** and notice the differences between *off* and *on*.

21. Click on **Use Occlusion** to see how this looks. If it doesn't look right, use the mouse wheel to zoom in and out to fix it.

22. Go through each of the options below **Read Sky Light** to see how it looks. In the *How it works...* section, I have explained each option. Run **Current Scene** (by pressing *F6*) to see how it looks in a game while you change the settings.

23. Click on **SSIL** at the top of **SDFGI** and click **Enabled**.

24. Go through each of these options and see how they look in the editor and game.

25. Open the **Project Settings** area (make sure the **Advanced Settings** button is on) and, under **Rendering**, click **Global Illumination**.

26. In the **Project Settings** area under **Rendering**, click **Environment** to see the **SSIL** properties.

How it works...

In this recipe, we created a new project by clicking on **3D Scene**, which added a **Node3D** root node. We renamed it `World`. You don't have to do that, but I wanted to rename the root node of my 3D project.

We added the **DirectionalLight3D** and **WorldEnvironment** nodes by clicking on the three vertical dots to open the **Sun and Environment** settings. We changed the position of the light source by changing **Position** under **Transform** in the **Inspector** area.

Then, we took the ship model that we saved to a folder when we extracted it from the ZIP file and moved the folder to the **World** node in the **Scene** tab. We added a **Camera3D** to the **World** scene and placed it in the boat so that we could see how the SDFGI options look when applied.

After, we went to the **Godot Asset Library** area to get a free script called **Free Look Camera** so that we could move the camera around the model to see how the lighting looks. We can use the *W*, *A*, *S*, and *D* keys to move and press and hold the right mouse button and move the mouse to position the view of the camera.

Next, we created a sphere mesh named `Orb` by adding **MeshInstance3D** to the scene. By changing the **Metallic** and **Roughness** values, we created a mirror-like surface for the sphere so that we could see how the lighting reflects off of the sphere.

Then, we moved the default **Editor** camera under the deck behind **Camera3D**, which we added earlier. After, we changed the viewport to show the default camera view and outside of the view so that we could see how SDFGI looks in the editor in real time.

Next, we checked out all of the properties in SDFGI. Using **Occlusion** reduces light leaking. **Bounce Feedback** is a multiplier that's applied to the light each time it bounces off of a surface. There are no performance impacts when using it.

When using brighter materials, anything over the default value of 0.5 could cause feedback loops, which could make everything white because of so much light. Cascades display SDFGI further away, keeping detail up close, but you will have a hit on performance.

If you have smaller levels, using one to four cascades will improve performance. **Min Cell Size** allows SDFGI updates to be more accurate up close with a higher hit on performance when using lower values.

Higher values decrease the performance hit and SDFGI is more diffuse. **Cascade 0 Distance** is linked to **Min Cell Size** and **Max Distance** (all three are linked). **Max Distance** is the maximum distance that SDFGI is visible. The **Y Scale 50% Compact** setting is used for better quality, while **100% Sparse** is used for very vertical games and how fast the camera moves on the *Y*-axis.

Energy is an SDFGI multiplayer such as **Bounce Feedback**. The higher values will be brighter. **Normal Bias** is for normal SDFGI probes. Higher values can reduce visible streaking artifacts on sloped surfaces but could increase light leaking. **Probe Bias** is the constant bias on SDFGI probes.

After, we enabled SSIL and checked out its properties. **Radius** is the distance that bounced lighting will travel. **Intensity** is a brightness modifier for SSIL. The higher the value, the brighter the light. **Sharpness** is the amount that SSIL is allowed to blur objects. **Normal Rejection** is used to avoid light leaking when only one side of an object is illuminated.

Then, we looked at the **Global Illumination** advanced settings. To improve performance with Voxel GI and SDFGI, turn on **Use Half Resolution**. **Voxel GI | Quality** can be set to **Fast** at lower quality (fewer cones) or **Slow** at higher quality (more cones). **SDFGI Probe Ray Count**, **Frames To Converge**, and **Frames To Update Lights** can also change the speed and quality settings.

Finally, we looked at the SSIL properties in the **Environment** advanced settings. Here, you can change the **Quality** property. **Half Size** is when SSIL is rendered at half size and upscaled before entering the scene. **Adaptive Target** has values of 0 to 1, where a value of 1 is high quality but slower while 0 has a speed and quality that's medium in quality.

Blur Passes is the number of blur passes when computing SSIL. A high number is smoother but slower. **Fadeout From** is the distance at which SSIL starts to fade out. **Fadeout To** is the distance at which SSIL is fully faded out.

Using Volumetric Fog to enhance your games

In this recipe, we will use Volumetric Fog in the scene from the previous recipe and go through each property and see what they do. Volumetric Fog reacts to light and shadow in real time throughout the scene. It makes your 3D scenes more realistic.

Getting ready

For this recipe, we will use the SDFGI scene that we made in the preceding recipe. You can also download the project from this book's GitHub repository.

Like the previous recipe, make sure the renderer is set to **Forward+**.

How to do it...

In this recipe, we will use the same scene from the previous recipe to add Volumetric Fog:

1. In the **Scene** tab, click on **WorldEnvironment**. Then, in the **Environment** options, click **Volumetric Fog** in the **Inspector** area.
2. To the right of **Enabled**, click **On**.
3. Move the slider of the **Density** property to the right and left to see its effects. After, click to the left of the slider to return to the default setting of 0.05.
4. Click on the white box to the right of **Albedo** to change the color of the fog.
5. Click on the black box to the right of **Emission** to change the light emitted from the fog.

6. Move the slider of **Emission Energy** to change the brightness of the emitted light. Change it back to the default setting of 1.

7. Move the slider of **GI Inject** to change the strength of **Global Illumination** in the **Albedo** color. Change it back to the default setting of 1.

8. Move the **Anisotropy** sliders around to change the direction of the light as it goes through the fog. Change it back to the default setting.

9. Let's move the **Length** slider to determine how far the Volumetric Fog is computed. Change it back to the default setting.

10. Move the **Detail Spread** slider to see how it looks. Change it back to the default setting.

11. Move the **Ambient Inject** slider to change the strength of the ambient light used in the Volumetric Fog. Change it back to the default setting.

12. Move the **Sky Affect** slider to 0 and then back to 1.

How it works...

In this recipe, we turned on **Volumetric Fog** and then moved the various sliders to change the density of the fog. Notice that the closer we came to the value of 1, the fog in the left viewport was closer to the camera. The opposite happened when the value was 0. Then, we set it back to its default to get some fog for the next step.

When we clicked the color box to the right of **Albedo**, we changed the color of the fog when the fog interacted with light. We also changed the **Emission** and **Emission Energy** properties. **Emission** is the light coming off of the fog, while **Emission Energy** is how much light is coming off of the fog.

We also changed **GI Inject** to look at how the strength of **Global Illumination** changes how the fog looks. A value of 0 will not change the fog. There is a slight performance hit when you set it above 0.

After, we changed the direction of the light when it goes through the Volumetric Fog. If a value is close to a value of 1, then the light is scattered forward. If the value is 0, then the light goes in all directions equally. If the value is close to –1, then the light is scattered backward.

Next, we changed the **Length** property. The higher the number, the greater the range; a lower number adds more detail. We also adjusted the **Detail Spread** property. If the value is higher, more detail is closer to the camera.

Then, we adjusted the **Ambient Inject** property to change the strength of the ambient light used in the Volumetric Fog. If the value is 0, there is no effect on the Volumetric Fog. There is a small performance hit when the value is over 0.

Finally, we moved the **Sky Affect** slider from 1 to 0 and then back to 1. When the value was 0, there was no fog in the scene except on the ship itself. This is because, at the default value of 1, the fog fully obscures the sky, while at 0, it doesn't but the fog on the ship is not affected.

Understanding the FogVolume node

The **FogVolume** node adds fog to a specific area. You can use many shapes to hold the fog, including a box, cones, cylinders, ellipsoids, as well as the world. In this recipe, we will create a **FogVolume** node and use it on the ship.

Getting ready

For this recipe, we will use the SDFGI scene that we used in the preceding two recipes. You can also download the project from this book's GitHub repository.

Like the previous recipes, make sure the renderer is set to **Forward+**.

How to do it...

In this recipe, we will create a **FogVolume** node and see how it looks:

1. Click **World** in the **Scene** tab and then click **+** to add the **FogVolume** node.

2. Enable **Volumetric Fog** in the **WorldEnvironment** node.

3. In the **Inspector** area, click **<empty>** to the right of **Material** and select **New FogMaterial**:

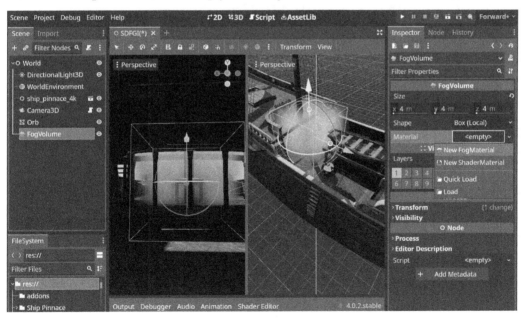

Figure 3.5 – New FogMaterial

4. Click on **FogMaterial** to the right of **Material** to open the **Properties** area.

5. Above **Shape**, change the box to **x 4m**, **y 4m**, **z 4m**.

6. Go to the **Height Falloff** property under **Emission** in the **Inspector** area. Left mouse click the box to the right of **Height Falloff** and drag it to the left until the number is 100 or more to see the fog on the ground.

7. Left mouse click the right of **Edge Fade** and drag it to the left and right to see the fog thin out when the value is high.

How it works...

In this recipe, we enabled **Volumetric Fog** so that we could see the fog in the cube. We added a **FogVolume** node to the scene and then added **New FogMaterial** to our **Material**. We changed the cube size to 2x2x2.

We also changed the value of **Height Falloff** to bring the fog to the ground. The **Density**, **Albedo**, and **Emission** properties do the same thing as the **Volumetric Fog** properties in the **WorldEnvironment** node. We changed the value of **Edge Fade** and noticed that the edge is thicker with a lower value and thinner with a higher value.

Working with particle nodes in Godot 4

In this recipe, we'll look at GPU-based particles node. We'll look at attractors, which attract particles toward the **GPUParticlesAttractorSphere3D** node, as well as collisions, where we create a ramp. When the particles hit the ramp, they collide and then fall down the ramp.

Next, we will create a second particle and use sub-emitters so that once the particles fall off the ramp or collide with the ramp, they change to the second particle. We will use trails to make a very basic explosion effect with the built-in **TubeTrailMesh**. Finally, we will look at the new **GPUParticles2D** node by making a cloud that shoots lighting using sub-emitters and trails.

Getting ready

For this recipe, we need to add a new **3D Scene** and save the scene as Particles. Click **View**, then **1 Viewport**. Rename **Node3D** to World and add a **WorldEnvironment** node to the **Scene** tab.

Download this free particle pack from Kenny here: https://www.kenney.nl/assets/particle-pack. We will use this later.

You can also download the project from this book's GitHub repository.

How to do it...

In this recipe, we will start by adding a **GPUParticles3D** node and then look at all the things we can do with particles in Godot 4:

1. Click the **World** node and then add a **GPUParticles3D** node to the **Scene** tab.

2. Click on **Process Material** and **Draw Passes** in the **Inspector** area to see the options for the properties.

3. Click **<empty>** to the right of **Pass 1** under **Draw Passes** and select **New SphereMesh** from the drop-down list.

4. Click **<empty>** to the right of **Process Material** under **Process Material** and select **New ParticleProcessMaterial** from the drop-down list:

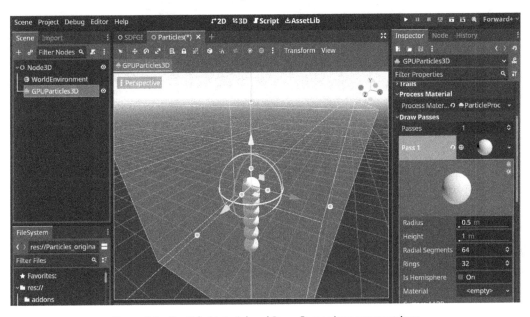

Figure 3.6 – Particle Material and Draw Passes Inspector settings

5. Click on **ParticleProcessMaterial** to the right of **Process Material** to open the options for **ParticleProcessMaterial**. Click **Emission Shape** and then left-click **Point** to change it to **Sphere**.

6. Click on the **World** node and click + to add a **GPUParticlesAttractorSphere3D** node. Right-click the node and rename it `AttractorSphere`.

7. Change the **GPUParticlesAttractorSphere3D** radius to 5m and **Strength** to 60. Now, move it around to see the particles moving toward the new node.

8. In the **Scene** tab, toggle off the visibility of the **AttractorSphere** node.

9. In **GPUParticles3D** in the **Inspector** area, click **Time** to open the options. Then, change the value of **Lifetime** to 2s and **Amount** to 64.

10. In the **Inspector** area, change the **Scale Min** and **Max** properties of the **GPUParticles3D | Process Material** property to 0.2. While we are here, click **Collision** to see the options and click **Disabled** to the right of **Mode**. Then, click **Rigid**.

11. Click **World** in the **Scene** tab and add a **GPUParticlesCollisionBox3D**. Right-click and rename this CollisionBox.

12. Click on **CollisionBox** in the **Scene** tab and change the **x**, **y**, and **z** values of **Size** to 8, 2, and 8, respectively. In the **Transform** area, change the **y** value to -3 and the **rotation** value of **z** to 30:

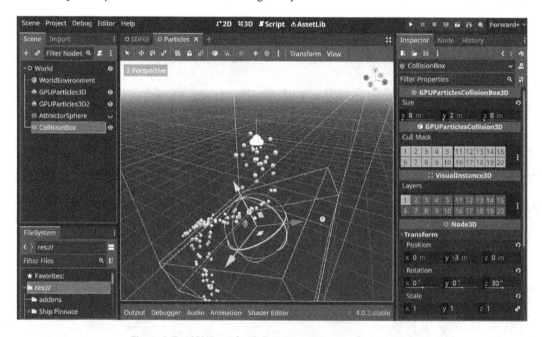

Figure 3.7 – GPUParticlesCollisionBox3D Inspector settings

13. Click on the **GPUParticles3D** node in the **Scene** tab and then click **Transform** in the **Inspector** area to change the value of **y** in **Position** to 2m.

14. Click on the **GPUParticles3D** node in the **Scene** tab and then press *Ctrl + D* (*Cmd + D* on Mac) to duplicate the node. Alternatively, you can right-click the node and click **Duplicate** in the drop-down list.

15. Click on the **GPUParticles3D2** node that we just created and, in the **Inspector** area, click on **Draw Passes** to open the options.

16. In **Pass 1**, click on the down arrow on the far right to open a list of new meshes. Select **New BoxMesh**.

17. Click on the original **GPUParticles3D** node and, at the top of the **Inspector** area, click **Assign...** to the right of **Sub Emitter**. Then, click **GPUParticles3D2**.

18. Go to the **Process Material** section and click **Sub Emitter** to see the options. Then, click **Disabled**, which is to the right of **Mode**, and select **At Collision**.

Trails

We are going to make a very basic explosion effect with the built-in **TubeTrailMesh** using particle trails. We will start by creating a new scene:

1. Let's create a new **3D Scene** by clicking the + button to the right of the **Particles** scene. Save the scene as Trails.

2. Add a **GPUParticles3D** node to the scene and click **Draw Passes** in the **Inspector** area.

3. Click **<empty>** to the right of **Pass 1** and select **New TubeTrailMesh** in the dropdown.

4. Left-click the tube that appeared where **<empty>** was and change **Radius** to .1m and **Section Length** to .1m:

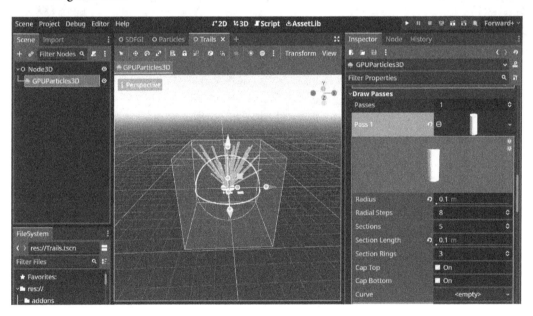

Figure 3.8 – Draw Passes Inspector settings

5. At the moment, we are still in **Draw Passes**. Click on **Material** and select **New StandardMaterial3D**. Left-click the material that appeared where **<empty>** used to be.

6. Click **Transform** to show the available options and click on **Use Particle Trails**.

7. Click **Process Material** in the **Inspector** area to see its properties. Click on **<empty>** and then **New ParticleProcessMaterial**. Then, left-click **ParticleProcessMaterial** where **<empty>** used to be to see its properties.

8. Click on **Direction** to open its properties and change **x** to 0 and **y** to 1.

9. Click on **Gravity** to open its properties and change **y** to 0.

10. Click on **Initial Velocity** to open its properties and change both **Velocity Min** and **Max** to 1:

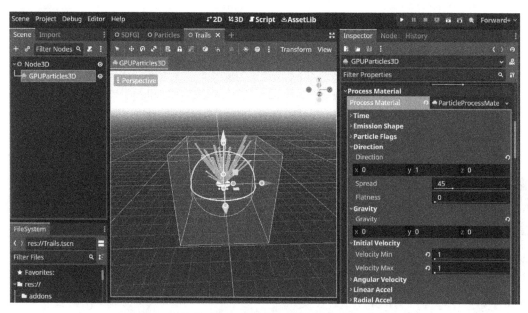

Figure 3.9 – Inspector settings for Process Materials

11. In the **Inspector** area, click **Trails** to open its properties. Then, click **Enabled** so that it is *on* and change **Length Secs** to 4s.

12. In the **Inspector** area, click **Time** to open its properties and change **Lifetime** to 5s.

13. In the **Inspector** area, change **Amount** to 50:

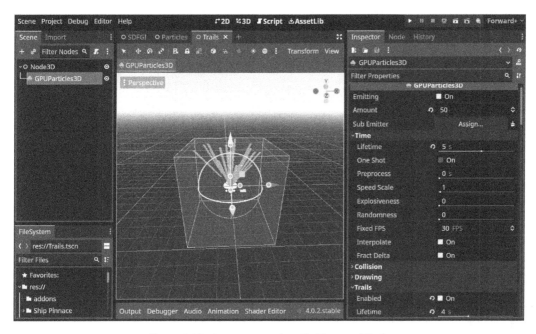

Figure 3.10 – Inspector settings for Time and Trails

Particles2D

In this part, we will make a cloud that shoots lighting using sub-emitters and trails with **GPUParticles2D**. We will start by creating a new scene:

1. Let's create a new **2D Scene** by clicking the + button to the right of the **Trails** scene. Save the scene as `Particles2D`.

2. Add **GPUParticles2D** to the scene. Rename it `Cloud`.

3. If you have not downloaded the free particle pack from Kenny, then go to the website in the *Getting ready* section and download it.

4. Once you've extracted and opened the `PNG(Transparent)` folder, move the `smoke_07.png` and `spark_05.png` files into the `res://` folder in Godot.

5. Click **Textures** under **Process Material** in the **Inspector** area, and drag the `smoke_07.png` file over to **<empty>** to add the texture.

6. Click **Process Material**, then click **<empty>** and select **New ParticleProcessMaterial** from the dropdown.

7. Left-click on **ParticleProcessMaterial**, which you just selected, to open its properties.

8. Click **Time** in the **ParticleProcessMaterial** properties and change the **Lifetime Randomness** property to `.2`.

9. Click **Emission Shape** and change **Point** to **Sphere** by clicking on **Point**. Change **Sphere Radius** to `150`.

10. Click **Direction** and change the **x** value to `0` and the **y** value to `1`.

11. Click **Initial Velocity** and change both **Velocity Min** and **Max** to `250`.

12. Click **Scale** and change **Scale Min** to `1` and **Scale Max** to `2`.

13. Click **Sub Emitter** and change the **Mode** property to **At End** and **Amount At End** to `20`. Turn on **Keep Velocity**.

14. Click **Collision** and change the **Mode** property to **Rigid**.

15. At the top of the **Inspector** area, change the **Amount** value to `100`.

16. Click **Time** to open the properties and then change the **Randomness** value to `.5`.

17. Add another **GPUParticles2D** node to the scene as a child of **Cloud**. Rename it `Lightning`.

18. Click on the **Cloud** node. Then, at the top of the **Inspector** area, click **Assign…**, which is to the right of **Sub Emitter**, and add the **Lightning** node you just created. Then, click on the **Lightning** node so that we can start to set up the sub-emitter.

19. Click **Textures**, which is under **Process Material** in the **Inspector** area, and drag the `spark_05.png` file to **<empty>**.

20. Click **Process Material** in the **Inspector** area to open its properties. Click **<empty>** and select **New ParticleProcessMaterial**. Click **ParticleProcessMaterial**, which you just added, to see its properties. Click on **Gravity** in the **Inspector** area and change the **y** value to `500`.

21. Click **Trails** in the **Inspector** area and click to the right of **Enabled**. Change **Lifetime** to `4`.

22. At the top of the **Inspector** area, change **Amount** to `1`. Then, click **Time** to open its properties. Change the value for **Lifetime** to `2` and the value of **Speed Scale** to `3`:

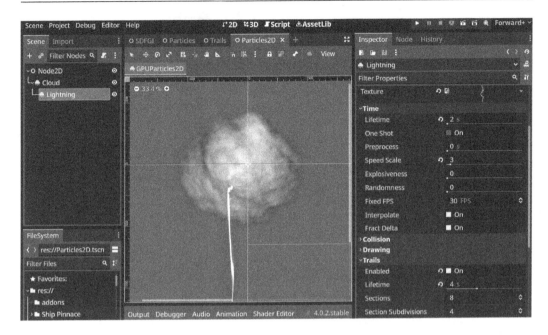

Figure 3.11 – Time and Trails Inspector settings for the Lightning node

How it works...

In this recipe, we added a **GPUParticles3D** node to the scene. After clicking on **GPUParticles3D** in the **Scene** tab, we looked in the **Inspector** area and clicked on **Process Material** and **Draw Passes** to show the options for these properties.

Then, we added **New SphereMesh** from the **Pass 1** drop-down box. We also added **New ParticleProcessMaterial** from the **Process Material** dropdown, we could see a sphere particle rendering eight particles per pass. If we wanted to have more particles per pass, we could change the **Amount** property located just under the **Emitting On** checkbox in the **Inspector** area. Finally, we changed the **Emission Shape** property so that the particles are rendered in a sphere instead of a point.

Next, we added a **GPUParticlesAttractorSphere3D** node and renamed it **AttractorSphere**. We changed the values of **Radius** and **Strength**. So long as the radius is touching the particles and the strength is high enough, the particles will go to the **AttractorSphere** node. Then, we toggled the visibility of the node *off* so that we could look at collisions.

We changed the particle amount to 64 and made the particles smaller at 0.2. We also increased the lifetime of the particles to see how **GPUParticleCollision** works. We went to **Collision** and changed it to **Rigid** from **Disabled** so that our collisions worked.

We also added a **GPUParticlesCollisionBox3D** and changed its name to **CollisionBox**. We made it a little bigger and set **Rotation** so that the particles hit the collision box and rolled down. We also moved the **GPUParticles3D** node higher so that the particles didn't sit on the slope we created.

We duplicated the **GPUParticles3D** node and changed the mesh to a box instead of a sphere so that we could see a difference when we turned on **Sub Emitter**. You could child the **GPUParticles3D2** node to the **GPUParticles3D** node, but this isn't required.

We went back to the **GPUParticles3D** node to add the new particle as a **Sub Emitter**. We set **Sub Emitter** to **At Collision** so that the new particle would appear when the first particle collides with something. If you change **Mode** to **At End**, the new particles will appear after they leave our ramp as they fall. If you change **Mode** to **Constant** and turn on **Keep Velocity**, it will change to a cube when it collides and will keep going down the ramp.

Trails

Next, we created a new scene and named it `Trails`. We added a **GPUParticles3D** node to the scene and clicked **Draw Passes** in the **Inspector** area to open its properties.

In **Pass 1**, we clicked **<empty>** to add a **New TubeTrailMesh**. We could have also selected **New RibbonTrailMesh** if we wanted to use a ribbon trail. Then, we changed the radius and section length to `.1m` to make it a little smaller.

In **Draw Passes**, we clicked the **Material** property and added a **New StandardMaterial3D**. After clicking on the material we just added, we went to the **Transform** property and clicked on **Use Particle Trails**. If you wish to add a texture, then click on **Albedo** and drag it into the **Texture** property.

We also added a new **ParticleProcessMaterial** and opened its properties. We changed the **Direction**, **Gravity**, and **Initial Velocity** values so that the tube goes up into the air.

We then changed the trails to make longer trails by adjusting the **Length Secs** and **Lifetime** properties. We added the number of particles that are emitted so that it could simulate an explosion.

Particles2D

In this final part, we created a new **2D Scene** and then added a **GPUParticle2D** node. We moved the two texture files that we wanted to use into Godot. We clicked on **Textures** under **Process Material** in the **Inspector** area and moved the `smoke_07.png` file to **<empty>** so that the particle texture looked like a storm cloud.

We changed the **Time, Emission Shape, Direction, Initial Velocity**, and **Scale** properties to make the cloud. We also turned on our **Sub Emitter** and added collision to set up our particle to use a sub-emitter later that will appear at the end of the cloud particle's life.

We made the cloud fuller by changing the **Amount** value and adding some randomness. We also created a new **GPUParticles2D** node as a child of the **Cloud** node and renamed it **Lightning**. In the **Cloud** node, we added the **Lightning** node as a **Sub Emitter**.

Next, we added the `spark_05.png` texture to the **Lightning** node we just added and changed the **y** value of **Gravity** to `500` so that the lightning would go down far enough past the cloud.

Finally, we turned on **Trails** and increased the lifetime of the lightning. We also changed the **Amount** property to `1` so that we only have one lightning bolt. Changing the **Speed Scale** property causes the lightning to go faster.

Using decals in your game

Decals are projected to a mesh, so you could use them for laser sight dots since it doesn't change the mesh they're projected on and can move. You can also use decals for when the player shoots a gun at a wall and bullet holes appear.

In this recipe, we will create a mesh and project the Godot icon onto it. We will make a wall and programmatically add the Godot icon to the wall so that you can add some bullet holes or spray paint tags, as a player could do in a game.

Getting ready

For this recipe, add a new **3D Scene** by clicking the + button to the right of the **Particles2D** scene. Then, save the scene as `Decals`.

You can also download the project from this book's GitHub repository.

How to do it...

Let's create a box mesh and project the Godot icon onto it so that you can use it for shadows or to add details to any background mesh:

1. Add a **Decal** node to the scene. Then, click **Textures** in the **Inspector** area to open its properties.
2. From the resource folder, drag the `icon.svg` file in the **FileSystem** tab to each of the **<empty>** boxes for **Albedo**, **Normal Orm**, and **Emission** in the **Textures** properties.
3. Click on **Node3D** and add a **MeshInstance3D** to the scene.
4. Click on **<empty>** to the right of the mesh in the **Inspector** area and select **New BoxMesh**. Click on **Transform** in the **Inspector** area to open the properties. Then, look to the right of **z** and click the chain icon to unlock the **Scale** settings. Change **x** to 3, **y** to 1, and **z** to 3:

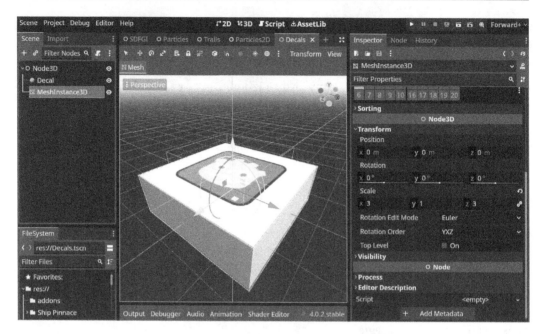

Figure 3.12 – MeshInstance3D Inspector Scale settings

5. Click on **Decal** in the **Scene** tab and then click **Parameters**, **Vertical Fade**, and **Distance Fade** in the **Inspector** area so that we can see what the properties do in the *How it works...* section.

Decals_World

We will make a wall and add a camera to use with the *Lightning_Decal* section. We will start by creating a new scene:

1. Let's create a new **3D Scene** and save it as Decals_World.

2. Rename **Node3D** to World. Then, add **Sun and World Environment** to the scene, as we did in the first recipe.

3. Click **World** and then add a **MeshInstance3D** to the scene. Rename it Ground.

4. In the **Inspector** area, click on <empty> to the right of **Mesh**. Click **New PlaneMesh** and then click on **Transform** in the **Inspector** area and change the **Scale** settings to x 10, y 10, and z 10.

5. Add a **Camera3D** to the **World** node in the **Scene** tab. Drag the free_look_camera.gd script to <empty> to the right of **Script** in the **Camera3D Inspector** area.

6. Click on **World** then add a **MeshInstance3D** to the scene and rename it Wall.

7. Click on **<empty>** to the right of the mesh and select **New BoxMesh**. Click on the **BoxMesh** property that was created to open its properties and click on **<empty>** to the right of **Material**. Then, select **New StandardMaterial3D**:

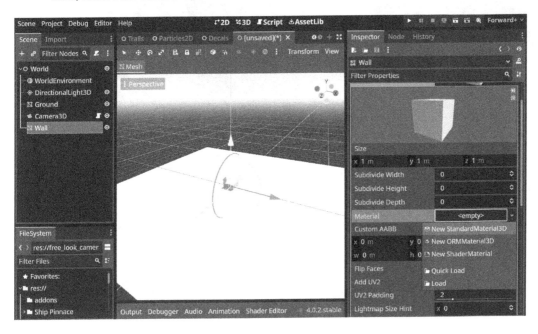

Figure 3.13 – Adding a New StandardMaterial3D to the wall

8. In the **Inspector** area, click on **Transform** under **Node3D** to open the properties. Under **Position**, change the **y** value to 2.46 and the **z** value to −5. Under **Scale**, make sure that you've clicked the link button on the right so that we can change each value separately. Change **x** to 15, **y** to 5, and **z** to 2.

9. In the top row, to the right of **View** and under the **Decals_World** tab, click on **Mesh** and select **Create Trimesh Static Body**:

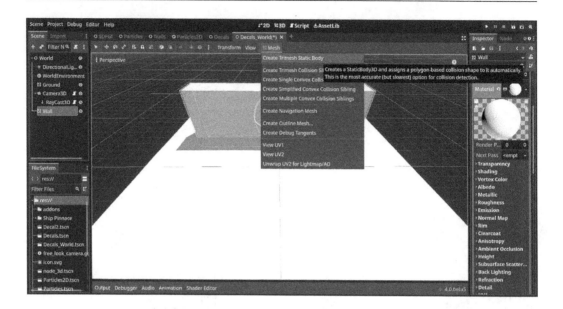

Figure 3.14 – Creating a Trimesh Static Body on the wall

10. Click **Camera3D** in the **Scene** tab and add a **RayCast3D** as a child to the camera. In the **Inspector** area, change the **Target Position** property of **y** to 0 and **z** to -20.

Lightning_Decal

In this part, we will create a lightning decal and a script so that we can see our lighting decals when we press the *spacebar* and point at the wall. We will start by creating a new scene:

1. Create a new **3D Scene** by clicking on the + button to the right of **Decals_World**. Save it as `Lightning_Decal`.

2. Add a **Decal** node to the scene. Click **Textures** in the **Inspector** area to open the texture's properties. Drag the `spark_05.png` file into **Albedo**, **Normal**, and **Emission**.

3. Change the **ESize x** value to 1, the **y** value to .356, and the **z** value to .471.

4. Click **Transform** in the **Inspector** area to open the properties. Change the **Rotation x** value to 90, the **Scale x** value to .1, the **Scale y** value to .5, and the **Scale z** value to .2. Save the scene.

5. Go back to the **Decals_World** scene and click on **RayCast3D**. Add a new script named `Player`.

6. Now, we are going to write some code that will get the **Lightning_Decal** node we just created. When the *spacebar* is pressed, the lightning PNG will be projected onto the wall. On *line 3*, drag **RayCast3D** in the **Scene** tab into the code after the equals (=) sign; it will apply $" . "$. Don't type that in because it won't work:

```
1    extends RayCast3D
2
3    @onready var raycast = $"."
4    @export var decal: PackedScene
5
6    func _unhandled_input(event):
7        if event.is_action_pressed("ui_select") and is_
colliding():
8            var new_decal = decal.instantiate()
9            raycast.get_collider().add_child(new_decal)
10           new_decal.global_transform.origin = raycast.get_
collision_point()
```

7. Click on **RayCast3D** in the **Scene** tab. Then, in the **Inspector** area, click on **<empty>** to the right of **Decal**. Select **Load** from the drop-down list and select `Lightning_Decal.tsn` to pack that scene into the variable decal in our code.

8. Click the **Run the Current Scene (F6)** icon. In the game window that appears, right-click and drag to move it and hit the *spacebar* to print the decal on the wall:

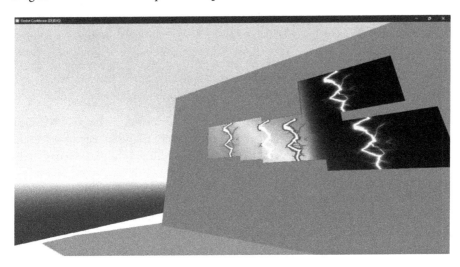

Figure 3.15 – Lightning decals on the wall

How it works...

In this recipe, we added a **Decal** node to the scene and added the Godot icon.svg file to the **Albedo**, **Normal**, **Orm**, and **Emission** properties. The **Albedo** or **Emission** properties must have a texture for the decal to be visible. The **Normal** and **Orm** textures add extra details to the texture.

Next, we added a **MeshInstance3D** to the scene. We opened the **Transform** properties in the **Inspector** area and clicked on the chain icon, which is to the right of **z**. We did this so that when we change the **Scale** values, they can have different values. We changed the **Scale** values to x 3, y 1, and z 3 to create a cube that is not as tall as its sides.

We also looked at the properties of the **Decal** node. In **Parameters**, the **Emission Energy** property changes the light intensity. The **Modulate** property changes the color of the decal. Finally, the **Albedo Mix** property blends the albedo color of the decal with the albedo color of the mesh.

Normal Fade will fade the decal if the angle of the decal and the target's surface is too large. The **Vertical Fade** property sets the fade as the surface goes over the center decal. The **Distance Fade** property sets how far away the decal will start fading before it disappears.

Then, we created a new scene and named it Decals_World. We added the **WorldEnvironment** and **DIrectionalLight3D** nodes. Then, we added a new **PlaneMesh** and named it Ground. We resized it to 10x10x10 so that we had some room to add a wall and a player to the scene later.

We added a **Camera3D** as a child and added the free_look_camera.gd script to the camera. We created a wall and adjusted its height and width. We moved back a bit so that our player has some room to move and shoot. We created a **Trimesh Static Body** on the wall so that we could detect collisions with ray casting.

We also added a **RayCast3D** node to **Camera3D** and changed the position of the raycast so that it points ahead of the player. We did this by changing the **y** position to 0 and the **z** position to -20.

Next, we created a new scene called Lightning_Decal and added the lightning PNG file to the **Albedo**, **Normal**, and **Emission** textures. We flipped the rotation of the **x** value to 90 so that the decal will face the wall when we add the decal to the wall. We adjusted the scale values so that the decal would be smaller.

After this, we went back to the Decals_World scene and added a script to the **RayCast3D** node. We created a variable named raycast equal to the **RayCast3D** node, and then a variable called decal as a PackedScene, where we hooked it up by loading the Lightning_Decal scene into the decal variable that we exported using @Export var decal: PackedScene so that we could see it in the **Inspector** area.

We also created an _unhandled_input event that looks for ui-select and whether the raycast is colliding with something. ui-select can be found under **Project Settings | Input Map** and is activated when the *spacebar* is pressed or joypad button 3 is pressed.

Finally, we instantiated a new decal and added it to the raycast. By doing this, the new decal is moved to where the raycast was when the *spacebar* is pressed:

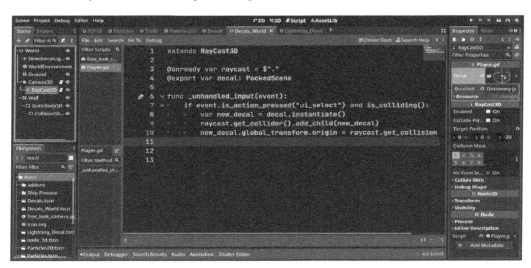

Figure 3.16 – Code for Player.gd and RayCast3D Inspector properties

We ran the current scene and pressed the *spacebar* to see the lightning decal project on the wall where our raycast was pointing. This is how you create bullet holes.

4

Practicing Physics and Handling Navigation in Godot 4

In this chapter, we start by looking at the effect that the **GPUParticlesCollisonHeightField3D** node has on 3D terrain. We will use the **GPUParticlesCollisonHeightField3D** node with some 3D terrain and create snow with particles to see how it interacts with the 3D terrain. With the new **CharacterBody2D** and **CharacterBody3D** that replaced kinematic bodies, we will create a 2D and 3D player.

We will see how easy scripting the **CharacterBody** is compared to Godot 3.x. We will look at the **NavigationServer** for 3D and 2D projects. Lastly, we will make a banner to show how the **SoftBody3D** nodes work.

In this chapter, we will cover the following recipes:

- Using Heightmap for 3D terrain
- Setting up and moving the **CharacterBody** in 2D
- Setting up and moving the **CharacterBody** in 3D
- Using the new **NavigationServer** for 3D
- Using **NavigationServer2D** for 2D projects
- Using **SoftBody** for 3D games

Technical requirements

For this chapter, you need the standard version of Godot 4.0 or later running on one of the following:

- Windows 64-bit or 32-bit
- macOS
- Linux 64-bit or 32-bit

- Android

- Web Editor

You can find the code and the files for the projects in this chapter on GitHub at `https://github.com/PacktPublishing/Godot-4-Game-Development-Cookbook/tree/main/Chapter%204`.

Using Heightmap for 3D terrain

In this recipe, we'll make a basic 3D scene with ground and cubes of various heights. We'll use the **GPUParticlesCollisonHeightField3D** node to add a 3D heightmap to the scene. We'll create snow using particles and see how the **GPUParticlesCollisonHeightField3D** node interacts with the particles on the ground and on top of the cubes in the scene.

Getting ready

For this recipe, open Godot 4 and start a new project called `Chapter 4`. In the **Scene** tab, click **3D** to add a 3D scene. Click on the word **Scene** in the top-left corner next to **Project**, then select **Save Scene As** and name it `Heightmap`.

How to do it...

In this recipe, we will create a 3D scene with cubes of various heights and snow using particles. When we add the **GPUParticlesCollisonHeightField3D** node, the snow will land on all of the surfaces no matter how tall:

1. Right-click on **Node3D** in the **Scene** tab and rename it `World`.

2. Left-click the three vertical dots to the left of the **Transform** View on the viewport toolbar.

3. Add the **Sun** and **Environment** nodes to the scene by left-clicking the **Add Environment to Scene** button at the bottom while holding down the *Shift* key.

4. Left-click on the **World** node and then click the + sign in the **Scene** tab. In the **Create New Node** window, type `mesh` in the **Search** box and then select **MeshInstance3D** to create the node in the scene.

5. Right-click the **MeshInstance3D** node in the **Scene** tab and rename it `Ground`.

6. In the **Inspector**, click on **<empty>** to the right of **Mesh** and select **New PlaneMesh**.

7. Left-click on the same place to open the properties of the **Ground** mesh.

8. In the **Inspector**, change the **Size** property of **x** and **y** to `15`.

9. Click on <empty> to the right of **Material** in the **Inspector** and select **New StandardMaterial3D** from the drop-down list.

10. Click on the same place that you did in *step 9* to open the **Material** properties.

11. In the **Material** properties, click **Albedo** and then click the white bar on the right of **Color**.

12. Leave the **R** value at 255. Change the **G** value to 0 and the **B** value to 0.

13. Make sure **Ground** in the **Scene** tab is still selected and then click + to add a new **MeshInstance3D**, as we did in *step 4.*

14. Click <empty> to the right of **Mesh** and select **New BoxMesh**.

15. Left-click on the same place to open the properties of the **BoxMesh**.

16. Click on <empty> to the right of **Material** in the **Inspector** and select **New StandardMaterial3D** from the drop-down list.

17. Left-click on the same place that you did in *step 16* to open the **Material** properties.

18. In the **Material** properties, click **Albedo** and then click the white bar on the right of **Color**.

19. Leave the **B** value at 255. Change the **G** value to 0 and the **R** value to 0.

20. Left-click on **Mesh**, which is to the right of the **Transform** View in the toolbar at the top of the viewport and select **Create Trimesh Static Body**.

21. You can click to the left of **MeshInstance3D** to hide the **StaticBody3D** and **CollisionShape3D** children we just added.

22. Click **MeshInstance3D**, which we just created, and then *Ctrl + D* to duplicate it four more times so that we have five cubes.

23. Move each of the cubes around to space them out. Click **Select Mode (Q)** located at the top left of the viewport with an icon that looks like a mouse pointer or press the *Q* button.

24. For each of the cubes, click on **Scale Mode (R)** located at the top of the viewport or press the *R* button and resize each cube to different sizes—for instance, some taller, some smaller, and others wider:

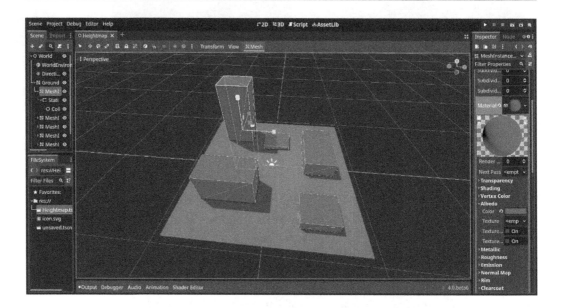

Figure 4.1 – Various cube sizes to demonstrate the Heightmap

25. Left-click on the **World** node and then click + in the **Scene** tab. In the **Create New Node** window, type GPU in the **Search** box and then select **GPUParticles3D** to create the node in the scene.

26. Right-click on **GPUParticles3D** and select **Rename** to rename this node Snow.

27. In the **Inspector**, under **Emitting**, change **Amount** to 500.

28. Click **Time** to open the properties and change **Lifetime** to 2 s.

29. In the **Inspector**, click **Process Material** to open its properties.

30. Click <empty> to the right of **Process Material** and select **New ParticleProcessMaterial**.

31. Left-click on **ParticleProcessMaterial**, which is in the same place as in *step 30*. This opens its properties.

32. Left-click **Emission Shape** to open its properties. To the right of **Shape**, left-click **Point** and select **Box**.

33. Change the **Box Extents** values on **x** and **z** to 5.

34. Left-click on **Direction** to see its properties and change the value of **x** to 0 and the value of **y** to −1.

35. Left-click on **Scale** to open its properties and change the values of **Scale Min** and **Scale Max** to 0.2.

36. Left-click **Collision** to open its properties and left-click **Disabled**, which is to the right of **Mode**, and select **Rigid** in the drop-down list.

37. Click on **Draw Processes** to open its properties.

38. Click on **<empty>** to the right of **Pass 1** and select **New SphereMesh**.

39. Left-click on **SphereMesh** to the right of **Pass 1**, which is in the same place as in *step 38*. This opens its properties.

40. Click on **<empty>** to the right of **Material** in the **Inspector** and select **New StandardMaterial3D** from the drop-down list.

41. In the **Inspector**, scroll down toward the bottom, and under **Node3D**, click **Transform** to open its properties.

42. Under **Position**, change the **y** value to `10`.

43. Under **Scale**, make sure the link icon to the right of the **z** value is clicked so that you can change each value individually. Then, change the **x** value to `1.8`, the **y** value to `3`, and the **z** value to `1.8`.

44. Left-click on the **World** node and then click on + in the **Scene** tab. In the **Create New Node** window, type `GPU` in the **Search** box and then select **GPUParticlesCollisionHeightField3D** to create the node in the scene.

45. In the **Size** properties, change the **x**, **y**, and **z** values to `20`. Notice that the snow is stopping on the different-sized cubes.

How it works...

We renamed the **Node3D** that was created when we added a 3D scene to **World**. Then, we added the **WorldEnvironment** and **DirectionalLight3D** nodes to the scene. If you hold down the *Shift* key and left-click on either of the buttons at the bottom, you can add both nodes at the same time. We have light in the scene so that we can see better.

We added a **MeshInstance3D** node as a child to **World**. We renamed the node **Ground**. We changed the size of the ground to 15 x 15 to give us some room to add cubes later. We added a new **StandardMaterial3D** so that we can change the color of the ground to red. We did that so that we can easily see the snow particles, which we will create later.

We added a **MeshInstance3D** node to the scene as a child of **Ground**. We added a new **BoxMesh** to the **Mesh** property and then added a new **StandardMaterial3D** to the **Material** property. In the **StandardMaterial3D** properties, we changed the **Albedo** material to the color blue.

We added a **StaticBody3D** and **CollisionShape3D** by clicking on **Create Trimesh Static Body** when we left-clicked on **Mesh**, which is to the right of the **Transform** View at the top of the Viewport. This is easier to do by only clicking on **Create Trimesh Static Body**.

We also clicked on the down arrow to the left of **MeshInstance3D** to hide the **StaticBody3D** and **CollisionShape3D** children because we will duplicate this cube later and it saves space in the **Scene** tab.

We duplicated the cube we created four times so that we have five cubes. We then moved them using **Select Mode (Q)** to space them out on the ground area. We changed to **Scale Mode (R)** to change the height and width of the cubes so that we can see after adding the Heightmap that the particles will stay on the top of each surface of the cube, no matter the height of the cube.

We created a **GPUParticles3D** as a child of the **World** node and renamed it **Snow**. In the **Inspector**, we changed the value of **Amount** to 500, and in the **Time** properties, we changed the **Lifetime** value to 2 s. The **Amount** value is how many particles we will emit, and the **Lifetime** value is how long the particles will last.

We clicked **Process Material** to see its properties. We added a new **ParticleProcessMaterial** to the **Process Material**. We changed **Emission Shape** to **Box** and changed the **Box Extents x** and **z** values to 5. This is so that the snow will fall in the same area as the ground. We changed the **Direction** property value of **y** to −1 so that the particles will fall downward. We changed the **Scale** property **Min** and **Max** values to 0.2 to decrease the size of the particles. We changed the **Collision** property **Mode** type to **Rigid** so that the **GPUParticlesCollisionHeightField3D** node will work.

We clicked on **Draw Passes** in the **Inspector** to see its properties. Then, we clicked on **<empty>** to the right of **Pass 1** and selected a new **SphereMesh** for the shape of our snow. We added a **StandardMaterial3D** to the **Material** property.

Toward the bottom of the **Inspector**, we clicked **Transform** to open its properties. We changed the **Position** property of **y** to 10 to raise the snow higher. We changed the **Scale x**, **y**, and **z** properties to expand the snow to cover the area of the ground. Remember to click the link icon, which is to the right of the **z** value. If you don't click that, all of the values will change to the one that you selected.

We left-clicked on the **World** node and then added a **GPUParticlesCollisionHeightField3D** node to the scene. We changed the **Size** property values to 20 on **x**, **y**, and **z**. This increased the area of the **GPUParticlesCollisionHeightField3D** node to cover the **Ground** node. Now, we can see the snow hitting the tops of the cubes when it collides with them, no matter how tall the cube is.

Setting up and moving the CharacterBody in 2D

In this recipe, we set up a 2D player character with the new **CharacterBody2D** node that replaced the kinematic bodies used in Godot 3.x. We will use free assets by Kenney for the player's idle, jump, fall, and walk animation.

The **CharacterBody2D** node has a basic default movement script that we will add to the player and modify the script to show the animations.

Getting ready

For this recipe, click the + sign to the right of the Heightmap scene we just completed to add a new scene. In the **Scene** tab, click on **Other Node**, and in the **Search** box that appears, type cha and select **CharacterBody2D**, then click the **Create** button. Now, we have **CharacterBody2D** as the base node for this scene. Click on the word **Scene** in the main menu next to **Project**, then select **Save Scene As** and name it `Player2D`.

Download Platformer Characters by Kenney from `https://www.kenney.nl/assets/` `platformer-characters` and extract it to a new folder.

How to do it...

We will create a player character using **CharacterBody2D** and use the default script that you can use to move the player:

1. In the **FileSystem** tab, right-click on **res://** and select **New Folder**. Name the folder `Art`.

2. After downloading the `Platformer Characters` files to a new folder, open the folder you created.

3. Open the `PNG` folder and then open the `Player` folder. You can use whichever one you want but I will use `Player` for this recipe.

4. Open the `Poses` folder and drag `player_idle`, `player_stand`, `player_fall.png`, `player_jump.png`, `player_walk1`, and `player_walk2` into the `Art` folder that we created in the **FileSystem** tab.

5. Left-click on the + sign above the **CharacterBody2D** node to bring up the **Create New Node** window.

6. In the **Search** box, type `anim` and select **AnimatedSprite2D**.

7. Click on **Animation** in the **Inspector**, then click on **<empty>** to the right of **Frames** and **New SpriteFrames**.

8. Left-click on **SpriteFrames**, which is now where **<empty>** was, so that we can see the **SpriteFrames Animations** at the bottom.

9. Under **Animations**, left-click on **Default** to rename the animation and type `idle`.

10. If the `Art` folder is not open, then double-click on the folder to open it.

11. Select `player_idle.png`, hold the *Shift* key, and then select `player_stand.png`. Drag the files into the space under **Animation Frames**.

12. Left-click on **5 FPS** located above **Filter Animations** to change **Speed** to `10`:

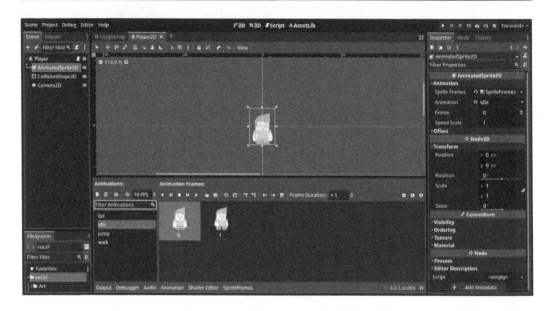

Figure 4.2 – Bottom panel: SpriteFrames animation

13. Under **Animations**, click the ⬚ icon to add a new animation.

14. Click **new_animation** and rename it `walk`.

15. Select `player_walk1.png`, hold the *Shift* key, and then select `player_walk2.png`. Drag the files into the space under **Animation Frames**.

16. Left-click on **5 FPS** located under **Walk** to change **Speed:** to `10`.

17. To see the animation running, click on the **Play selected animation from start** button located four icons to the right of 10 FPS above the first animation sprite or press *Shift + D*.

18. Click on the ⬚ icon, then click **new_animation** and rename it `jump`.

19. Select the `player_jump.png` file in the `Art` folder and drag it into the space under `Animation Frames`.

20. Left-click on **5 FPS** located under `walk` to change **Speed** to `10`.

21. Click on the ⬚ icon, then click **new_animation** and rename it `fall`.

22. Select the `player_fall.png` file in the `Art` folder and drag it into the space under **Animation Frames**.

23. Left-click **5 FPS** located under `walk` to change **Speed** to `10`.

24. To look at the other animations in the **Inspector**, left-click on **walk**, which is to the right of **Animation**, and select **idle** in the drop-down list of animations. You can also click on the animation in the **SpriteFrames** editor and run the animation.

25. Left-click on **CharacterBody2D** in the **Scene** tab.

26. Left-click on the + sign above the **CharacterBody2D** node to bring up the **Create New Node** window.

27. In the **Search** box, type `coll` and select **CollisionShape2D** to create a **CollisionShape2D** node.

28. In the **Inspector,** for **CollisionShape2D**, click **<empty>** to the right of **Shape** and select **New CapsuleShape2D**.

29. Using the dots at the bottom and on the right, resize the **CapsuleShape2D** to fit the player.

30. Resize the **CapsuleShape2D**:

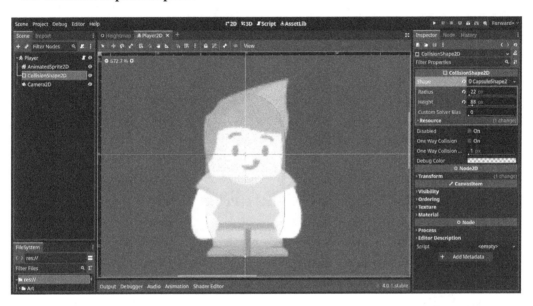

Figure 4.3 – Resizing the CapsuleShape2D

31. Left-click on the + sign above the **CharacterBody2D** node to bring up the **Create New Node** window.

32. In the **Search** box, type `cam` and select **Camera2D** to create a **Camera2D** node.

33. In the **Inspector,** to the right of **Enabled**, left-click on **On**.

34. Right-click **CharacterBody2D** in the **Scene** tab and select **Rename** and then rename it `Player`.

35. In the **Inspector,** at the bottom, to the right of **Script**, click on **<empty>** and select **New Script**.

36. In **Path**, name the file `Player.gd`. Click on the **Template** checkbox to the right of **Template**. Notice to the right of **Template** is **CharacterBody2D Basic Movement**. Click **Create** at the bottom:

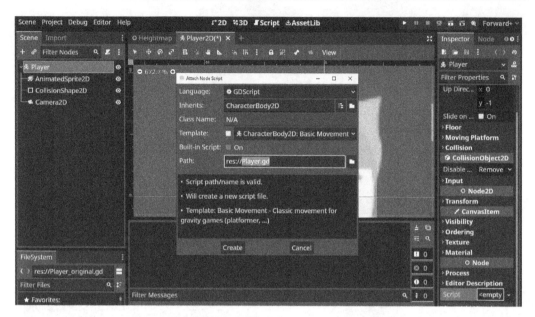

Figure 4.4 – CharacterBody2D Basic Movement template

37. Click the + sign to the right of **Player2D**, then in the **Scene** tab, left-click **Node2D**.

38. Click on the word **Scene** in the main menu next to **Project**, then select **Save Scene As** or press *Ctrl* + *Shift* + *S* and name it Platform2D.

39. In the **FileSystem** tab, grab the Player2D.tscn file and drag it into the scene.

40. Grab the Icon.svg file in the **FileSystem** tab and drag it into the scene. Position and stretch the icon under the player so that we have a platform.

41. Left-click on the + sign above the **Node2D** node to bring up the **Create New Node** window.

42. In the **Search** box, type static and select **StaticBody2D** to create a **StaticBody2D** node as a child of **Icon**.

43. Left-click on the + sign above the **Node2D** node to bring up the **Create New Node** window.

44. In the **Search** box, type coll and select **CollisionShape2D** to create a **CollisionShape2D** node as a child of **StaticBody2D**.

45. In the **Inspector** for **CollisionShape2D**, click <empty> to the right of **Shape** and select **New RectangleShape2D**.

46. Use the dots at the top, bottom, right, and left to resize the **RectangleShape2D** to fit the **Icon** we are using as a platform:

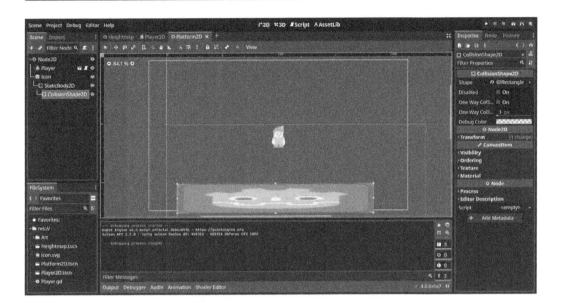

Figure 4.5 – Platform with RigidBody2D and CollisionShape2D

47. Click on **Script** at the top of the screen to see the `player.gd` script.

48. Under `var gravity = ProjectSettings.get_setting("physics/2d/default_gravity")` on *line 8*, enter the following code:

```
9 @onready var animated_sprite = $AnimatedSprite2D
```

49. We will add the following to the `func _physics_process(delta):` function:

```
11 func _physics_process(delta):
12    # Add the gravity.
13    if not is_on_floor():
14       velocity.y += gravity * delta
15       if velocity.y <= 0:
16          animated_sprite.animation = "jump"
17       else:
18          animated_sprite.animation = "fall"
19    else:
20       if velocity.x == 0:
21          animated_sprite.animation = "idle"
22       else:
23          animated_sprite.animation = "walk"
24    # Handle Jump.
25    if Input.is_action_just_pressed("ui_accept") and is_on_
floor():
```

```
26        velocity.y = JUMP_VELOCITY
27
28    # Get the input direction and handle the movement/
deceleration.
29    # As good practice, you should replace UI actions with
custom gameplay actions.
30    var direction = Input.get_axis("ui_left", "ui_right")
31    if direction:
32        velocity.x = direction * SPEED
33        if velocity.x < 0:
34            animated_sprite.flip_h = true
35        elif velocity.x > 0:
36            animated_sprite.flip_h = false
37
38    else:
39        velocity.x = move_toward(velocity.x, 0, SPEED)
40
41    move_and_slide()
```

In the **Platform2D** scene, click the **Run the current scene** button in the upper-right corner of the editor or hit the *F6* key. Use the arrow keys to move the player and the *spacebar* to jump.

How it works...

We created a new folder called Art under the **FileSystem** tab so that we can place our player_idle, player_stand, player_walk1, and player_walk2 PNG files that we downloaded in the *Getting ready* section of this recipe.

We added **AnimatedSprite2D** as a child node to CharacterBody2D so that we can add idle and walk animations for our player.

We added a new **SpriteFrames** to **Frames** in the **AnimatedSprite2D Inspector**. We renamed **default** to **idle**. We dragged the player_idle.png and player_stand.png files at the same time by holding *Shift* after selecting the first PNG file. As long as the second PNG file is right behind the first, it will select both. If the files are spread out, you can hold down the *Ctrl* (*Cmd* on Mac) button and select each file.

We then added a new animation named **walk**. Dragging player_walk1.png and player_walk2.png into **Animation Frames**, we created a walking animation. We added a jump and fall animation by creating a new animation and dragging the PNG files into the respective animations.

We changed all of the animation speeds to 10 to make it look better. Lastly, we looked at the animations by clicking the **Play selected animation from start** button in the animation editor or pressing *Shift* + *D*. To change which animation is showing, click to the right of **Animation** in the **Inspector** to select the animation you want to see.

We selected the **CharacterBody2D** parent node so that we could add a **CollisionShape2D** node as a child. We added the **CollisionShape2D** and resized it to fit the player. We also added a **Camera2D** node as a child of the **CharacterBody2D** node. In the **Inspector**, we left-clicked on **On** in the **Enabled** property. Now, if we run the current scene (by pressing *F6*), the camera will center on the player we just created.

We renamed the **CharacterBody2D** parent node **Player**. We added a new script called `Player.gd`. We saw that when we created the script, there was a default template called **CharacterBody2D Basic Movement** that already has very basic movement code that we can use without writing code from scratch.

We created a new scene called **Platform2D**. We dragged the **Player2D** scene into the **Platform2D** scene to use the player in this scene. We dragged the `Icon.svg` file into the scene and then stretched it so that there is room for the player to run. We added a **StaticBody2D** as a child to the `Icon.svg` file so that it will react to physics. We then added a **CollisionShape2D** as a child to the **StaticBody2D** to give the player something to stand on.

We edited the `Player.gd` script to get the animations to work. We added an `@onready` annotation to *line 9* to assign the **AnimatedSprite2D** node to the `animated_sprite` variable. *Lines 15-18* check to see if the `velocity.y` value is negative and, if so, then it shows the jump animation.

If it is positive, then it shows the fall animation. *Lines 19-23* check to see if the `velocity.x` value is 0, in which case it shows the idle animation, but if it's not, then it shows the walk animation. *Lines 33-36* check to see if the `velocity.x` value is less than 0 or going to the left, then flip the animation by assigning `true` to `flip_h`.

If the `velocity.x` value is greater than 0 or going to the right, then show the default animation by assigning `false` to `flip_h`. We clicked **Run** in the **Platform2D** scene to see how it looks.

Setting up and moving the CharacterBody in 3D

In this recipe, we set up a third-person 3D player character prototype with the new **CharacterBody3D** node. We will create a scene with ground and the player prototype, for which we use a **CapsuleMesh** with a **BoxMesh** for the gun. We place a camera behind the player for a third-person perspective. We add to the **CharacterBody3D** node the new **CharacterBody3D: Basic Movement** template found in the **Template** section when creating a new script.

Getting ready

For this recipe, click the + sign to the right of the **Platform2D** scene we just completed to add a new scene. In the **Scene** tab, click **3D Scene**. Right-click on **Node3D** and select **Rename** in the drop-down list and rename it `World`. Click on the word **Scene** in the main menu next to **Project**, then select **Save Scene As** and name it **Ground3D**.

How to do it...

Let's create a world scene with ground and a player with a camera following the player:

1. Left-click the three vertical dots on the left of the **Transform** View on the Viewport toolbar.

2. Add the **Sun** and **Environment** nodes to the scene by left-clicking the **Add Environment to Scene** button at the bottom while holding down the *Shift* key.

3. Left-click on the **World** node and then the + sign in the **Scene** tab. In the **Create New Node** window, type `mesh` in the **Search** box and then select **MeshInstance3D** to create the node in the scene.

4. Right-click the **MeshInstance3D** node in the **Scene** tab and rename it `Ground`.

5. In the **Inspector**, click on <**empty**> to the right of **Mesh** and select **New PlaneMesh**.

6. Left-click on the same place to open the properties of the **Ground** mesh.

7. In the **Inspector**, change the **Size** property of **x** and **y** to `20`.

8. Left-click on **Mesh**, which is to the right of the **Transform** View in the toolbar above the Viewport.

9. Select **Create Trimesh Static Body** from the drop-down list.

10. Click the + sign to the right of the **Ground3D** scene we just completed to add a new scene. In the **Scene** tab, click **Other Node**, and in the **Search** box that appears, type `cha` and select **CharacterBody3D**, then click the **Create** button.

11. Right-click on **CharacterBody3D** and select **Rename** from the drop-down list to rename it `Player`.

12. Click on the word **Scene** in the main menu next to **Project**, then select **Save Scene As** and name it `Player3D`.

13. Left-click on the **Player** node and then the + sign in the **Scene** tab. In the **Create New Node** window, type `mesh` in the **Search** box and then select **MeshInstance3D** to create the node in the scene.

14. Right-click on **MeshInstance3D** and select **Rename** from the drop-down list and rename it `Body`.

15. In the **Inspector**, click on <**empty**> to the right of **Mesh** and select **New CapsuleMesh**.

16. Left-click on the **Player** node and then the + sign in the **Scene** tab. In the **Create New Node** window, type `mesh` in the **Search** box and then select **MeshInstance3D** to create the node in the scene.

17. Right-click on **MeshInstance3D** and select **Rename** from the drop-down list to rename it `Gun`.

18. In the **Inspector**, click on <**empty**> to the right of **Mesh** and select **New BoxMesh**.

19. Left-click **Scale Mode (R)** on the toolbar above the viewport or press the *R* key.

20. Shape the **BoxMesh** into a long rectangle and position it in the middle and to the right side of the body by left-clicking **Select Mode (Q)** or pressing the *Q* key:

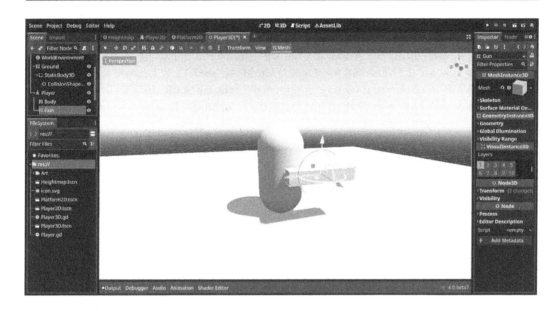

Figure 4.6 – BoxMesh shape and position

21. Left-click on the **Player** node and then the + sign in the **Scene** tab. In the **Create New Node** window, type `coll` in the **Search** box and then select **CollisionShape3D** to create the node in the scene.

22. Click on **<empty>** to the right of **Shape** in the **Inspector** and select **New CapsuleShape3D**.

23. Left-click on the **Player** node and then the + sign in the **Scene** tab. In the **Create New Node** window, type `cam` in the **Search** box and then select **Camera3D** to create the node in the scene.

24. Click on **Camera3D** in the **Scene** tab, making sure **Select Mode (Q)** is selected. Left-click and drag the blue **z** arrow so that the camera is behind the player.

25. Use the green **y** arrow to pull the player up so that its **y** value is `1`. Or, you could click **Transform** in the **Inspector** and change the **y** value in **Position** to `1`.

26. Click on the **Player** node, and in the **Inspector**, at the bottom, click **<empty>** on the right of **Script** and select **New Script** from the drop-down list.

27. In the **Path,** change the name of the script to `Player3D.gd` and click on the **Template** checkbox to the right of **Template** if it isn't already checked. Notice to the right of **Template:** is **CharacterBody3D: Basic Movement**, then click **Create**.

28. Click on the **Ground3D** scene, and in the **FileSystem** tab, select `Player3D.tsn` and drag it to **World** in the **Scene** tab.

29. In the **Ground3D** scene, click the **Run the current scene** button in the upper-right corner of the editor or hit the *F6* key. Use the arrow keys to move the player and the spacebar to jump.

How it works...

We added **DirectionalLight3D** and **WorldEnvironment** to the scene by clicking on the three vertical dots in the toolbar above the Viewport. We added a **MeshInstance3D** and assigned the type of the mesh as **PlaneMesh**. We renamed it **Ground** and created a **Trimesh Static Body** by left-clicking on **Mesh** in the toolbar, which added a **StaticBody3D** and **CollisionShape3D** to the **Ground** so that our player won't fall through the ground.

We created a new **CharacterBody3D** scene and named it **Player3D**. We added a **MeshInstance3D** node as a child to the **CharacterBody3D** and gave it a **CapsuleMesh**, then we renamed it **Body**. We added another **MeshInstance3D** and shaped it into a small rectangle and moved it to the middle and to the right of the body capsule to simulate a gun. We also renamed the rectangle **Gun**.

We created a **CollisionShape3D** for the **Body** to detect collisions. We created a **Camera3D** and then moved it behind the player so that we have a third-person game instead of a first-person one. The camera follows the player wherever it goes because it is a child of the **Player** node.

We moved the player up to ground level by changing the **y Transform** value to 1 in the **Inspector** or by selecting **Select Mode (Q)**. We did this so that when we use this scene in the **Ground3D** scene, it will be on the ground and not in the middle.

We added a new script to the **Player** node that includes the **CharacterBody3D: Basic Movement** template and named it `Player3D.gd`. As long as the script is on a **CharacterBody3D**, the template will be available to use instead of writing your own code from scratch.

You can use the template for a quick basic movement system that allows the player to move left, right, up, and down, along with the ability to jump. You can change the `SPEED` and `JUMP_VELOCITY` constant variables to move faster and jump higher. The `gravity` variable in the template is tied to the default gravity setting in **Project Settings**.

This means it is using the same gravity value as **RigidBody** nodes. You will want to change the variable input direction to joysticks or to different keys besides just the arrow keys. We dragged the `Player3D.tsn` scene into the **Ground3D** scene from the **FileSystem** tab to the **Scene** tab. Then, we ran the current scene to see how the movement and jump felt.

Using the new NavigationServer for 3D

In this recipe, we will create a scene with obstacles and create a **CharacterBody3D** capsule to navigate from one end of the world to the other. We will use the **NavigationRegion3D** node to set up the area on the map where we can travel. We will use **NavigationAgent3D** on the **CharacterBody3D** to interact with **NavigationRegion3D** to move along the navigation path.

Getting ready

For this recipe, click the + sign to the right of the **Player3D** scene we just completed to add a new scene. In the **Scene** tab, click **3D Scene**. Right-click on **Node3D** and select **Rename** in the drop-down list and rename it World. Click on the word **Scene** in the main menu next to **Project**, then select **Save Scene As** and name it NavServer3D.

How to do it...

First, we will create an area with obstacles so that we can set up an area that we can travel in on the map:

1. Left-click the three vertical dots on the left of the **Transform** View on the Viewport toolbar.

2. Add the **Sun** and **Environment** nodes to the scene by left-clicking the **Add Environment to Scene** button at the bottom while holding down the *Shift* key.

3. Left-click on the **World** node and then the + sign in the **Scene** tab. In the **Create New Node** window, type mesh in the **Search** box and then select **MeshInstance3D** to create the node in the scene.

4. Right-click the **MeshInstance3D** node in the **Scene** tab and rename it Ground.

5. In the **Inspector**, click on <empty> to the right of **Mesh** and select **New PlaneMesh**.

6. Left-click on the same place to open the properties of the **Ground** mesh.

7. In the **Inspector**, change the **Size** property of **x** and **y** to 20.

8. Left-click on **Mesh**, which is to the right of the **Transform** View in the toolbar above the Viewport.

9. Select **Create Trimesh Static Body** from the drop-down list.

10. Click on <empty> to the right of **Material** in the **Inspector** and select **New StandardMaterial3D** from the drop-down list.

11. Click on the same place that you did in *step 10* to open the **Material** properties.

12. In the **Material** properties, click **Albedo** and then click the white bar to the right of **Color**.

13. Leave the **R** and **G** values at 255. Change the **B** value to 60.

14. Left-click on the down arrow on the left of **Ground** in the **Scene** tab to hide the child nodes of **Ground**.

15. Left-click on the **World** node and then the + sign in the **Scene** tab. In the **Create New Node** window, select the white node at the very top of **Matches** under the **Search** box.

16. Right-click on the white node and select **Rename** from the drop-down list and rename it Walls.

17. Left-click on **Walls** in the **Scene** tab and then the + sign in the **Scene** tab. In the **Create New Node** window, type mesh in the **Search** box and then select **MeshInstance3D** to create the node in the scene.

18. Right-click the **MeshInstance3D** node in the **Scene** tab and rename it `Wall`.

19. In the **Inspector**, click on **<empty>** to the right of **Mesh** and select **New BoxMesh**.

20. Left-click on **Mesh**, which is to the right of the **Transform** View at the top of the Viewport, and select **Create Trimesh Static Body**.

21. Using **Scale Mode (R)** and **Select Mode (Q)**, resize and position the walls around the edges of the ground. After the first wall is positioned, press *Ctrl + D* on that wall and move on to the next wall, and continue until the walls look like the ones shown in *Figure 4.7*:

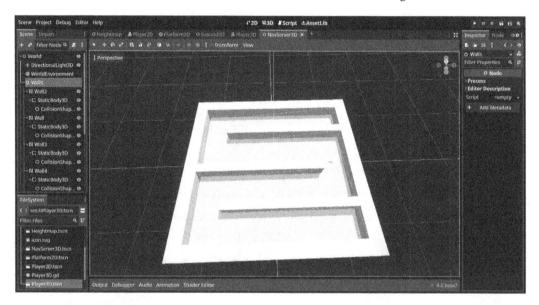

Figure 4.7 – Wall positions for a navigation path

22. Click the arrow to the left of the white **Walls** node in the **Scene** tab to hide the child nodes of **Wall**.

23. Left-click on **World** in the **Scene** tab, then the + sign in the **Scene** tab. In the **Create New Node** window, type `nav` in the **Search** box and then select **NavigationRegion3D** to create the node in the scene.

24. Left-click the **Ground** and **Walls** nodes in the **Scene** tab and drag them onto the **NavigationRegion3D** node.

25. In the **Inspector**, to the right of **NavMesh**, click on **<empty>** and select **New NavigationMesh**.

26. To the right of the **Transform** View, in the toolbar above the Viewport, left-click on **Bake NavMesh**.

27. Left-click on the **World** node and then the + sign in the **Scene** tab. In the **Create New Node** window, type `char` in the **Search** box and then select **CharacterBody3D** to create the node in the scene.

28. Left-click on the **CharacterBody3D** node and then the + sign in the **Scene** tab. In the **Create New Node** window, type `mesh` in the **Search** box and then select **MeshInstance3D** to create the node in the scene.

29. In the **Inspector**, click on <empty> to the right of **Mesh** and select **New CapsuleMesh**.

30. Left-click on the **CharacterBody3D** node and then the + sign in the **Scene** tab. In the **Create New Node** window, type `coll` in the **Search** box and then select **CollisionShape3D** to create the node in the scene.

31. Click on <empty> to the right of **Shape** in the **Inspector** and select **New CapsuleShape3D**.

32. Left-click on the **CharacterBody3D** node and then the + sign in the **Scene** tab. In the **Create New Node** window, type `nav` in the **Search** box and then select **NavigationAgent3D** to create the node in the scene.

33. Left-click on the **CharacterBody3D** node, and in the **Inspector**, click **Transform** to open the properties.

34. Change the **Position x** value to 8.5, the **y** value to 1, and the **z** value to 8.

35. Left-click on **World** in the **Scene** tab then the + sign in the **Scene** tab. In the **Create New Node** window, type `cam` in the **Search** box and then select **Camera3D** to create the node in the scene.

36. In the **Inspector**, click **Transform** to see the properties.

37. In **Position**, change the value of **y** to 14.

38. In **Rotation**, change the value of **x** to -90.

39. Left-click on the **CharacterBody3D** node in the **Scene** tab.

40. In the **Inspector**, at the bottom, to the right of **Script**, click on <empty> and select **New Script**.

41. In the **Attach Node Script** window to the right of **Path**, change the name of the script to `PathAI`, and to the right of **Template**, click the check mark to get rid of the template. It should say **Empty** now:

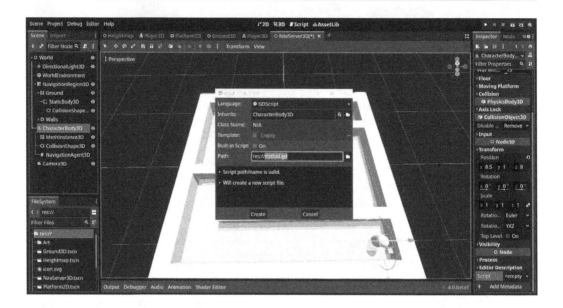

Figure 4.8 – Attach Node Script window

42. Click on the **Create** button to create the new script.

43. Enter the following code to the empty `PathAI` script:

```
1    extends CharacterBody3D
3    const SPEED = 15
5    @onready var nav_agent = $NavigationAgent3D
7    var target = Vector3(8.5, 1, -7)
9    func _ready():
10        nav_agent.set_target_position(target)
12   func _physics_process(delta):
13        if nav_agent.is_target_reachable():
14            var next_location = nav_agent.get_next_path_
position()
15            var direction = global_transform.origin.
direction_to(next_location).normalized() * SPEED
16            global_position += direction * delta
17            move_and_slide()
```

44. In the **NavServer3D** scene, click the **Run the current scene** button in the upper-right corner of the editor or hit the *F6* key:

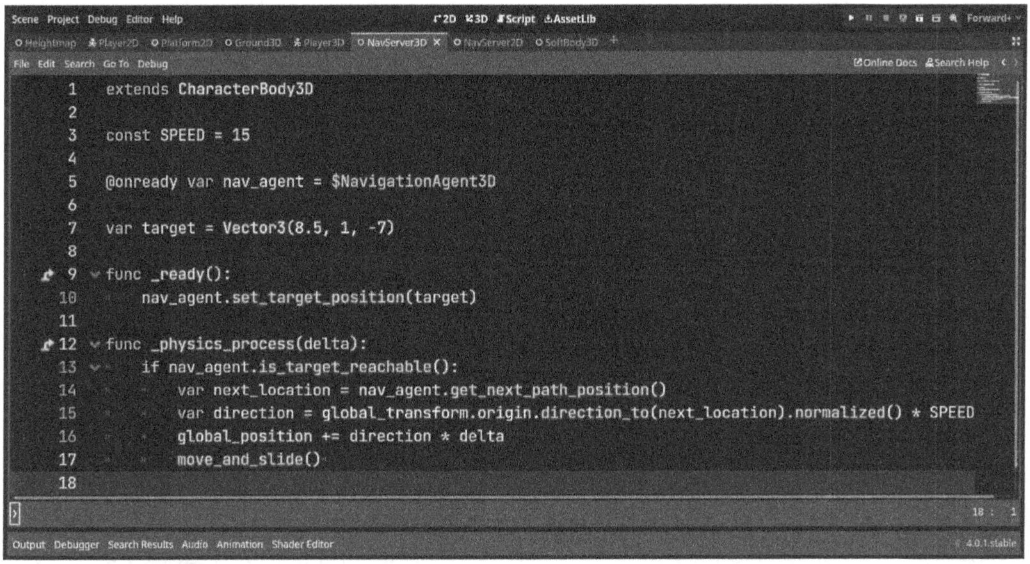

```gdscript
1    extends CharacterBody3D
2
3    const SPEED = 15
4
5    @onready var nav_agent = $NavigationAgent3D
6
7    var target = Vector3(8.5, 1, -7)
8
9  ∨ func _ready():
10       nav_agent.set_target_position(target)
11
12 ∨ func _physics_process(delta):
13  ∨     if nav_agent.is_target_reachable():
14             var next_location = nav_agent.get_next_path_position()
15             var direction = global_transform.origin.direction_to(next_location).normalized() * SPEED
16             global_position += direction * delta
17             move_and_slide()
18
```

Figure 4.9 – PathAI script for CharacterBody3D

How it works...

We added **DirectionalLight3D** and **WorldEnvironment** to the scene by clicking on the three vertical dots in the toolbar above the Viewport. We added a **MeshInstance3D** and assigned the type of the mesh as **PlaneMesh**.

We renamed it **Ground** and created a **Trimesh Static Body** by left-clicking on **Mesh** in the toolbar, which added a **StaticBody3D** and **CollisionShape3D** to the **Ground** so that our player won't fall through the ground. We added a **StandardMaterial3D** to the ground so that we could change the color of the ground.

We changed the color to yellow so that we can see the area we can navigate and where we can't. Then, we hid the child nodes of **Ground** so that we can have more room in the **Scene** tab.

We created a container to hold our wall by selecting the white node in the **Create New Node** window that comes up when we select the + sign in the **Scene** tab. We renamed it **Walls**. We added a **MeshInstance3D** as a child of the **Walls** container and added a **BoxMesh** to it so that we don't get an error when we add a **Trimesh Static Body**. We created a **Trimesh Static Body** on it so that it will react to physics.

We renamed it **Wall**, and using **Scale Mode (R)** and **Select Mode (Q)**, we resized and positioned the walls around the edges of the ground. We duplicated **Wall** by pressing *Ctrl + D* on the wall and resized and repositioned the walls until they looked like those shown in *Figure 4.7*. Now, we have a navigational path that we can use.

We closed the **Walls** container that we created to give us more room in the **Scene** tab. We created a **NavigationRegion3D** node as a child to **World**. We selected the **Ground** and **Walls** nodes and moved them onto **NavigationRegion3D** so that **Ground** and **Walls** are a child of **NavigationRegion3D**. We selected **New NavigationMesh** for **NavMesh** in the **Inspector**. We clicked **Bake NavMesh** in the toolbar above the viewport to show a navigation path that we will use later.

We created a **CharacterBody3D** as a child to this node we created a **MeshInstance3D** and gave that a capsule shape. We clicked **CharacterBody3D** to add a **CollisionShape3D** as a child to **CharacterBody3D** and gave the **CollisionShape3D** a capsule shape. We clicked on **CharacterBody3D** to add a **NavigationAgent3D** as a child of **CharacterBody3D**. We will use this to interact with the **NavigationRegion3D** that we created. We clicked on **CharacterBody3D**, and in the **Inspector**, we changed the **Transform Position** values to start the **CharacterBody3D** in the bottom-right corner.

We created a **Camera3D** node. We moved the camera up 14 on the *y* axis and rotated the camera so that it looks down on the whole scene. Now, when we run the current scene, we can see something.

We created a new empty script called `PathAI` with no **CharacterBody3D** template so that we can code the capsule to move from the bottom of the screen to the top using the **NavigationRegion3D** and **NavigationAgent3D** nodes.

We added code to the `PathAI` script. In *line 3*, we have a constant variable named SPEED set to 5. In *line 5*, we use `@onready` on the `nav_agent` variable that references the **NavigationAgent3D** node, which is a child of the **CharacterBody3D** node.

In *line 7*, we created a variable named `target` and gave it a `Vector3` location, which is in the top-right corner of the scene that we want to navigate. In *lines 9-10*, the `_ready()` function, we set the target location of `nav_agent` to the `target` variable. In *lines 12-17* in the `_physics_process(delta)` function, we first checked to see if it was reachable, and if so, then we created a `next_location` variable equal to `nav_agent.get_next_position()`.

This is how the **CharacterBody3D** is going to move a step. We created a variable called `direction` that references `global_transform_origin`, which is where the **CharacterBody3D** is currently located.

`direction_to(next_location).normalized() * SPEED` calculated the next location to move to by using the `next_location` variable in *line 14*. We used `.normalized()` to set the vectors at a value of 1, then we multiplied the `speed` variable to move it at the speed desired.

Line 16 moved the **CharacterBody3D** by updating **global_position** by multiplying the `direction` variable with delta, which is the time elapsed in one frame. In *line 17*, `move_and_slide()` actually moved the **CharacterBody3D**. Then, we ran **Current Scene** (by pressing *F6*) to see the **CharacterBody2D** navigate to the target.

Using NavigationServer2D for 2D projects

In this recipe, we are going to create a background using a **MeshInstance2D** and four **Shape2D** instances as walls. We will create a **CharacterBody2D** with a **NavigationAgent2D** node to interact with the **NavigationRegion2D** node that we will add as a parent to the background so that we can create a navigational area where the player can move. We will create a script to move the **CharacterBody2D** to a target location on the opposite side of the map.

Getting ready

For this recipe, click the + sign to the right of the **NavServer3D** scene we just completed to add a new scene. In the **Scene** tab, click **2D Scene**. Click on the word **Scene** in the top-left corner next to **Project**, then select **Save Scene As** and name it NavServer2D.

How to do it...

Let's create a background and walls as a child to the **NavigationRegion2D** node:

1. Left-click on the **Node2D** node and then the + sign in the **Scene** tab. In the **Create New Node** window, type nav in the **Search** box and then select **NavigationRegion2D** to create the node in the scene.
2. In the **Inspector,** to the right of **Navigation Polygon**, click on **<empty>** and select **New NavigationPolygon.**
3. Left-click on the **NavigationRegion2D** node and then the + sign in the **Scene** tab. In the **Create New Node** window, type mesh in the **Search** box and then select **MeshInstance2D** to create the node in the scene.
4. Right-click the **MeshInstance2D** node in the **Scene** tab and rename it Background.
5. In the **Inspector**, click on **<empty>** to the right of **Mesh** and select **New BoxMesh.**
6. Left-click on the same place to open the properties of the **Background** mesh.
7. In the **Inspector**, change the **Size** property of **x** and **y** to 100.
8. In the **Inspector**, left-click on **Transform** to show the transform properties.
9. To the right of **Position**, change the **x** value to 600px and the **y** value to 340px.
10. To the right of **Scale**, left-click the link icon so that the link is gray and broken.
11. Change the value of **x** to 12 and the value of **y** to 7 in **Scale**.
12. Left-click on the **NavigationRegion2D** node and then the + sign in the **Scene** tab. In the **Create New Node** window, type sprite in the **Search** box and then select **Sprite2D** to create the node in the scene.
13. Right-click the **Sprite2D** node in the **Scene** tab and rename it Wall.

14. In the **FileSystem** tab, drag `icon.svg` into **<empty>** to the right of **Texture** in the **Inspector**.

15. Click on **Transform** in the **Inspector** to show the **Properties** values.

16. To the right of **Position**, change the **x** value to `219px` and the **y** value to `142px`.

17. To the right of **Scale**, left-click the link icon so that it is gray, then change the **x** value to `1.75` and the **y** value to `1`.

18. Left-click on the **Wall** node we just added and then the **+** sign in the **Scene** tab. In the **Create New Node** window, type `static` in the **Search** box and then select **StaticBody2D** to create the node as a child of the **Wall** node.

19. While **StaticBody2D** is still selected, click on the **+** sign in the **Scene** tab. In the **Create New Node** window, type `coll` in the **Search** box and then select **CollisionShape2D** to create the node in the scene.

20. In the **Inspector** to the right of **Shape**, click **<empty>** and select **New RectangleShape2D** from the drop-down list and adjust the shape to cover the whole **Sprite2D Wall**.

21. Click on the **Wall** node in the **Scene** tab and then *Ctrl + D* to duplicate the wall.

22. Click on **Transform** in the **Inspector** to see the properties of the **Wall2** node.

23. Change the **Position** value of **x** to `346.5px` and the value of **y** to `446px`.

24. To the right of **Scale**, click on the link icon to turn it gray, then change the **x** value to `3.66` and the **y** value to `1`.

25. Click on the **Wall2** node in the **Scene** tab and then *Ctrl + D* to duplicate the wall.

26. Click on **Transform** in the **Inspector** to see the properties of the **Wall3** node.

27. Change the **Position** value of **x** to `680px` and the value of **y** to `143px`.

28. To the right of **Scale**, click on the link icon to turn it gray, then change the **x** value to `3.98` and the **y** value to `2.28`.

29. Click on the **Wall3** node in the **Scene** tab and then *Ctrl + D* to duplicate the wall.

30. Click on **Transform** in the **Inspector** to see the properties of the **Wall4** node.

31. Change the **Position** value of **x** to `970px` and the value of **y** to `471px`.

32. To the right of **Scale**, click on the link icon to turn it gray, then change the **x** value to `1.28` and the **y** value to `2.08`.

33. Click on the **NavigationRegion2D** node, and to the right of the view in the toolbar above the viewport, there are three buttons: **Create Points**, **Edit Points**, and **Erase Points**. Click on **Create Points** and click in the top-left corner, and click around the area the default camera can see and also around the walls:

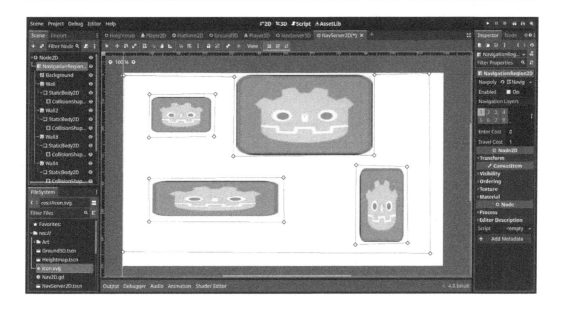

Figure 4.10 – Setting up the navigation path in the scene

34. Left-click on the **Node2D** node and then the + sign in the **Scene** tab. In the **Create New Node** window, type `char` in the **Search** box and then select **CharacterBody2D** to create the node in the scene.

35. Click on **Transform** in the **Inspector** to see the properties of the **CharacterBody2D** node.

36. Change the **Position** value of **x** to `13px` and the value of **y** to `18px`.

37. Left-click on the **CharacterBody2D** node and then the + sign in the **Scene** tab. In the **Create New Node** window, type `sprite` in the **Search** box and then select **Sprite2D** to create the node in the scene.

38. In the **FileSystem** tab, drag `icon.svg` into **<empty>** to the right of **Texture** in the **Inspector**.

39. Click on **Transform** in the **Inspector** to see the properties of the **Sprite2D** node.

40. To the right of **Scale**, click on the link icon to turn it gray, then change the **x** value to `.16` and the **y** value to `.21`.

41. Left-click on the **CharacterBody2D** node and then the + sign in the **Scene** tab. In the **Create New Node** window, type `coll` in the **Search** box and then select **CollisionShape2D** to create the node in the scene.

42. Click **<empty>** to the right of **Shape** and select **New CapsuleShape2D**.

43. Left-click on the **CharacterBody2D** node and then the + sign in the **Scene** tab. In the **Create New Node** window, type `nav` in the **Search** box and then select **NavigationAgent2D** to create the node in the scene.

44. Left-click on the **CharacterBody2D** node, and at the bottom of the **Inspector**, click on **<empty>** to the right of **Script**, then select **New Script**.

45. In the **Attach Node Script** window to the right of **Path**, change the name of the script to Nav2D. Check to the right of **Template** to see if it is empty. If it is not, then click the check mark to get rid of the template. It should say **Empty** now.

46. Click on the **Create** button to create the new script.

47. Enter the following code to the empty Nav2D.gd script:

```
1    extends CharacterBody2D
3    const SPEED = 100
5    @onready var nav_agent = $NavigationAgent2D
7    @export var target = Vector2(1125, 525)
9    func _ready():
10       nav_agent.set_target_position(target)
12   func _physics_process(delta):
13       if nav_agent.is_target_reachable():
14           var next_location = nav_agent.get_next_path_
position()
15           var direction = global_transform.origin.direction_
to(next_location).normalized() * SPEED
16           global_position += direction * delta
17           move_and_slide()
```

48. In the **NavServer2D** scene, click the **Run the current scene** button in the upper-right corner of the editor or hit the *F6* key.

How it works...

We added a **NavigationRegion2D** node to the scene and added a new **NavigationPolygon** in the **Navpoly** property. We added a **MeshInstance2D** node as a child of the **NavigationRegion2D** node and renamed it **Background**. We added a **BoxMesh** to the **Mesh** property. We changed the **Size** values of **x** and **y** to 100.

We opened the **Transform** properties in the **Inspector** to change the **Position x** value to 600px and the **y** value to 340px to center it so that the default camera can see the background. We left-clicked the link icon so that we can change both **x** and **y** values to the values we want. We changed the **Scale** of value **x** to 12 and **y** to 7 so that it covers the area that the default camera will show.

We made our first wall shape by creating a **Sprite2D** as a child of the **NavigationRegion2D** node and renaming it Wall. We dragged the icon.svg file into **<empty>** to the right of **Texture** in the **Inspector** so that we can see it. We changed the **Position** value of **x** to 219 and the value of **y** to 142.

Then, we changed the values of **Scale** of the wall to **x** – 1.75 and **y** to 1. Clicking on the **Wall** node, we added a **StaticBody2D** as a child of **Wall**. Then, we added a **CollisionShape2D** as a child to **StaticBody2D** with a new **RectangleShape2D**, which will cover the area of the **Wall** node.

We duplicated the **Wall** node and changed its position three times so that we have a total of four walls. This is so that we have some walls in between the start position of our **CharacterBody2D** that we will build later and a target position we will program the **CharacterBody2D** to navigate to.

Then, we clicked the **NavigationRegion2D** node and noticed that in the toolbar above the viewport on the right of **View** are three buttons, which we used to add the navigation area to be used by our **CharacterBody2D** that we will create next. *Figure 4.10* shows where to add the points.

We created a **CharacterBody2D** as a child of **Node2D**. We changed the **x** and **y** positions in **Transform** so that they will start in the top left-hand corner. We added a **Sprite2D** as a child of **CharacterBody2D** and added the icon.svg file to the **Texture** property so that we can see it.

We scaled it down to .16 on **x** and .21 on **y** so that it will be smaller than the walls and fit through some of the narrower paths. We added a **CollisionShape2D** as a child of **CharacterBody2D** and used a **CapsuleShape2D** for the **Shape** property. Then, we added a **NavigationAgent2D** as a child of **CharacterBody2D** so that it can react with the **NavigationRegion2D** and move in the navigation path we set up previously.

We created a new script and named it Nav2D.gd. We did not include the **CharacterBody2D** default template. In *line 3*, we created a constant variable named SPEED and set its value to 100. In *line 5*, we used @onready on the nav_agent variable that references the **NavigationAgent2D** node, which is a child of the **CharacterBody2D** node.

In *line 7*, we used @export so that we can change the target location in the **Inspector**. The variable target is equal to Vector2(1125, 525), which is located on the far-right side of the screen. In *lines 9-10*, the _ready() function, we set the target location of nav_agent to the variable target.

In *lines 12-17*, in the _physics_process(delta) function, we first checked to see if it was reachable, and if so, then we created a next_location variable equal to nav_agent.get_next_position(). This is how the **CharacterBody2D** is going to move a step. We created a variable called direction that references global_transform_origin, which is where the **CharacterBody2D** is currently located.

direction_to(next_location).normalized() * SPEED calculated the next location to move to by using the next_location variable in *line 14*. We used .normalized() to set the vectors at a value of 1, then we timed the speed to move it at the speed desired. *Line 16* moves the **CharacterBody2D** by updating global_position by multiplying the direction variable with delta, which is the time elapsed in one frame.

In *line 17*, move_and_slide() actually moved the **CharacterBody2D**. We ran **Current Scene** (by pressing *F6*) to see the **CharacterBody2D** navigate to the target. If you want, you can change the target values in the **Inspector** to see it pick a path to get to the new target.

Using SoftBody for 3D games

In this recipe, we will create a banner using **SoftBody3D**. We are going to create a ground with two poles that we will attach to the banner, and when we play the scene the banner will fall, and you can see how the **SoftBody3D** reacts.

Getting ready

For this recipe, click the + sign to the right of the **NavServer2D** scene we just completed to add a new scene. In the **Scene** tab, click **3D Scene**. Click on the word **Scene** in the main menu next to **Project**, then select **Save Scene As** and name it `SoftBody3D`. Right-click **Node3D** and select **Rename**, and rename it `World`.

How to do it...

Let's first create a basic area with the ground and two poles along with a camera:

1. Left-click the three vertical dots on the left of the **Transform** View on the Viewport toolbar.

2. Add the **Sun** and **Environment** nodes to the scene by left-clicking the **Add Environment to Scene** button at the bottom while holding down the *Shift* key.

3. Left-click on the **World** node and then the + sign in the **Scene** tab. In the **Create New Node** window, type `mesh` in the **Search** box and then select **MeshInstance3D** to create the node in the scene.

4. Right-click the **MeshInstance3D** node in the **Scene** tab and rename it `Ground`.

5. In the **Inspector**, click on <empty> to the right of **Mesh** and select **New PlaneMesh**.

6. Left-click on the same place to open the properties of the **Ground** mesh.

7. In the **Inspector**, change the **Size** property of **x** and **y** to `10`.

8. Left-click on the **World** node and then the + sign in the **Scene** tab. In the **Create New Node** window, type `mesh` in the **Search** box and then select **MeshInstance3D** to create the node in the scene.

9. Right-click the **MeshInstance3D** node in the **Scene** tab and rename it `Pole`.

10. In the **Inspector**, click on <empty> to the right of **Mesh** and select **New CylinderMesh**.

11. Left-click on the same place to open the properties of **CylinderMesh**.

12. Change the **Top Radius** and **Bottom Radius** property values to `.2m` on each.

13. Change the **Height** property value to `6m`. If the pole is below the ground, then click and drag the **y** arrow to bring it level with the ground.

14. Scroll down in the **Inspector** and click on **Transform** to open the properties.

15. Change the **Position** property of the **y** and **z** values to 3.

16. Left-click on **Mesh**, which is to the right of the **Transform** View in the toolbar at the top of the Viewport, and select **Create Trimesh Static Body**.

17. Click on **Pole** and then *Ctrl + D* to duplicate the **Pole** we just created.

18. Scroll down in the **Inspector** and click on **Transform** to open the properties.

19. Change the **Position** property of the **z** value to 0.

20. Left-click on the **World** node and then the + sign in the **Scene** tab. In the **Create New Node** window, type soft in the **Search** box and then select **SoftBody3D** to create the node in the scene.

21. In the **Inspector**, click on <empty> to the right of **Mesh** and select **New PlaneMesh**.

22. Left-click on the same place to open the properties of the **PlaneMesh**.

23. Change the **Size** properties of the **x** value to 2.6m and the **y** value to 1.5m.

24. Change the **Subdivide Width** value to 7 and the **Subdivide Depth** value to 7.

25. Change **Orientation** to **Face X**.

26. In the **Inspector**, click on <empty> to the right of **Material** right under **Orientation** and select **New StandardMaterial3D**.

27. Left-click on the same place to open the properties of the **StandardMaterial3D**.

28. Click on **Transparency** to open its properties.

29. To the right of **Cull Mode**, select **Disabled** in the drop-down list.

30. Click on **Albedo** to open its properties.

31. Click on the white box to the right of **Color**.

32. In the **Hex** field, enter 89ffff.

33. Using **Select Mode (Q)**, click on the **y** arrow and move the banner up in between the two poles so that the bottom of the banner is even with the tops of the poles.

34. Click on the bottom-left and bottom-right dots, which are also touching the poles.

35. Place the banner above the poles and attach the banner to the two poles:

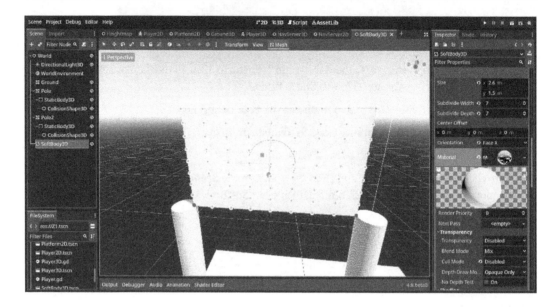

Figure 4.11 – Banner placement

36. At top of the **Inspector**, change the value **of Simulation Precision** to 10.

37. Change the value of **Total Mass** to 0.

38. Change the value of **Linear Stiffness** to .01.

39. Left-click on the box to the right of **Pinned Points** to see the two points we clicked on in *step 34*.

40. In the **Inspector**, click **Attachments** and then on the down arrows to the left of 0 and 1 to see the properties of each attachment.

41. In 0, click on **Assign**, which is to the right of **Spatial Attachment Path**, and select **CollisionShape3D** in **Pole**.

42. In 1, click on **Assign**, which is to the right of **Spatial Attachment Path**, and select **CollisionShape3D** in **Pole2**.

43. Left-click on the **World** node and then the + sign in the **Scene** tab. In the **Create New Node** window, type cam in the **Search** box and then select **Camera3D** to create the node in the scene.

44. In the **Inspector**, change the value of **FOV** to 100.

45. Click on **Transform** to see its properties.

46. Change the **Position** values of **x** to 5 and **y** to 1.

47. Change the **Rotation** value of **y** to 90.

48. In the **SoftBody3D** scene, click the **Run the current scene** button in the upper-right corner of the editor or hit the *F6* key.

How it works...

We added the **WorldEnvironment** and **DirectionalLight3D** nodes to the scene. If you hold down the *Shift* key and left-click either button at the bottom, you can add both nodes at the same time. We added a **MeshInstance3D** node as a child to **World**. We renamed the node **Ground**. We changed the size of the ground to 10 x 10 to give us some room to add two poles.

We created two poles that will hold up our banner. We created a **MeshInstance3D**, renamed it **Pole**, and added a **CylinderMesh**. We opened the **CylinderMesh** properties in the **Inspector** and changed the values of **Top Radius** and **Bottom Radius** to .2m. We changed the **Height** value to 6m and made sure the bottom of the pole was set on the ground. In the **Transform** section of the **Inspector**, we changed the **y** and **z Position** values to 3.

We created a **Trimesh Static Body** by left-clicking on **Mesh** located to the right of the **Transform View** in the toolbar at the top of the Viewport. This added a **StaticBody3D** and a **CollisionShape3D** to interact with the physics engine. Then, we duplicated the pole and changed its **Transform z** value to 0 to move it over so that we could put the banner in between the two poles.

We created a **SoftBody3D** node, and for the **Mesh**, we selected a **PlaneMesh** to simulate the fabric of a banner. We changed the size so that it could fit in between the two poles. We changed the **Subdivide Width** and **Subdivide Depth** values to give the banner flexibility. We changed the **Orientation** value to **Face X** so that the banner can be seen along the *x* axis.

We added a new **StandardMaterial3D** to **Material** so that we can see a banner. In the **Transparency** properties, we disabled **Cull**. Since we used a **PlaneMesh** for the **Mesh**, only one side can be seen by default. When we disabled **Cull**, we could then see both sides of the banner. We clicked **Albedo** and changed the color of the material so that we can see the banner more easily.

We dragged the banner to the top of the poles so that the bottom of the banner could attach to each pole. When we run the scene after we are done, the banner will fall down so that we can see how the **SoftBody3D** banner reacts to gravity.

Changing the values of **Simulation Precision**, **Total Mass**, and **Linear Stiffness** makes the banner flexible. **Simulation Precision** can affect performance while improving the simulation, so when making your own projects, you might want to try values until it feels right.

We only clicked on the box to the right of **Pinned Points** to show you the points that were added when we clicked on the bottom two dots to connect the banner to the poles.

We clicked **Attachments** in the **Inspector** to see the properties. We clicked the down arrows to the left of 0 and 1 to show the two points we added that connected the banner to the two poles. In 0, we assigned the **CollisionShape3D** of **Pole** to the left point, which was the first point we clicked on. In 1, we assigned the **CollisionShape3D** of **Pole2** to the right point, which was the second point we clicked on. 0 and 1 in **Attachments** correspond to 0 and 1 in **Pinned Points**, which we looked at previously.

We added a **Camera3D** node so that we can see the scene when we run the current scene. We changed the **FOV** value to 100 so that the camera can see more of the scene from its position. We changed the rotation value of **y** to 90 so that the camera can see the banner. Then, we clicked the **Run the current scene** button to see how the banner reacts when it falls while it is connected to each pole.

5

Playing with Shaders in Godot 4

In this chapter, we start with looking at the **Shader Creation** dialog to create shaders and also look at the new features in the shader language in Godot 4. We will examine how to use **Global Uniforms** and **Instance Uniforms** with shaders. With visual shaders, we start by looking at the **Visual Shaders Context** menu.

We will work with **Integer** and **Comment** nodes. We create nodes using **Texture3D** and **CurveTexture**. We look at the **Billboard** and **UVFunc** nodes. We play with the **Sky Shader** mode to create sky shaders. We will examine the **Fog Shader** mode to see what we can do with it.

In this chapter, we will cover the following recipes:

- Creating shaders with the **Shader Creation** dialog
- Exploring **Uniform Arrays** in the Godot 4 shader language
- How to use **Global Uniforms**
- Using **Instance Uniforms** with shaders
- Exploring the **Visual Shaders Context** menu
- Working with **Integer** and **Comment** nodes
- Creating nodes using **Texture3D** and **CurveTexture**
- Using the **Billboard** node
- Using the **UVFunc** node
- Improving the **Sky Shader** mode
- What the **Fog Shader** mode can do

Technical requirements

For this chapter, you need the standard version of Godot 4.0 or later running on one of the following:

- Windows 64-bit or 32-bit

- macOS

- Linux 64-bit or 32-bit

- Android

- Web Editor

You can find the code and project files for the projects in this chapter on GitHub at `https://github.com/PacktPublishing/Godot-4-Game-Development-Cookbook/tree/main/Chapter%205`.

Creating shaders with the Shader Creation dialog

In this recipe, we take a look at the new **Shader Creation** dialog and the options you can select when you create shaders in Godot 4 such as **Spatial**, **Canvas Item**, **Particles**, **Sky**, and **Fog**.

Getting ready

For this recipe, open Godot 4 and start a new project called `Chapter 5`. In the **Scene** tab, click **3D** to add a 3D scene. Click on **Scene** in the main menu next to **Project**, then select **Save Scene As**, and name it `Creationdialog`.

How to do it...

Let's add a **PlaneMesh** to the scene and then add a new **ShaderMaterial** in the **Material** property where we can create a shader and see the new **Shader Creation** dialog:

1. Left-click on the **Node3D** node and then press the + sign in the **Scene** tab. In the **Create New Node** window, type `mesh` in the **Search** box and then select **MeshInstance3D** to create the node in the scene.

2. In the **Inspector**, click on <empty> to the right of the mesh and select **New PlaneMesh**.

3. Left-click on the same place to open the properties of **MeshInstance3D**.

4. Click on <empty> to the right of **Material** in the **Inspector** and select **New ShaderMaterial** from the drop-down list.

5. Click on <empty> to the right of **Shader** in the **Inspector** and select **New Shader** from the drop-down list. A **Create Shader** dialog box appears:

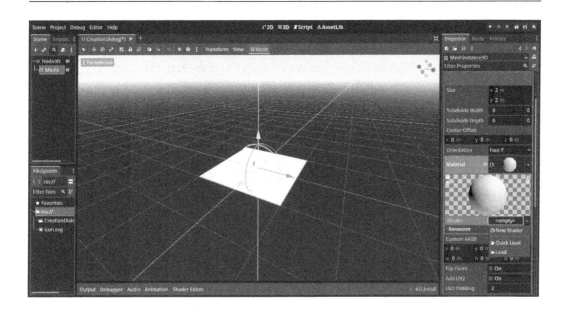

Figure 5.1 – Material Shader location in the Inspector

6. Left-click the down arrow to the right of **Type: Shader** to select either a **Shader** or a **VisualShader** to create.

7. Left-click the down arrow to the right of **Mode: Spatial** to select **Spatial**, **Canvas Item**, **Particles**, **Sky**, and **Fog**:

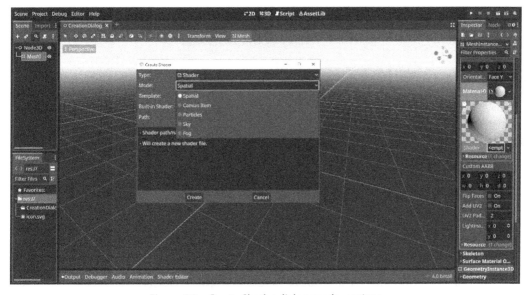

Figure 5.2 – Create Shader dialog mode: options

8. Left-click the down arrow to the right of **Template: Default** to select either a **Default** or an **Empty** script.

9. Below that, see the **Built-in Shader** button and **Path:** where the script is saved.

How it works...

We created a new **MeshInstance3D**, and for the **Mesh** property, we selected a **PlaneMesh**. For the **Material** property, we selected a new **ShaderMaterial**, and in the **Shader** property, we selected **New Shader** from the drop-down to bring up **the Create Shader** dialog.

We look at the **Create Shader** dialog box and its options. In **Type:**, we can select **Shader** or **VisualShader**. **Shader** is selected when you want to program a shader using shader language. **VisualShader** is selected when you want to use visual shaders where you program shaders with a visual editor.

Selecting the **Spatial** mode is for shading 3D objects. The **Canvas Item** selection is for shading 2D objects. The **Particles** selection is used to calculate particle properties such as color, position, and rotation for both 2D and 3D. The **Sky** selection is used for drawing sky backgrounds and updating radiance cubemaps, which are used for image-based lighting. The **Fog** selection is used to define how fog is added or subtracted in an area with **FogVolume** or volumetric fog.

We see in **Template:** that we can start the shader script with a default template or an empty shader script. Below **Template:** is the checkbox for **Built-in Shader**. **Path:** is where you can edit the name of the shader.

Exploring Uniform Arrays in the Godot 4 shader language

In this recipe, we create a shader on a **MeshInstance3D** that uses the new Uniform Array, which is a `Vector3` array and holds three colors—red, green, and blue—in the array.

Getting ready

For this recipe, open Godot 4 and open the project from the last recipe, called `CreationDialog`.

How to do it...

Let's use the new **Uniform Arrays** and structs in the shader language with the plane we created in the last recipe:

1. Left-click on **MeshInstance3D** in the **Scene** tab.

2. Click on <empty> to the right of **Material** in the **Inspector** and select **New ShaderMaterial** from the drop-down list.

3. Click on <empty> to the right of **Shader** in the **Inspector** and select **New Shader** from the drop-down list, as shown in *Figure 5.1*.

4. To the right of **Path:**, rename `CreationDialog.gdshader` to `Recipe2.gdshader` and click the **Create** button.

5. Left-click on **Recipe2.gdshader**, which is to the right of **Shader** in the **Inspector**.

6. In the **Shader Editor**, at the bottom, enter the following code:

```
1    shader_type spatial;
2
3    uniform vec3 array[3];
4
5    void fragment() {
6        ALBEDO = array[2];
7    }
```

7. In the **Inspector** under **Shader Parameters | Array**, click the + **Add Element** button three times to match the array size:

- In the 0 position, change the x value to 1

- In the 1 position, change the y value to 1

- In the 2 position, change the z value to 1:

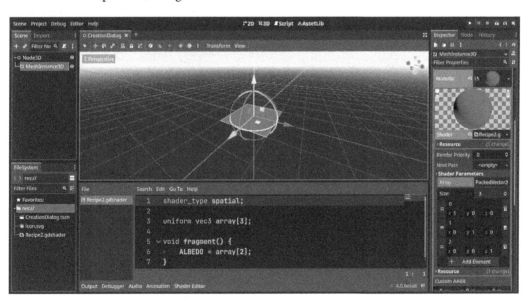

Figure 5.3 – The Shader parameters in the Inspector

How it works...

We left-clicked on **MeshInstance3D** so that we can add a shader. In the **Material** properties in the **Inspector**, we selected a new **ShaderMaterial** from the drop-down list that appeared when we clicked on <empty>. In the **Material** properties in the **Inspector**, we clicked on <empty> to the right of **Shader** to bring up the **Shader Creation** dialog. We changed the name of the shader script to Recipe2 and then left-clicked on **Recipe2.gdshader** so that we could see the gdshader script.

We wrote the shader code. In *line 1*, we see that the shader_type value is spatial, which is for 3D. In *line 3*, we used the new **Uniform Array**. We created a uniform Vector3 array that holds three values. In the fragment function, we assign **ALBEDO** to the array, pointing to [2], which is the last value in the array.

After we changed the values in the **Inspector**, we could come back and change these values to [0] and [1]. Remember to add a semicolon at the end of each line so that you don't get any errors. The Shader language is different from GDScript.

We looked in the **Inspector** for shader parameters that appear because we created the Vector3 array. We clicked on the **+ Add Element** button at the bottom of **Size** so that we can change the three Vector3 values.

In the first position of this array, [0], we changed the x value to 1. This will change the **MeshInstance3D** to the color red. In the second position of this array, [1], we changed the y value to 1. This will change the **MeshInstance3D** to the color green. In the third position of the array, [2], we changed the z value to 1. This will change the **MeshInstance3D** to the color blue.

How to use Global Uniforms

In this recipe, we go into **Project Settings** and create a Shader **Global Uniform** that is a red color. We create a **PlaneMesh** and call the Shader **Global Uniform** from a shader script to change the plane color to red, then we create a script and change the color to blue using GDScript.

Getting ready

For this recipe, open Godot 4 and open the project from the last recipe, called CreationDialog.

How to do it...

We start by removing the Recipe2.gdshader script from **MeshInstance3D** and then create the global shader:

1. Left-click on **MeshInstance3D**, and in the **Inspector** in the **Material** section, click on the **Set to default** icon to the right of **Shader** and to the left of **Recipe2.gdshader**, as seen in *Figure 5.3* just below the blue ball.

2. Click on **Output** on the bottom panel of the editor to the right of the **FileSystem** tab.

3. Click on **Project** in the main menu located on the top left of the editor.

4. Select **Project Settings** in the drop-down list.

5. Select the **Shader Globals** tab.

6. In the **Name** field, type Red.

7. In the **Type** field, select **Color**.

8. Click on the **Add** button.

9. Left-click on the black bar on the right of **Red** and change the **R** value to 255:

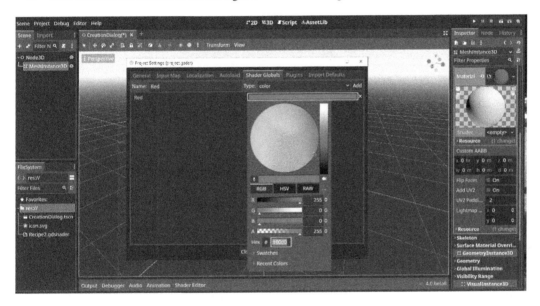

Figure 5.4 – The Shader Globals tab

10. Click on the **Close** button.

11. Click on the **Set to default** icon to the right of **Shader** and then on **<empty>** to the right of **Shader** in the **Inspector** and select **New Shader** from the drop-down list.

12. To the right of **Path:**, rename **CreationDialog.gdshader** Recipe3.gdshader and click the **Create** button.

13. Left-click on **Recipe3.gdshader**, which is to the right of **Shader** in the **Inspector**.

14. In the **Shader Editor**, at the bottom, enter the following code.

```
1    shader_type spatial;
2
3    global uniform vec4 Red;
```

```
4
5    void fragment() {
6        ALBEDO = Red.xyz;
7    }
```

15. Left-click on the **Node3D** node and then press the + sign in the **Scene** tab. In the **Create New Node** window, type cam in the **Search** box and then select **Camera3D** to create the node in the scene.

16. Left-click on **Transform** in the **Inspector** and change the **Position y** value to 1 and the **z** value to 3.

17. Left-click on **Node3D** in the **Scene** tab.

18. In the **Inspector**, click on **<empty>** to the right of **Script** and select **New Script**.

19. In **Path**, rename the script Recipe3.gd:

```
1 extends Node3D
2
3 func _ready():
4    RenderingServer.global_shader_parameter_set("Red", Color.
BLUE)
```

20. In the CreationDialog scene, click the **Run the current scene** button in the upper-right corner of the editor or hit the *F6* key.

How it works...

We removed the Recipe2.gdshader script from **MeshInstance3D** so that we can use a new script. We clicked on **Output** at the bottom panel of the editor so that we don't see the **Shader Editor** since we removed it.

We opened **Project Settings**, located in the **Project** menu of the editor. We selected the **Shader Globals** tab to add a new global shader. We named the shader Red and selected **Color** as the **Type** value. Then, we clicked on the **Add** button and left-clicked the black bar that appeared and changed the **R** value to 255 so that it was red. We clicked the **Close** button to close the **Project Settings** window.

We looked in the **Material** properties in the **Inspector**, and we clicked on **<empty>** to the right of **Shader** to bring up the **Shader Creation** dialog. We changed the name of the shader script to Recipe3 and then left-clicked on **Recipe3.gdshader** so we could see the gdshader script.

In *line 1*, we saw that the shader_type value is spatial, which is for 3D. In *line 3*, we used the **vec4 Global Uniform** to get the **Red** global shader that we set up earlier. In the fragment function, we assign **ALBEDO** to the **Red** global shader that we set up in **Project Settings**. We see the plane is red in the scene.

We added a **Camera3D** to the scene and changed its **Transform** position so that it is behind and above the **MeshInstance3D**. We can see it change its color when we run the scene after we create a new GDScript script and add the code.

We created a new script on the **Node3D** node called `Recipe3.gd`. In the `_ready()` function, we call the `global_shader_parameter_set` method in RenderingServer. We use Red and `Color.BLUE` as parameters. Red gets the global shader we set up and `Color.BLUE` changes the shader to use the color blue.

We click the **Run the current scene** button and see the **MeshInstance3D** is now blue. If you take the script off of Node3D and click on 3D in the **Workspaces** section of the editor (the top center) to look at the scene, you can see the **MeshInstance3D** is back to the color red because the shader is not overwritten now.

Using Instance Uniforms with shaders

In this recipe, we will create two instance uniform variables—`color` and `alphachannel`—in a shader script. We see that the variables that we created can now be seen in **Inspector** and changed from there, not from the script.

Getting ready

For this recipe, click the + sign to the right of the **CreationDialog** scene we just completed to add a new scene. In the **Scene** tab, click **3D Scene**. Click on **Scene** in the top-left corner next to **Project**, then select **Save Scene As**, and name it `InstanceUniforms`.

How to do it...

Let's add **MeshInstance3D** with a PlaneMesh and then write a shader script with the two **Instance Uniforms**:

1. Left-click on the **Node3D** node and then press the + sign in the **Scene** tab. In the **Create New Node** window, type `mesh` in the **Search** box and then select **MeshInstance3D** to create the node in the scene.

2. In the **Inspector**, click on **<empty>** to the right of **Mesh** and select **New PlaneMesh**.

3. Left-click on the same place to open the properties of the **MeshInstance3D**.

4. Click on **<empty>** to the right of **Material** in the **Inspector** and select **New ShaderMaterial** from the drop-down list.

5. Click on **ShaderMaterial**, then click on **<empty>** to the right of **Shader** in the **Inspector** and select **New Shader** from the drop-down list.

6. To the right of **Path:**, rename `InstanceUniforms.gdshader` to `Recipe4.gdshader` and click the **Create** button.

7. Left-click on **Recipe4.gdshader**, which is to the right of **Shader** in the **Inspector**.

8. In the **Shader Editor**, at the bottom, enter the following code.

```
1    shader_type spatial;
2
3    instance uniform vec3 color;
4    instance uniform float alphachannel = 1;
5
6    void fragment() {
7        ALBEDO = color.xyz;
8        ALPHA = alphachannel;
9    }
```

9. In the **Inspector**, at the bottom of the **GeometryInstance3D** section, click on **Instance Shader Parameters**. If you don't see this, then click on the **CreationDialog** tab and then go back to the **Instance Uniforms** tab.

10. In the **Color** section, change the **x** value to 1 and the **y** value to 1.

11. Change the value of `Alphachannel` to .1.

How it works...

We created a new **MeshInstance3D**, and for the **Mesh** property, we selected a **PlaneMesh**. For the **Material** property, we selected a new **ShaderMaterial**, and in the **Shader** property, we selected **New Shader** from the dropdown to bring up the **Create Shader** dialog. We changed the name to `Recipe4.gdshader`.

We left-clicked on **Recipe4.gdshader** in the **Inspector** to bring up the **Shader Editor**. *Line 1* states that this shader is `spatial`, which is for 3D. In *line 3*, we created an Instance Uniform that is a `Vector3` array called `color`. We used a `Vector3` array because of the red, green, and blue values of a color. In *line 4*, we created an Instance Uniform that is a float called `alphachannel`.

With this, we can give a float value to the `alphachannel` Instance Uniform of the color. If we set it at 0, you can see through it. In the `fragment` function on *line 7*, we set the **ALBEDO** value of the **MeshInstance3D** to the Instance Uniform color. In *line 8*, we set the **ALPHA** value to the `alphachannel` Instance Uniform. These now show up in the **Inspector** under **Instance Shader Parameters**, where we can change the values.

We looked at **Instance Shader Parameters** in the **Inspector** at the bottom of the **GeometryInstance3D** section. We changed the **Color x** and **y** values to 1 to make it yellow. We changed the `alphachannel` value to .1, and now we can see through it.

Exploring the Visual Shaders Context menu

In this recipe, we use visual shaders to change the color of the panel to yellow with **Vector3Parameter** and **ColorOp**, which we create using the **Visual Shaders Context** menu.

Getting ready

For this recipe, click the + sign to the right of the `InstanceUniforms` scene we just completed to add a new scene. In the **Scene** tab, click **3D Scene**. Click on **Scene** in the top-left corner next to **Project**, then select **Save Scene As**, and name it `VSContextMenu`.

How to do it...

We start with **MeshInstance3D** with a **PlaneMesh** and then create a visual shader:

1. Left-click on the **Node3D** node and then press the + sign in the **Scene** tab. In the **Create New Node** window, type `mesh` in the **Search** box and then select **MeshInstance3D** to create the node in the scene.

2. In the **Inspector**, click on **<empty>** to the right of **Mesh** and select **New PlaneMesh**.

3. Left-click on the same place to open the properties of the **MeshInstance3D**.

4. Click on **<empty>** to the right of **Material** in the **Inspector** and select **New ShaderMaterial** from the drop-down list.

5. Click on **ShaderMaterial**, then click on **<empty>** to the right of **Shader** in the **Inspector** and select **New Shader** from the drop-down list.

6. To the right of **Type:**, click the down arrow on the far right and select **VisualShader**, then click the **Create** button.

7. Click **VSContextMenu.tres** to the right of **Shader**.

8. In the bottom panel where **Output** is on the left, on the far right, click the **Expand Bottom Panel** (*Shift + F12*) button:

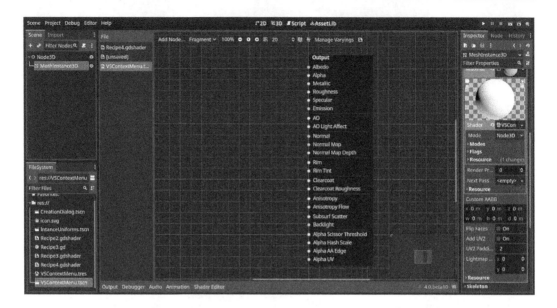

Figure 5.5 – Visual Shader fullscreen

9. Right-click on anywhere outside of the **Output** box to bring up the **Create Shader Node** menu and select **Color | Common | ColorOp**, then press the **Create** button:

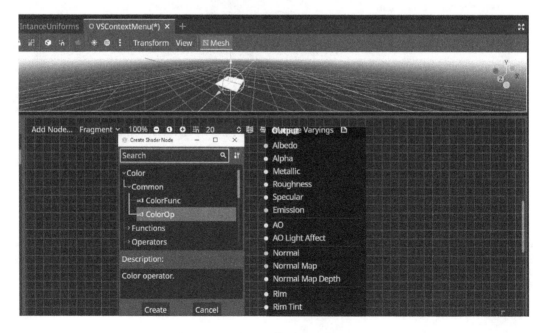

Figure 5.6 – Create Shader Node menu

10. In **ColorOp** to the right of **Op**, click the down arrow.

11. To the left of **a**, left-click on 0,0,0, then click on **y**, and change the value to 1.

12. Left-click on the dot on the right side and drag it to the dot to the left of **Albedo**.

13. Left-click on **ColorOp** to select the node. Right-click on **ColorOp** to see the new **Visual Shaders Context** menu and select **Add Node** at the top of the menu:

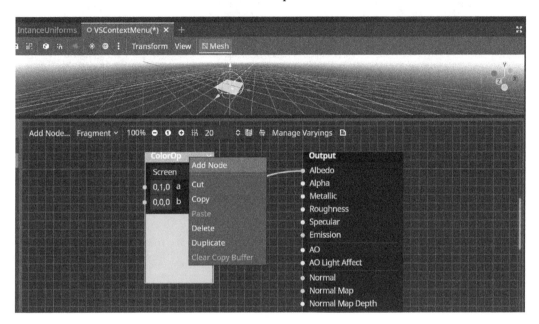

Figure 5.7 – Visual Shaders Context menu

14. In the **Create Shader Node** menu, select **Vector | Variables | Vector3Parameter**.

15. In the **Vector3Parameter** node to the right of **Qualifier**, left-click on the down arrow on the far right and select **Instance** from the drop-down list.

16. For the **Default Value Enabled:** value, check the **On** checkbox.

17. In **Default Value:**, change the x value to 1.

18. In the **Vector3Parameter** node, left-click on the dot on the right side and drag it to **b** in the **ColorOp** node:

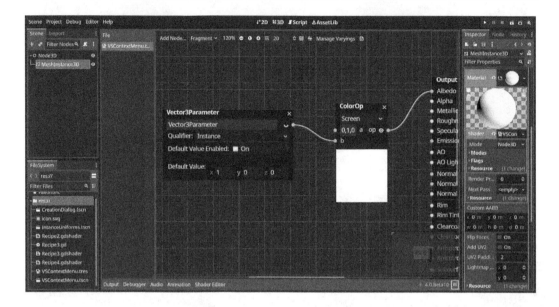

Figure 5.8 – Vector3Parameter node

19. Click on the button at the bottom right of the viewport to see that the **MeshInstance3D MeshPlane** is yellow as well as **Material** in the **Inspector**.

How it works...

We created a new **MeshInstance3D**, and for the **Mesh** property, we selected a **PlaneMesh**. For the **Material** property, we selected a new **ShaderMaterial**, and in the **Shader** property, we selected **New Shader** from the dropdown to bring up the **Create Shader** dialog. In the **Create Shader** dialog, we selected **VisualShader** as the type of shader we want to create. We clicked **VSContextMenu.tres** to the right of **Shader** to open the **Visual Shader** screen and then clicked the **Expand Bottom Panel** (*Shift + F12*) button to see it in fullscreen.

We clicked anywhere outside of the **Output** node to bring up the **Create Shader Node** menu, where we selected **ColorOp**. We clicked on the down arrow to the right of 0, 0, 0 **a op** to unhide the shader. Then, we clicked on 0, 0, 0 to change the value of **y** to 1. We clicked on the dot on the right side of the **ColorOp** node and dragged it to the dot to the left of **Albedo**. This connects **ColorOp** to **Albedo** for the shader. The color of our **MeshInstance3D** is now green. We can confirm that by clicking on the button at the bottom right of the viewport.

We left-clicked on the **ColorOp** node to select that node. The **ColorOp** node should be highlighted in blue. We right-clicked on the very top of **ColorOp** to see the new **Visual Shaders Context** menu and selected **Add Node** at the top of the menu to add the **Vector3Parameter** node. The other new things in the new **Visual Shaders Context** menu are **Cut**, **Copy**, **Paste**, **Delete**, **Duplicate**, and **Clear**

Copy Buffer. In some nodes, such as the **Vector3Parameter** node, there is an option to convert parameters in to constants.

For the **Vector3Parameter** node's **Qualifier** value, we selected **Instance**. We enabled **Default Value Enabled:** by checking the **On** checkbox. A **Default Value** box appeared, and we changed the value of **x** to 1. Then, we connected the **Vector3Parameters** node by dragging the dot on the right of this node to the **ColorOp** node's dot on the left of **b**. Then, we clicked the button on the bottom right of the viewport to confirm the **MeshInstance3D** is yellow.

The **ColorOp** node displays an error that it can't show the result retrieved from the **Instance** parameter, which means there is no preview color shown in the **ColorOp** node. The **MeshInstance3D** changed from green to yellow.

Working with Integer and Comment nodes

In this recipe, we use the **IntConstant**, **IntFunc**, and **IntOp** nodes to input values that will connect to a **VectorCompose** node, which will connect to the **Albedo** material of the **MeshInstance3D PlaneMesh**. We also use the **Comment** node to group all of the **Integer** nodes together and type a comment about the nodes.

Getting ready

For this recipe, we will stay in VSContextMenu from the last recipe. In the **Material** section in the **Inspector**, to the right of **Shader**, click on the counterclockwise circle to the left of the VSContextMenu. tres file to make the field empty. Click on <**empty**> and select **New Shader** from the drop-down list. In the **Type** section, select **Visual Shader** and then name it IntComNodes.

How to do it...

To see how the **Integer** nodes work, we are going to create more than you would normally use and also use the new **Comment** node:

1. Click on the **Distraction Free Mode** (*Ctrl* + *Shift* + *F11*) button located just to the left of the word **Inspector** at the top of the **Inspector**.

2. Right-click anywhere to the left of the **Output** node in the Visual **Shader Editor** and type vectorc or go to **Vector** | **Common** | **VectorCompose** and then select **VectorCompose** from the **Create Shader Node** menu. Click the **Create** button.

3. Under **VectorCompose**, make sure Vector3 is selected. If not, click on the down arrow on the right and select Vector3 from the drop-down list.

4. Left-click and drag the dot on the right to the dot to the left of **Albedo** in the **Output** node.

5.   Right-click anywhere to the left of **VectorCompose** node in the Visual **Shader Editor** and type int or go to **Scaler** | **Variables** | **IntConstant** and then select **IntConstant** from the **Create Shader Node** menu.

6.   Left-click on 0 and change the value to 1.

7.   Press *Ctrl* + *D* twice so that we have three **IntConstant** nodes, each with a value of 1.

8.   Move all three nodes to the left. We will add more nodes that will go between these nodes and the **VectorCompose** node, so leave some space, as shown in *Figure 5.9*.

9.   Right-click anywhere to the left of the **VectorCompose** node and to the right of the three **IntConstant** nodes in the Visual **Shader Editor**. Type int or go to **Scaler** | **Common** | **IntFunc**, then select **IntFunc** from the **Create Shader Node** menu. Click the **Create** button.

10. Left-click on **Sign** below **IntFunc** to bring up the drop-down list and then select **Abs**.

11. Press *Ctrl* + *D* one time and move both of the **IntFunc** nodes to the right of the top two **IntConstant** nodes, as shown in *Figure 5.9*.

12. Connect the dot on the right side of the **IntConstant** node to the dot on the left side of the **IntFunc** node for both copies.

13. For **IntConstant** | **IntFunc** in the middle, connect the dot on the right to the **y** value in **VectorCompose**.

14. Right-click anywhere to the left of the **VectorCompose** node and to the right of the three **IntConstant** nodes in the Visual **Shader Editor**. Type int or go to **Scaler** | **Common** | **IntOp**, then select **IntOp** from the **Create Shader Node** menu. Click the **Create** button.

15. Press *Ctrl* + *D* one time and move one of the **IntOp** nodes to the right of the top two **IntFunc** nodes and the other under the middle **IntFunc** node.

16. The operator for the top node should be **Add**. Connect the right dot of the top **IntFunc** node to **b** in the **IntOp** node.

17. Connect the right dot of the top **IntOp** node to **x** in the **VectorCompose** node.

18. Left-click on **Add** in the **InOp** node at the bottom and select **Subtract** in the drop-down list of operators.

19. Connect the right dot of the bottom **IntConstant** node to **b** in the **IntOp** node.

20. Connect the right dot of the bottom **IntOp** node to **z** in the **VectorCompose** node.

21. Right-click anywhere to the top left of the three **IntConstant** nodes in the Visual **Shader Editor**. Type comm or go to **Special** | **Comment**, then select **Comment** from the **Create Shader Node** menu. Click the **Create** button.

22. Click on the arrow in the bottom-right corner and drag it to cover all of the **IntConstant**, **IntFunc**, and **IntOp** nodes that we created.

23. Right-click on the word **Comment** in the **Comment** node, and at the bottom, select **Select Comment Description**.

24. Left-click in the box that pops up and type `Three int values going into VectorCompose then to Albedo:`

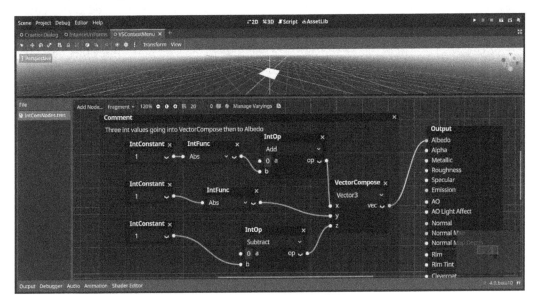

Figure 5.9 – IntConstant, IntFunc, and IntOp nodes

How it works...

We clicked on the **Distraction Free Mode** (*Ctrl + Shift + F11*) button to give us some room to create and move the visual shaders we are going to use in this recipe while also viewing the plane mesh. You could click **Expand Bottom Panel** (*Shift + F12*) to only see the Visual **Shader Editor**.

We right-clicked to the left of the **Output** node to bring up the **Create Shader Node** menu and selected the **VectorCompose** node by typing `vectorc` or went to **Vector | Common | VectorCompose** in the **Create Shader Node** menu. We checked to see that `Vector3` was selected, and if it was not, we selected it by clicking on the down arrow on the right and selecting it in the drop-down list.

We left-clicked the dot on the right side of the node and dragged it to the dot next to **Albedo** in the **Output** node. After we add nodes to connect to the **x**, **y**, and **z** inputs of the **VectorCompose** node, it will output to the **Albedo** material of the **PlaneMesh** and change its color.

We right-clicked to the left of the **VectorCompose** node to bring up the **Create Shader Node** menu and selected the **IntConstant** node by typing `int` or went to **Scaler | Variables | IntConstant** in the **Create Shader Node** menu. We changed the value to `1` by left-clicking on `0` to highlight it and then entering `1`.

We duplicated this node two times by making sure the **IntConstant** node was selected and then using *Ctrl + D*. We then had three **IntConstant** nodes each with a value of 1, which we moved over to the left side, leaving space between them and the **Output** node so that we could add more nodes to place between them.

We right-clicked to the left of the **VectorCompose** node and to the right of the three **IntConstant** nodes in the Visual **Shader Editor**. We typed int or went to **Scaler | Common | IntFunc** and then selected **IntFunc** from the **Create Shader Node** menu. We left-clicked on **Sign** below **IntFunc** to bring up a drop-down list and then selected **Abs**, which is the absolute value of the parameter.

The **Negate** option negates the value of the parameter. **Sign** extracts the sign of the parameter. **Bitwise NOT** returns the Bitwise NOT operation on the integer. We duplicated it one time, giving us two nodes. We connected it to the top **IntConstant** node and to the middle **IntConstant** node. We connected the middle **IntConstant** and **IntFunc** nodes to the **y** value of the **VectorCompose** node. The **PlaneMesh** was now green.

We right-clicked to the left of the **VectorCompose** node and to the right of the three **IntConstant** and **IntFunc** nodes in the Visual **Shader Editor**. We typed int or went to **Scaler | Common | IntOp**, then selected **IntOp** from the **Create Shader Node** menu. We duplicated the **IntOp** node once and moved one to the top and the other to the bottom. The one on the top has the **Add** operator.

The top **IntConstant** -> **IntFunc** node's right dot is connected to the **b** value of the top **IntOp** node. For the bottom **IntOp** node, we left-clicked on **Add** to select **Subtract** from the drop-down list. The list shows mathematical operators such as **Add**, **Subtract**, **Multiply**, **Divide**, and **Remainder**, just to name a few.

We selected **Subtract** so that after we connect the **IntOp** node on the bottom to the **z** value of the **VectorCompose** node, the **z** value would be 0. The Vector3 values going into the **Albedo** material of the **PlaneMesh** are 1 for **x** and **y** and 0 for **z**, which produce the color yellow, as we have seen in previous recipes.

We right-clicked to the top left of the three **IntConstant** nodes in the Visual **Shader Editor**. We typed comm or went to **Special | Comment**, then selected **Comment** from the **Create Shader Node** menu. We clicked on the arrow in the bottom-right corner and dragged it to cover all of the nodes we created.

We right-clicked on **Comment** in the **Comment** node, and at the bottom, we saw **Set Comment Title** and **Set Comment Description**. We selected the **Set Comment Description** option from the drop-down list and entered some text. You can change the title too if you wish. If you left-click on **Comment** at the top and hold then move the mouse, everything in the **Comment** node moves as a group.

Creating nodes using Texture3D and CurveTexture

In this recipe, we will add a **CurveTexture** node to the `IntComNodes.tres` visual shader file. We will use the **CurveTexture** node to control how much alpha we have on **MeshInstance3D**.

Getting ready

For this recipe, we will stay in `VSContextMenu` from the last recipe. If you'd like to keep the recipes separate, then continue with the rest of the *Getting ready* section. Otherwise, use the existing `IntComNodes.tres` visual shader. Right-click on the `IntComNodes` visual shader file and select **Duplicate** from the drop-down list.

In the popup that appears, change the name to `CurveTexture.tres` and left-click on the **Duplicate** button. In the **Inspector**, in the **Material** section, click on the counterclockwise circle to the right of **Shader**. Click on <**empty**> to the right of **Shader** and select **Load** from the drop-down menu. Select `CurveTexture.tres`, then click the **Open** button.

How to do it...

Let's add a **CurveTexture** node and hook it up to the **Alpha** channel in the Visual **Shader Editor**:

1. Right-click anywhere to the left of the **Output** node and not in the **Comment** section from the last recipe.

2. In the **Search** box, type `cur` and select **CurveTexture**.

3. Left-click the **Create** button.

4. Left-click on the blue dot on the right side of the **CurveTexture** node and drag it to the blue dot to the left of **Alpha** in the **Output** node.

5. In the **CurveTexture** node, click on <**empty**> and select **New CurveTexture**.

6. In the **Inspector**, click on <**empty**> to the right of **Curve**. If the **Inspector** is not visible, exit **Distraction Free Mode** by pressing *Ctrl + Shift + F11*.

7. Left-click on **New Curve**.

8. In the **CurveTexture** node, right-click and select **Add Point** from the popup.

9. Left-click the point and drag it to the `1` instance on the left side.

10. In the **CurveTexture** node, right-click and select **Add Point** from the popup.

11. Left-click the point and drag it to the 1 instance on the bottom-right side:

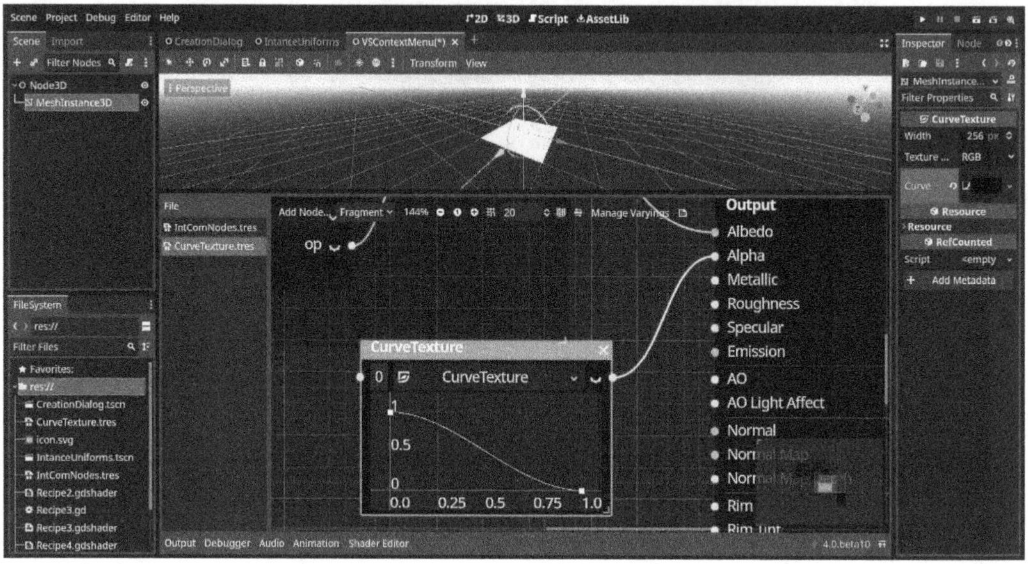

Figure 5.10 – CurveTexture node

12. Left-click on the point on the top left and drag down and up.

How it works...

We right-clicked to the left of the **Output** node and under the **Comment** node. In the **Create Shader Node** menu, we clicked on **CurveTexture** located in **Textures| Functions** by entering cur in the **Search** box. We dragged the blue dot on the right side of the **CurveTexture** node to the blue dot to the right of **Alpha** in the **Output** node.

We clicked on **<empty>** and selected **New CurveTexture**. This added properties of **CurveTexture** in the **Inspector**. In the **Inspector**, we clicked on **<empty>**, which was to the right of **Curve**. We left-clicked **New Curve** to add a curve texture to the **CurveTexture** node.

We added two points to the **CurveTexture** node and positioned them at the 1 instance on the top left and the 1 instance on the bottom right. To see it change the **Alpha** value, we left-clicked on the top right point and pulled it down to 0, which made the **MeshInstance3D** disappear. We then brought the same point back to 1, and the **MeshInstance3D** appeared.

Using the Billboard node

In this recipe, we will create a **MeshInstance3D** with a **BoxMesh**. We use the visual shader **Billboard** node so that the **MeshInstance3D** will always face the camera.

Getting ready

For this recipe, click + to the right of the VSContextMenu scene we just completed to add a new scene. In the **Scene** tab, click **3D Scene**. Click on the word **Scene** in the top-left corner next to **Project**, then select **Save Scene As**, and name it Billboard.

How to do it...

Let's create **MeshInstance3D** and then add the visual shader:

1. Left-click on the **Node3D** node and then press the + sign in the **Scene** tab. In the **Create New Node** window, type mesh in the **Search** box and then select **MeshInstance3D** to create the node in the scene.

2. In the **Inspector**, click on **<empty>** to the right of **Mesh** and select **New BoxMesh**.

3. Left-click on the same place to open the properties of the **MeshInstance3D**.

4. Click on **<empty>** to the right of **Material** in the **Inspector** and select **New ShaderMaterial** from the drop-down list.

5. Click on **<empty>** to the right of **Shader** in the **Inspector** and select **New Shader** from the drop-down list.

6. To the right of **Type:**, click the down arrow on the far right and select **VisualShader**.

7. Name the shader Billboard.tres and then click the **Create** button.

8. Left-click on **Transform** in the **Inspector**.

9. In **Transform**, left-click on the link icon to the right of **z** under **Scale** and change the **z** value to .2.

10. Click Billboard.tres to the right of **Shader**.

11. In the **Shader Editor** on the top and to the right of **Add Node**, left-click on **Fragment**.

12. Select **Vertex** from the drop-down list.

13. Right-click to the left of the **Output** node.

14. In the **Search** box of the **Create Shader Node** menu, type get.

15. Select **GetBillboardMatrix** located in **Transform | Functions**.

16. Left-click the **Create** button.

17. In the **GetBillboardMatrix** node for **Billboard Type**, make sure **Enabled** is selected on the right. If not, left-click and select **Enabled** from the drop-down list.

18. In the **GetBillboardMatrix** node, check the **On** checkbox for **Keep Scale**.

19. Left-click the orange dot on the bottom right and drag it to the orange dot labeled **Model View Matrix** in the **Output** node:

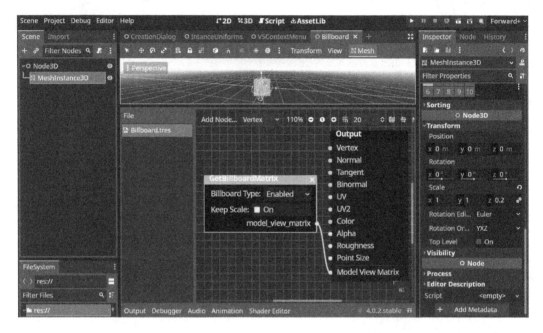

Figure 5.11 – GetBillboardMatrix node

20. Move your mouse cursor into the viewport.

21. Press and hold the scroll wheel of the mouse, then move the mouse around, and notice that one face of the **BoxMesh** follows the camera.

How it works...

We created a new **MeshInstance3D**, and for the **Mesh** property, we selected a **BoxMesh**. For the **Material** property, we selected a new **ShaderMaterial**, and in the **Shader** property, we selected **New Shader** from the drop-down to bring up the **Create Shader** dialog. For **Type:**, we selected **Visual Shader** and named it `Billboard.tres`.

We left-clicked **Transform** in the **Inspector**. We changed the scale of the box by left-clicking the link icon to the right of **z** under **Scale** in the **Transform** section in the **Inspector**. The values in **Scale** should be **x** 1, **y** 1, and **z** .2. We did this so that we can see more of a side of the box so that when we add the shader, we will notice that one side of the **BoxMesh** will follow the camera.

We clicked on `Billboard.tres` located to the right of **Shader** in the **Inspector** to see the visual shader in the **Shader Editor**. On the top left of the **Shader Editor**, we clicked on **Fragment** and selected **Vertex** from the drop-down list. We right-clicked to the left of the **Output** node to bring up the **Create Shader Node** menu, then typed `get` in the **Search** box. We selected **GetBillboardMatrix** located in **Transform | Functions**.

We changed the settings in the **GetBillboardMatrix** node. To the right of **Billboard Type**, we made sure **Enabled** was selected. If it wasn't, then we left-clicked what was selected, and from the drop-down list, we selected **Enabled**. We checked the **On** checkbox to the right of **Keep Scale**. We left-clicked the orange dot on the bottom right of the **GetBillboardMatrix** node and dragged it to the orange dot on the bottom of the **Output** node named **Model View Matrix**.

We moved the mouse cursor into the viewport around **MeshInstance3D**. We pressed and held the mouse wheel while we moved the mouse around to see that the face of the **MeshInstance3D** that is looking at the camera will always look at the camera, no matter where we move the camera.

Using the UVFunc node

In this recipe, we use the **UVFunc** node with the **Texture2D** node to scale and pan the `icon.svg` picture using visual shaders.

Getting ready

For this recipe, click + to the right of the **Billboard** scene we just completed to add a new scene. In the **Scene** tab, click **2D Scene**. Click on **Scene** in the top-left corner next to **Project**, then select **Save Scene As**, and name it `UVFunc`.

How to do it...

We will move the `icon.svg` file into the scene and then add a **ShaderMaterial** in the **CanvasItem** property:

1. Left-click and hold the left mouse button, then drag `icon.svg` anywhere in the viewport.

2. In the **CanvasItem** section of the **Inspector**, left-click on **Material**.

3. Click on **<empty>** to the right of **Material** and select **New ShaderMaterial**.

4. Left-click on **ShaderMaterial** to the right of **Material**.

5. Click on **<empty>** to the right of **Shader** and select **New Shader**.

6. To the right of **Type**, select **Visual Shader**.

7. To the right of **Mode**, select **Canvas Item**.

8. To the right of **Path name**, rename the file `UVFunc.tres`, and then click the **Create** button.

9. Left-click `UVFnc.tres` in the **Inspector** to see the shader in the **Shader Editor**.

10. Right-click anywhere to the left of the **Output** node in the **Shader Editor**.

11. In the **Create Shader Node** menu, type `texture2D` and left-click **Texture2D** in **Textures | Functions**.

12. Left-click the **Create** button.

13. In the **Texture2D** node, click on **Texture** at the top and select **Texture2D** from the drop-down list.

14. Left-click on the dot on the right side of the node and drag it to the dot to the left of **Color** in the **Output** node.

15. Right-click anywhere to the left of the **Texture2D** node in the **Shader Editor**.

16. Click **Add Node** from the popup.

17. In the **Create Shader Node** menu, type `uvf` and left-click **UVFunc** in **Textures | Common**.

18. Left-click the **Create** button.

19. Left-click on the dot on the right side of **UV** in the **UVFunc** node and drag it to the dot to the left of **UV** in the **Texture2D** node.

20. In the **UVFunc** node, left-click to the left of **scale** and then enter `.5, .5`.

21. In the **UVFunc** node, left-click to the left of **pivot** and then enter `.25 , .25`:

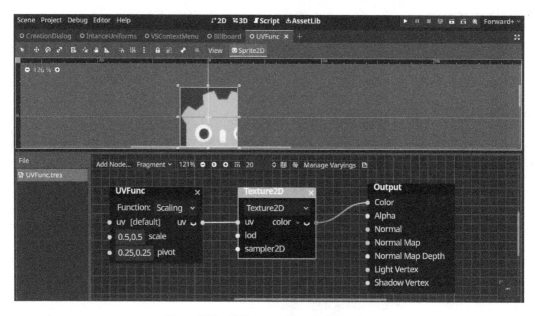

Figure 5.12 – UVFunc and Texture2D nodes

22. In the **UVFunc** node to the left of **Function**, left-click on **Scaling** and look at the icon in the viewport.

23. In the **UVFunc** node to the left of **Function**, left-click on **Panning** and look at the icon in the viewport.

How it works...

We dragged the `icon.svg` file into the viewport. In the **CanvasItem** section of the **Inspector**, we left-clicked on **Material** and then on <**empty**> to the right of **Material** so that we could create a new shader material. We selected **New ShaderMaterial** from the drop-down list.

Then, we left-clicked on **ShaderMaterial**, which appeared in the place of <**empty**> to reveal its properties. We left-clicked on <**empty**> to the right of **Shader** and selected **New Shader**. We made sure that it was a visual shader and that it was a **Canvas Item** type—these should have been the default. In the **Path** field, we named the shader `UVFunc.tres`.

We clicked on `UVFunc.tres`, which is on the left of **Shader** in **Material** in the **CanvasItem** section of the **Inspector**. This shows the **Shader Editor** on the bottom panel under the viewport. We right-clicked in the **Shader Editor** to the left of the **Output** node. We selected the **Texture2D** node by searching for `texture2d` and selecting **Texture2D** under **Textures | Functions** and then left-clicking on the **Create** button.

In the **Texture2D** node, we clicked on **Texture** at the top and selected **Texture2D** from the drop-down list. Then, we left-clicked and dragged the dot on the right side of **Color** in the **Texture2D** node to the dot on the left of **Color** in the **Output** node.

We added the **UVFunc** node by right-clicking anywhere to the left of the **Texture2D** node and clicking **Add Node** in the popup. In the **Search** box, we typed `uvf` and clicked on **UVFunction**, located in **Textures | Common**. Then, we left-clicked on the **Create** button. We left-clicked on the dot on the right side of **UV** in the **UVFunc** node and dragged it to the dot to the left of **UV** in the **Texture2D** node.

In the **UVFunc** node, we changed the **x** and **y** values of **Scale** to `.5` each and the **x** and **y** values of **Offset** to `.25` each. We changed the **Function** values to **Scaling** and **Panning** to see how the `icon.svg` file changed. Change the values to something different to see what happens.

Improving the Sky Shader mode

In this recipe, we are going to create a custom sky using the **Sky Shader** mode in the Visual **Shader Editor**. Using sky shaders in Godot 4, you can update the sky in real time to create dynamic skies.

Getting ready

For this recipe, click on the + sign to the right of the **UVFunc** scene we just completed to add a new scene. In the **Scene** tab, click **3D Scene**. Click on **Scene** in the top-left corner next to **Project**, then select **Save Scene As**, and name it `SkyShader`.

How to do it...

First, we will add the **WorldEnvironment** node to the **Scene** tab so that we can create a shader on **Sky Material**:

1. Left-click on the three vertical dots in the toolbar above the viewport and left-click on **Add Environment to Scene**.

2. Left-click on the **WorldEnvironment** node in the **Scene** tab.

3. In the **Inspector**, left-click on **Environment** to the right of **Environment** to open its properties.

4. Left-click on **Sky** in the **Inspector** to open its properties.

5. Left-click on **Sky** to the right of the **Sky** property in the **Inspector**.

6. To the right of **Sky Material**, right-click on **ProceduralSkyMaterial**.

7. Select **New ShaderMaterial** from the drop-down list.

8. To the right of **Sky Material** in the **Inspector**, left-click on **ShaderMaterial** to see its properties.

9. Click on **<empty>** to the right of **Shader** and select **New Shader**.

10. To the right of **Type**, select **Visual Shader**.

11. To the right of **Mode**, select **Sky**.

12. To the right of **Path**, name the file `SkyShader.tres`, and then click the **Create** button.

13. Left-click `SkyShader.tres` to see the shader in the **Shader Editor**.

14. Right-click anywhere to the left of the **Output** node in the **Shader Editor**.

15. Click **Add Node** from the popup.

16. In the **Create Shader Node** menu, type `mix` and left-click **Mix** under **Scalar | Functions**.

17. Left-click the **Create** button.

18. Left-click on **Scalar** and select **Vector3Scalar** from the drop-down list.

19. Left-click the dot on the right side of the **Mix** node and drag it to the dot to the left of **Color** in the **Output** node.

20. Right-click anywhere to the left of the **Mix** node in the **Shader Editor.**

21. Click **Add Node** from the popup.

22. In the **Create Shader Node** menu, type `smo`, and left-click **SmoothStep** under **Scalar | Functions**.

23. Left-click the **Create** button.

24. Left-click on `0` to the left of **edge0** and change the value to `-.2`.

25. Left-click on `1` to the left of **edge1** and change the value to `.4`.

26. Left-click the dot on the right side of the **SmoothStep** node and drag it to the dot to the left of **Weight** in the **Mix** node.

27. Right-click anywhere to the left of the **SmoothStep** node in the **Shader Editor.**

28. Click **Add Node** from the popup.

29. In the **Create Shader Node** menu, type `dot`, and left-click **Dot** under **Vector | Functions.**

30. Left-click the **Create** button.

31. Left-click on 0, 0, 0 to the left of **a** and change the **y** value to 2.

32. Left-click the dot on the right side of the **DotProduct** node and drag it to the dot to the left of **x** in the **SmoothStep** node.

33. Right-click anywhere to the left of the **DotProduct** node in the **Shader Editor.**

34. Click **Add Node** from the popup.

35. In the **Create Shader Node** menu, type `eye`, and left-click `EyeDir` under **Input | Sky.**

36. Left-click the **Create** button.

37. Left-click the dot on the right side of the **eyedir Input** node and drag it to the dot to the left of **b** in the **DotProduct** node.

38. Right-click anywhere to the left of the **Output** node and above the **SmoothStep** node in the **Shader Editor.**

39. Click **Add Node** from the popup.

40. In the **Create Shader Node** menu, type `vec`, and left-click **Vector3Constant** under **Vector | Variables** at the bottom of the drop-down list.

41. Left-click the **Create** button.

42. Left-click 0 in **x** and change the value to .2.

43. Left-click 0 in **y** and change the value to .4.

44. Left-click 0 in **z** and change the value to .9.

45. Left-click the dot on the right side of the **Vector3Constant** node and drag it to the dot to the left of **b** in the **Mix** node.

46. Right-click anywhere to the left of the **Output** node and above the **Vector3Constant** node in the **Shader Editor.**

47. Click **Add Node** from the popup.

48. In the **Create Shader Node** menu, type `col`, and left-click **Light1Color** under **Input | Sky** at the bottom of the drop-down list.

49. Left-click the **Create** button.

50. Left-click the dot on the right side of the **Light1Color Input** node and drag it to the dot to the left of **a** in the **Mix** node:

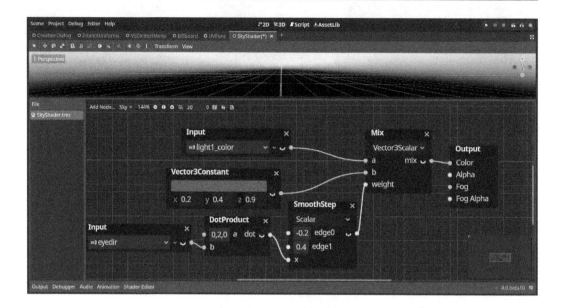

Figure 5.13 – SkyShader.tres

How it works...

We clicked on the three vertical dots to add the **WorldEnvironment** node to the **Scene** tab. In the **Inspector**, we left-clicked on **Environment** to open its properties. In the **Inspector**, we left-clicked on **Sky** to open its properties. In the **Inspector** underneath **Sky** is **SkyMaterial**. We right-clicked on **ProceduralSkyMaterial** and selected **New ShaderMaterial** from the drop-down list.

We left-clicked on **ShaderMaterial** located on the right of **Sky Material** in the **Inspector**. Now, we can see its properties. We clicked on <**empty**> located to the right of **Shader** and selected **New Shader**. When we created a new shader, we made sure that the type was a visual shader, and that the **Mode** setting was **Sky**. In the **Path** field, we named the shader SkyShader.tres.

We left-clicked SkyShader.tres to see the shader in the **Shader Editor**. We added a **Mix** node on the left side of the **Output** node. We left-clicked on **Scalar** and selected **Vector3Scalar** from the drop-down list. We dragged the dot on the right side of the **Mix** node to the dot to the left of **Color** on the **Output** node.

We added a **SmoothStep** node to the left of the **Mix** node and moved the node down toward the bottom-left corner of the **Mix** node to give us some room to create new nodes later. We left-clicked on 0 to the left of **edge0** and changed the value to -.2. Then, we left-clicked on 1 to the left of **edge1** and changed the value to .4. We left-clicked the dot on the right side of the **SmoothStep** node and dragged it to the dot to the left of **Weight** in the **Mix** node.

We added a **DotProduct** node to the left of the **SmoothStep** node. We left-clicked on **0,0,0** to the left of **a** and changed the **y** value to 2. We left-clicked the dot on the right side of the **DotProduct** node and dragged it to the dot to the left of **x** in the **SmoothStep** node. We added an **eyedir Input** node to the left of the **DotProduct** node. We left-clicked the dot on the right side of the **eyedir Input** node and dragged it to the dot to the left of **b** in the **DotProduct** node.

We added a **Vector3Constant** node above the **SmoothStep** node and to the left of **b** of the **Mix** node. We changed the **x** value to . 2, the **y** value to . 4, and the **z** value to . 9. This gave us a blue-sky color. We left-clicked the dot on the right side of the **Vector3Constant** node and dragged it to the dot to the left of **b** in the **Mix** node.

We then added a **Light1Color Input** node above the **Vector3Constant** node. We left-clicked the dot on the right side of the **Light1Color Input** node and dragged it to the dot to the left of **a** in the **Mix** node. We now have a blue sky using visual shaders.

What the Fog Shader mode can do

In this recipe, we are going to create custom fog in the **FogVolume** node using visual shaders. We will make a greenish fog, which could be used for a poisonous area in a game.

Getting ready

For this recipe, click the + sign to the right of the **UVFunc** scene we just completed to add a new scene. In the **Scene** tab, click **3D Scene**. Click on **Scene** in the top-left corner next to **Project**, then select **Save Scene As**, and name it FogShader.

How to do it...

First, we will add a **FogVolume** node to the **Scene** tab and then add a visual shader to **Material**:

1. Left-click on the three vertical dots in the toolbar above the viewport and left-click on **Add Environment to Scene**.
2. Left-click on the **WorldEnvironment** node in the **Scene** tab.
3. In the **Inspector**, left-click on **Environment** to the right of **Environment** to open its properties.
4. Left-click on **Volumetric Fog** in the **Inspector** to open its properties.
5. Check the **On** checkbox to the right of **Enabled**.
6. To the right of **Density**, change the value to 0.
7. Left-click on the **Node3D** node and then the + sign in the **Scene** tab. In the **Create New Node** window, type fog in the **Search** box and then select **FogVolume** to create the node in the scene.

8. In the **Inspector**, click on **<empty>** to the right of **Material** and select **New ShaderMaterial**.

9. In the **Inspector**, click on **ShaderMaterial** to the right of **Material** to open the **ShaderMaterial** properties.

10. In the **Inspector**, click on **<empty>** to the right of **Shader** and select **New Shader**.

11. To the right of **Type**, select **Visual Shader**.

12. To the right of **Mode**, select **Fog**.

13. To the right of **Path**, name the file `FogShader.tres` and then click the **Create** button.

14. Left-click `FogShader.tres` in the **Inspector** to see the shader in the **Shader Editor**.

15. Right-click anywhere to the left of the **Output** node in the **Shader Editor**.

16. In the **Create Shader Node** menu, type `col` and left-click **ColorConstant** under **Color | Variables** in the drop-down list.

17. Left-click the **Create** button.

18. Left-click on the white box and enter `65ff39` in the box to the right of **Hex**.

19. Left-click on the dot on the right side of the **ColorConstant** node and drag it to the dot on the left side of **Albedo**.

20. Right-click anywhere to the left of the **Output** node in the **Shader Editor**.

21. In the **Create Shader Node** menu, type `floa` and left-click **FloatConstant** under **Scalar | Variables** at the bottom of the drop-down list.

22. Left-click the **Create** button.

23. Left-click on `0` and change the value to `2`.

24. Left-click on the dot on the right side of the **FloatConstant** node and drag it to the dot on the left side of **Density**:

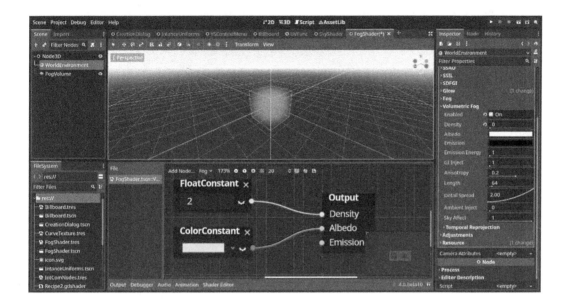

Figure 5.14 – FogShader.tres

How it works...

We clicked on the three vertical dots to add the **WorldEnvironment** node to the **Scene** tab. In the **Inspector**, we left-clicked on **Environment** to the right of **Environment** to open its properties. In the **Inspector**, we left-clicked on **Volumetric Fog** to open its properties. We checked the **On** checkbox to the right of **Enabled** to use volumetric fog. We changed the value of **Density** to 0 because we are going to use a shader for our fog.

We created a **FogVolume** node in the **Scene** tab. We clicked on <empty> to the right of **Material** in the **Inspector** and selected **New ShaderMaterial**. We clicked on **ShaderMaterial** to open its properties. In the **Inspector**, we saw <empty> on the right of **Shader**, and we clicked on it to bring up the **Create Shader** dialog box. We checked to see that the **Type** value was **Visual Shader**, the **Mode** value was **Fog**, and in the **Path** field, we changed the name to FogShader.tres. We left-clicked FogShader. tres in the **Inspector** to see the shader in the **Shader Editor**.

We created a **ColorConstant** node in the visual **Shader Editor**. We clicked on the white box and changed the **Hex #** value to 65ff39. This gave us a green color. We left-clicked the dot on the right side of the **ColorConstant** node and dragged it to the dot on the left of **Albedo** in the **Output** node. We created a **FloatConstant** node and changed its value to 2. We left-clicked the dot on the right side of the **FloatConstant** node and dragged it to the left of **Density**.

6

Importing 3D Assets in Godot 4

In this chapter, we will start by connecting the Blender and FBX2glTF paths to Godot 4 in **Editor Settings**. We will then import blend files into Godot 4 and see how the models change in Godot when they're updated in Blender. Because Godot does not have FBX support, we will import a `FBX2glTF.exe` file, which we are going to download from GitHub.

This file is going to change the FBX file into a glTF file so that we can use FBX files. We will also import a glTF file into Godot. Finally, we will use the **Import** dialog to extract a `.tres` file from a texture and add that texture to the copy of the glTF file we downloaded previously.

In this chapter, we will cover the following recipes:

- Importing Blender blend files into Godot 4
- Importing FBX files into Godot 4
- Importing glTF files into Godot 4
- Using the **Import** dialog

Technical requirements

For this chapter, you need the standard version of Godot 4.0 or later running on one of the following operating systems:

- Windows 64-bit or 32-bit
- macOS
- Linux 64-bit or 32-bit
- Android
- Web Editor

You can find the code and the project files for the projects in this chapter on GitHub: `https://github.com/PacktPublishing/Godot-4-Game-Development-Cookbook/tree/main/Chapter%206`.

Blender can be downloaded for free here: `https://www.blender.org/download`.

Importing Blender blend files into Godot 4

In this recipe, we will connect the Blender path to Godot 4 in **Editor Settings**. We will import a blend file into Godot and change the file in Blender to see that the imported file changes in Godot without having to reimport the file.

Getting ready

For this recipe, open Godot 4 and start a new project called `Chapter 6`. In the **Scene** tab, click **3D** to add a 3D scene. Click on **Scene** in the main menu next to **Project**, then select **Save Scene As**, and name it `Blend`.

How to do it...

In this recipe, we will start by connecting the Blender path to Godot 4 in **Editor Settings**:

1. In the main menu, at the top left of Godot, select **Editor | Editor Settings**.
2. On the left, under **Filter Settings | FileSystem**, click **Import**.
3. Click on the folder icon to the far right of **Blender 3 Path**:

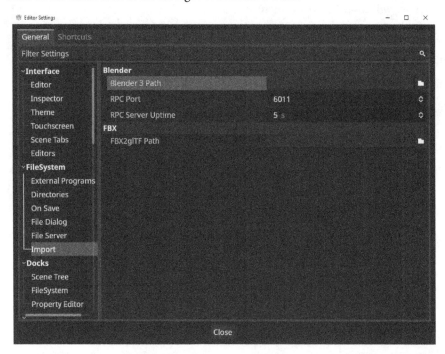

Figure 6.1 – Editor Settings

4. Select the correct path where you installed Blender 3 and then click the **Close** button.

5. Download **Lefty jack Truck 3D Model** from `https://www.cadnav.com/3d-models/model-53400.html`.

6. Extract the files from the ZIP file to anywhere on your computer.

7. Double-click the `cadnav.com_model` folder that you just extracted from the ZIP file.

8. Click and drag the `Model_G0402A160` folder into the **FileSystem** tab in Godot.

9. Click on the arrow to the left of the `Models_G0402A160` folder in the **FileSystem** tab.

10. Click and drag the **LeftyJ_Truck.blend** scene onto **Node3D** in the **Scene** tab.

11. Press *Ctrl + S* to save the scene.

12. In the **FileSystem** tab, right-click the **LeftyJ_Truck.blend** scene and select **Show in File Manager** from the drop-down list at the bottom.

13. In the window that appears, double-click on the **LeftyJ_Truck** blend file.

14. In Blender, which just popped up, click on the **Texture Paint** workspace to the right of the Blender menu on the top bar:

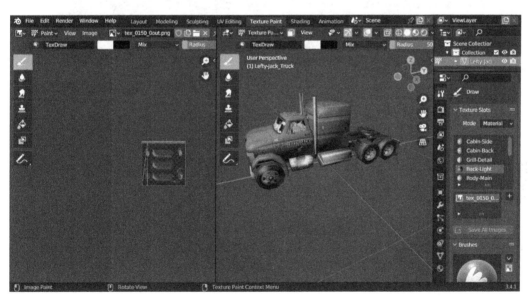

Figure 6.2 – Texture Paint workspace

15. Using the mouse wheel, scroll in to see the model better.

16. Move the mouse cursor, which is now a big circle, over to the back cab of the truck and click the left mouse button and paint the side of the back cab.

17. On the top bar, in the main menu, click **File** and select **Save** from the drop-down list, or press *Ctrl + S* in Windows or *Cmd + S* on Mac.

18. Click anywhere in Godot:

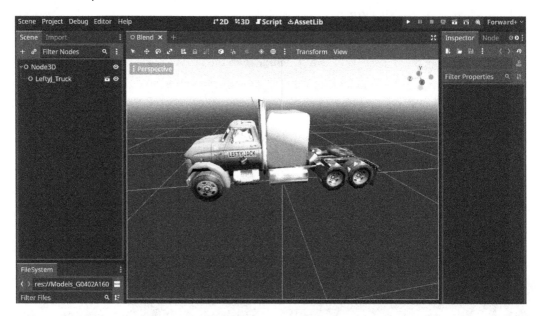

Figure 6.3 – Blender 3 Path in Godot's Editor Settings

19. On the top bar, in the main menu, click **File** and select **Quit** from the drop-down list.

20. When Blender asks whether you want to save your changes before closing, select **Save**.

21. Restart Godot and click anywhere inside it.

How it works...

In this recipe, we went to the main menu in Godot, which can be found in the top left of the **Editor** area. We clicked on **Editor** and then **Editor Settings**. In **Filter Settings**, on the left-hand side of the pop-up window, then under **FileSystem**, we clicked **Import**. Then, we clicked on the folder icon on the far right of **Blender 3 Path** under Blender. Finally, we selected the correct path that Blender 3 installed.

Next, we went to https://www.cadnav.com/ to download a blend file called **Lefty jack Truck 3D Model**. We extracted the files in the ZIP folder to wherever we wanted. I have a folder called 3D Assets in my **Documents** folder where I extract 3D models – you can extract it to your desktop or anywhere you like.

We double-clicked on the cadnav.com_model folder to open the folder. Then, we clicked and dragged the Model_G0402A160 folder into the **FileSystem** tab in Godot. We clicked on the arrow to the left of the `Model_G0402A160` folder to show the contents of the folder. Then, we clicked and dragged the `LeftyJ_Truck.blend` scene onto **Node3D** in the **Scene** tab to see the model in the viewport. We saved the scene by pressing *Ctrl + S* on our keyboard.

After, we right-clicked the `LeftyJ_Truck.blend` scene in the **FileSystem** area and selected **Show in File Manager** from the drop-down list at the bottom. This brought up the `Models_ G0402A160` folder window in the `Chapter 6` Godot project. In the window that appeared, we double-clicked on the **LeftyJ_Truck** blend file to open the file in Blender.

Once we were in Blender, we went to the **Texture Paint** workspace, which is to the right of the Blender menu on the top bar. We used the mouse wheel to zoom in to see the model better. We painted the back cab by moving the mouse cursor, which became a big circle, over the back cab of the truck and then pressed the left mouse button. We then saved the file and clicked on Godot. When we clicked on Godot, we saw an importing assets window open briefly because we changed that file in Blender.

Finally, we selected **File** and then **Quit** from the drop-down list in Blender. Blender asked whether we wanted to save our changes before we exited. We selected **Save**. When we restarted Godot, we clicked anywhere in Godot and the model with the changes appeared.

Importing FBX files into Godot 4

In this recipe, we are going to download the `FBX2glTF.exe` file from GitHub and connect it to **FBX2glTF Path** in **Editor Settings**. We will download and import an FBX file into Godot.

Getting ready

For this recipe, click the + button to the right of the **Blend** scene we just completed to add a new scene. In the **Scene** tab, click **3D Scene**. Click on **Scene** in the main menu next to **Project**, then select **Save Scene As**, and name it `FBX`.

How to do it...

First, let's download the `FBX2glTF.exe` file from GitHub and connect it to Godot:

1. Go to `https://github.com/godotengine/FBX2glTF/releases/tag/ v0.12.9-p2` and select `FBX2glTF.exe`.

2. Save the file somewhere you will remember it.

3. In the main menu, on the top left of Godot, select **Editor | Editor Settings**.

4. On the left of **Filter Settings | FileSystem**, click **Import**.

5. Click on the folder icon to the far right of **FBX2glTF Path**, as shown in *Figure 6.1*.

6. Select the `FBX2glTF.exe` file that you just downloaded and click the **Close** button.

7. Go to https://polyhaven.com/a/wooden_table_02 and, to the right of **4K**, click on the down arrow to open the drop-down list:

Figure 6.4 – FBX file type

8. Select **ZIP** and click on all the **PNG** files you wish to include in the download. Then, click **Download**.

9. Extract the ZIP file to your Godot Chapter 6 project folder or a new folder on your computer. Then, drag the textures folder and the wooden_table_02_4k.fbx file into the **FileSystem** tab.

10. Press *Ctrl + S* (*Cmd + S* on Mac) to save the scene and reboot Godot.

11. In Godot, click and drag wooden_table_02_4k.fbx onto **Node3D** in the **Scene** tab.

How it works...

In this recipe, we went to GitHub to download the FBX2glTF.exe file. We went to the main menu in Godot, in the top left of the **Editor** area. We clicked on **Editor** and then **Editor Settings**. In **Filter Settings**, on the left-hand side of the pop-up window, under **FileSystem**, we clicked **Import**. After, we clicked on the folder icon on the far right of **FBX2glTF Path** under Blender. We selected the path where the FBX2glTF.exe file was installed.

Next, we went to Poly Haven and downloaded wooden_table_02_4k.fbx, which is the FBX version of Wooden Table 02. We clicked on all of the PNG texture files. If we hadn't included these PNG files, it would not have worked. We extracted the contents of the ZIP file into the Godot Chapter 6 folder. We could have also created a new folder and extracted its contents in the new folder and then dragged the `textures` folder, along with the `wooden_table_02_4K.fbx` file, into the **FileSystem** tab in Godot.

When the files are imported, we will see some errors and a red **x** by the `wooden_table_02_4K.fbx` file, but don't worry – we saved the scene and then rebooted Godot. The FBX file now doesn't have a red **x**. Finally, we clicked and dragged the `wooden_table_02_4k.fbx` file onto **Node3D** in the **Scene** tab.

Importing glTF files into Godot 4

In this recipe, we are going to download and import a glTF file into Godot. This is the format that is supported by Godot by default.

Getting ready

For this recipe, click the + button to the right of the **FBX** scene we just completed to add a new scene. In the **Scene** tab, click **3D Scene**. Click on **Scene** in the top-left corner next to **Project**, then select **Save Scene As**, and name it `glTF`.

How to do it...

In this recipe, we will download the glTF format of `Wooden Table 02` from the previous recipe:

1. Go to `https://polyhaven.com/a/wooden_table_02` and, to the right of **4K**, click on the down arrow to open the drop-down list:

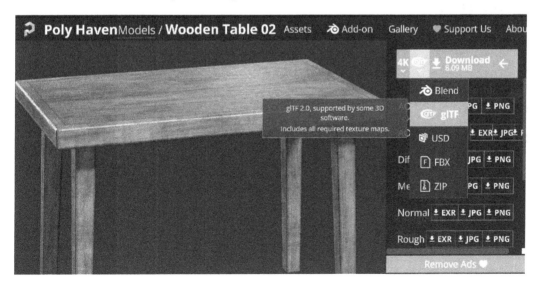

Figure 6.5 – glTF file type

2. Select **glTF**, then click **Download**.

3. Extract the ZIP file to your Godot `Chapter 6` project folder or a new folder on your computer. Then, drag the `textures` folder and the `wooden_table_02_4k.gltf` file into the **FileSystem** tab.

4. In Godot, click and drag `wooden_table_02_4k.gltf` onto **Node3D** in the **Scene** tab.

How it works...

In this recipe, we went to Poly Haven and downloaded `wooden_table_02_4k.gltf`, which is the glTF version of `Wooden Table 02`.

We extracted the contents of the ZIP file into the Godot `Chapter 6` folder. We could have also created a new folder and extracted its contents into the new folder and then dragged the `textures` folder, along with the `wooden_table_02_4K.gltf` file, into the **FileSystem** tab in Godot.

Finally, we clicked and dragged the `wooden_table_02_4k.gltf` file onto **Node3D** in the **Scene** tab.

Using the Import dialog

In this recipe, we are going to duplicate the wooden table that we used in the previous recipe and download an **Old Wood Floor** texture. Using the **Import** dialog, we are going to extract the `old_wood_floor.tres` file from the `old_wood_floor_1K.gltf` file we downloaded. Then, we will use that texture for the texture of the wooden table.

Getting ready

For this recipe, click the + button to the right of the **glTF** scene we just completed to add a new scene. In the **Scene** tab, click **3D Scene**. Click on **Scene** in the top-left corner next to **Project**, then select **Save Scene As**, and name it `Import`.

How to do it...

First, we will download the **Old Wood Floor** texture from Poly Haven and then extract the `.tres` file:

1. Go to `https://polyhaven.com/a/old_wood_floor` and, to the right of **1K**, click on the down arrow to open the drop-down list:

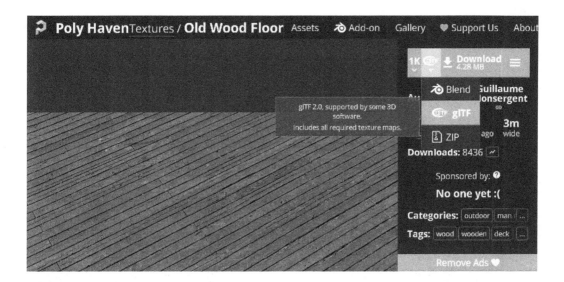

Figure 6.6 – The Old Wood Floor texture

2. Select **glTF**, then click **Download**.

3. Extract the ZIP file to your Godot Chapter 6 project folder or a new folder on your computer, then drag the textures folder and the old_wood_floor_1k.gltf file into the **FileSystem** tab.

4. In Godot, right-click in the **FileSystem** tab and select **New Folder** from the drop-down list. Name this new folder materials.

5. Go to https://polyhaven.com/a/wooden_crate_01 and, to the right of **1K**, click on the down arrow to open the drop-down list.

6. Select **glTF**, then click **Download**.

7. Extract the **ZIP** file to your Godot Chapter 6 project folder or a new folder on your computer, then drag the textures folder and the wooden_crate_01_4k.gltf file into the **FileSystem** tab.

8. Click wooden_crate_01_4k.gltf and hold and drag it onto **Node3D** in the **Scene** tab.

9. Click on old_wood_floor_1k.gltf in the **FileSystem** tab.

10. Click on the **Import** tab to the right of the **Scene** tab.

11. Click on the **Advanced** button on the bottom right-hand side of the **Import** tab.

12. In the **Advanced Import Settings** pop-up window, click on the **Materials** tab.

13. In the **Materials** tab, click on old_wood_floor.

14. In the **Advanced Import Settings** pop-up window, click on **Actions** above the **Scene**, **Meshes**, and **Materials** tabs. This can be found at the top left-hand side of the window.

15. After clicking **Actions**, click **Set Mesh Save Paths**.

16. Click on the `materials` folder and then click on the **Select This Folder** button. After, click on the **Set Paths** button.

17. In the **Advanced Import Settings** pop-up window, click on **Actions** above the **Scene**, **Meshes**, and **Materials** tabs. This can be found at the top left-hand side of the window:

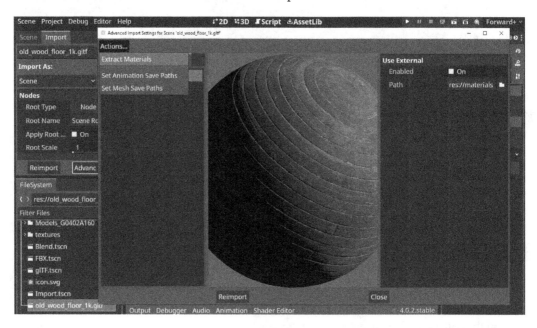

Figure 6.7 – Extract Materials

18. After clicking **Actions**, click **Extract Materials**.

19. Click the `materials` folder and click on the **Select This Folder** button.

20. Click on the **Extract** button. Then, click on the **Close** button.

21. In the **FileSystem** tab, click on `wooden_crate_01_4k.gltf`.

22. In the **Import** tab, click the **Advanced** button.

23. In the **Advanced Import Settings** pop-up window, click on the **Materials** tab.

24. In the **Materials** tab, click on `wooden_crate_01`.

25. On the far right-hand side, check the **On** checkbox to the right of **Enabled**.

26. Click on the folder to the far right of **Path** under **Enabled**.

27. Double-click on the `materials` folder.

28. Click on `old_wood_floor.tres` and then click the **Open** button.

29. Click the **Reimport** button at the bottom of the **Advanced Import Settings** pop-up window.

30. If you don't see a change, save the scene and reboot Godot.

How it works...

In this recipe, we went to Poly Haven and downloaded `old_wood_floor_1k.gltf`. We extracted the contents of the ZIP file into the Godot `Chapter 6` folder. We could have also created a new folder and extracted its contents into the new folder or an existing folder.

Then, we dragged the `textures` folder, along with the `old_wood_floor_1k.gltf` file, into the **FileSystem** tab in Godot. We created a new folder called `materials` so that we had a place to extract the `.tres` file we got from `old_wood_floor_1k.gltf`.

We went back to Poly Haven and downloaded `wooden_crate_01_4k.gltf`. We extracted the contents of the ZIP file just like we did with `old_wood_floor_1k.gltf`. We clicked and dragged `wooden_crate_01_4k.gltf` onto **Node3D** in the **Scene** tab. At this point, we could see the crate with its default texture.

Next, we clicked on `old_wood_floor_1k.gltf` in the **FileSystem** tab and then clicked on the **Import** tab, which is to the right of the **Scene** tab, and clicked the **Advanced** button to bring up the **Advanced Import Settings** pop-up window. In the **Advanced Import Settings** pop-up window, we clicked on the **Materials** tab and clicked on `old_wood_floor`.

After that, we checked the **On** checkbox to the right of **Enabled** and clicked on the folder to the far right of **Path** under **Enabled**. We double-clicked the `materials` folder so that we could use it for the `.tres` file that we extracted from `old_wood_floor`.

Then, we clicked **Actions** in the **Advanced Import Settings** pop-up window to select **Set Mesh Save Paths** from the drop-down list. We clicked on the `materials` folder and then clicked on the **Select This Folder** button. We did this so that any mesh data that we extract will be saved to the `materials` folder. Then, we clicked the **Set Paths** button.

Next, we clicked **Actions** in the **Advanced Import Settings** pop-up window to select **Extract Materials** from the drop-down list. We clicked the `materials` folder and clicked on the **Select This Folder** button. After, we clicked on the **Extract** button to extract the `old_wood_floor.tres` file from `old_wood_floor_1K.gltf`.

Then, we clicked on `wooden_crate_01_4k.gltf` in the **FileSystem** tab. This is where we added the texture that we extracted from `old_wood_floor_1K.gltf` and added it to `wooden_crate_01_4k.gltf`. We clicked the **Advanced** button in the **Import** tab to bring up the **Advanced Import Settings** pop-up window.

Finally, we clicked on `wooden_crate_01`, which is located under the **Materials** tab, so that we could check the **On** checkbox to the right of **Enabled**. Under **Path**, we selected the `materials` folder to find `old_wood_floor.tres` and clicked on the **Open** button to select it. After, we clicked on the **Reimport** button at the bottom of the **Advanced Import Settings** pop-up window to add the `old_wood_floor.tres` texture that we extracted from `old_wood_floor_1K.gltf`. The **Old Wood Floor** texture should now be applied to the wooden crate. If this didn't happen for you, save the scene and reboot Godot.

7

Adding Sound and Music to Your Game

Godot 4 fixed some audio issues, such as popping, resampling behavior, and performing sound operations simultaneously.

In this chapter, we are going to use the **AudioStreamPlayer** node to play constant music no matter where the player is located. We will also set up a repeated gunshot SFX to show off Godot 4's built-in polyphonic support.

We will use the **AudioStreamPlayer2D** node to see how to create directional sound. When the player comes close to an object, they will be able to hear it. In the last recipe, we will use the **AudioStreamPlayer3D** node to create directional sound in a 3D environment.

In this chapter, we will cover the following recipes:

- Working with **AudioStreamPlayer**
- Exploring directional sound in 2D
- Using directional sound in 3D

Technical requirements

For this chapter, you need the standard version of Godot 4.0 or later running on one of the following:

- Windows 64-bit or 32-bit
- macOS
- Linux 64-bit or 32-bit
- Android
- Web Editor

You can find the code and the project files for the projects in this chapter at GitHub: `https://github.com/PacktPublishing/Godot-4-Game-Development-Cookbook/tree/main/Chapter%207`.

Working with AudioStreamPlayer

In this recipe, we will use the **AudioStreamPlayer** node to play constant rain SFX or music, no matter where the player goes in the game. We will also use another **AudioStreamPlayer** node to create SFX of a gunshot to show off the new polyphonic support, which allows you to repeat the same sound multiple times on top of itself, using one **AudioStreamPlayer** node without any distorting sounds.

Getting ready

For this recipe, open Godot 4 and start a new project called `Chapter 7`. In the **Scene** tab, click **2D** to add a 2D scene. Click on **Scene** in the main menu next to **Project**, then select **Save Scene As**, and name the scene `AudioStreamPlayer`.

How to do it...

Let's download our gunshot SFX and music before we add the **AudioStreamPlayer** node to the scene:

1. Go to `https://pixabay.com/sound-effects/search/background` and download the `Soft Rain Ambient` file. If you have your own MP3, WAV, or OGG files or find a different file on this website that you like, you can use that file instead.

2. Extract the file onto the **FileSystem** tab in Godot.

3. Go to `https://www.videvo.net/sound-effect/gun-shot-single-shot-in-pe1097906/246309` and download the `Loud Gunshot` WAV or MP3 file.

4. Extract the file into the **FileSystem** tab in Godot.

5. Left-click on + above **Node2D** in the **Scene** tab to bring up the **Create New Node** window. In the **Search** box, type `audio` and select **AudioStreamPlayer** at the bottom of the list.

6. Left-click on the **Node2D** node and then + in the **Scene** tab. In the **Create New Node** window, type `mesh` in the **Search** box and then select **MeshInstance2D** to create the node in the scene. Left-click the **Create** button.

7. Right-click the **MeshInstance2D** node in the **Scene** tab and rename it `Background`.

8. In the **Inspector** window, click on **<empty>** to the right of **Mesh** and select **New BoxMesh**.

9. Left-click on the same place to open the properties of the **Background** mesh.

10. In the **Inspector** window, change the **Size** property of **x** to `100` and **y** to `100`.

11. In the **Inspector** window, left-click on **Transform** to show the transform properties.

12. To the right of **Position**, change the **x** value to 600px and the **y** value to 340px.

13. To the right of **Scale**, left-click the link icon so that the link is gray and broken.

14. Change the value of **x** to 12 and the value of **y** to 7 in **Scale**.

15. Left-click on the **Node2D** node and then + in the **Scene** tab. In the **Create New Node** window, type button in the **Search** box and then select **Button**.

16. Left-click the **Create** button.

17. Left-click and drag on the bottom-right dot to make the button bigger. Move the button inside the viewable background area.

18. In the **Inspector** window, click on the empty box under **Text** and enter Gun Shot.

Figure 7.1 – The background and button placement

Left-click on **AudioStreamPlayer** in the **Scene** tab.

19. In the **FileSystem** tab, left-click, hold, and drag soft-rain-ambient-111154.mp3 (or .WAV) to <**empty**> to the right of **Stream** in the **Inspector** window.

20. In the **Inspector** window, check the checkbox to the right of **Autoplay**.

21. Left-click on the **Button** in the **Scene** tab.

22. In the **Inspector** window at the bottom, left-click <**empty**> to the right of **Script**.

23. Left-click **New Script** from the drop-down list.

24. In **Path**, rename the script Gunshot.gd.

25. Left-click the **Create** button.

26. Left-click on the **Button** in the **Scene** tab.

27. Left-click the **Node** tab located to the right of the **Inspector** tab.

28. Toward the top left, click `pressed()`.

29. At the bottom left, click the **Connect** button.

30. Left-click the **Connect** button in the window that pops up.

31. Left-click on + above **Node2D** in the **Scene** tab to bring up the **Create New Node** window.

32. In the **Search** box, type `audio` and select **AudioStreamPlayer** at the bottom of the list.

33. Left-click on **AudioStreamPlayer2** in the **Scene** tab.

34. In the **FileSystem** tab, left-click, hold, and drag `GunShotSnglShotIn PE1097906.wav` to **<empty>** to the right of **Stream** in the **Inspector** window.

35. Left-click `1`, which is located to the right of **Max Polyphony** in the **Inspector** window, and change it to `10`.

36. Left-click **Script**, which is to the right of **3D** in the top-middle area in Godot.

37. In the `Gunshot` script, copy the following code:

```
1  extends Button
2
3  @onready var audio = $"../AudioStreamPlayer2"
4
5  func _on_pressed():
6      audio.play()
```

38. In the **AudioStreamPlayer** scene, click the **Run the current scene** button in the upper-right corner of the editor or hit the *F6* key.

We click on the button and hear the gunshots and the rain at the same time, and no matter how fast we click the button, we don't get any distortion.

How it works...

We went to Pixaby and downloaded `Soft Rain Ambient` to show that the music or ambient sound effect will play, no matter where a player is in the game. You can download a different free file on the website, or you can use your own WAV, MP3, or OGG Vorbis files. We extracted the file onto the **FileSystem** tab in Godot.

We went to `https://www.videvo.net/` and downloaded `Loud Gunshot`. We are going to attach a **AudioStreamPlayer** node to a button, and when we click it, it will play the gunshot sound effect. We extracted the file into the **FileSystem** tab in Godot.

We added the **AudioStreamPlayer** node to the **Scene** tab. We added a **MeshInstance2D** node as a child of the **Node2D** node and renamed it `Background`. We added a BoxMesh to the **Mesh** property. We changed the **Size** values of the **x** and **y** to `100`.

We opened the **Transform** properties in the **Inspector** window to change the **Position x** value to `600px` and the **y** value to `340px`, centering it so that the default camera could see the background. We left-clicked the link icon so that we can change both the **x** and **y** values to the values we want. We changed the scale of the **x** value to `12` and **y** to `7` so that it covers the area that the default camera will show.

We left-clicked on the **Node2D** node and then + in the **Scene** tab to add a button as a child of **Node2D**. We left-clicked and dragged the bottom-right dot that surrounds the button to make the button bigger. Then, we moved the button into the viewable background area. We typed `Gun Shot` in the empty box under the word **Text** in the **Inspector** window.

We left-clicked on **AudioStreamPlayer** in the **Scene** tab so that we could see its **Inspector** properties. In the **FileSystem** tab, we left-clicked and dragged the `soft-rain-ambient-111154.mp3` file to **<empty>** to the right of **Stream** in the **Inspector** window. If you downloaded a different file or file type, use that instead. Then, we checked the checkbox to the right of **Autoplay** in the **Inspector** window to turn it on. Now, when we run the current scene, the file will play.

We left-clicked on the **Button** node in the **Scene** tab to see its properties in the **Inspector** window. At the bottom, we left-clicked **<empty>** to the right of **Script** and selected **New Script**. We named this script `Gunshot.gd` and left-clicked the **Create** button to create it.

We left-clicked **Button** in the **Scene** again so that we can add a signal to the button. We left-clicked on the **Node** tab, which is to the right of the **Inspector** tab. Toward the top of the list of signals, we left-clicked `pressed()` and then left-clicked the **Connect** button. A window appeared, and we left-clicked the **Connect** button to hook up the signal to the script.

We added another **AudioStreamPlayer** node to use with the gunshot audio that we downloaded. We left-clicked on **AudioStreamPlayer2** to show the properties in the **Inspector** window. We dragged `GunShotSnglShotIn PE1097906.wav` to **<empty>** to the right of **Stream** in the **Inspector** window.

We changed the value of **Max Polyphony** to `10` in the **Inspector** window. This is the number of sounds **AudioStreamPlayer2** can play at the same time. Clicking on the button really fast will play the full gunshot file each time, without cutting out when the next gunshot is fired by clicking the button again.

We clicked the script in the **Workspaces** part of Godot to add code to the `Gunshot.gd` script. In *line 3*, we entered `@onready var audio = $"../AudioStreamPlayer2"` in case you got an error and then deleted `$"../AudioStreamPlayer2"` after =. Then, in the **Scene** tab, we left-clicked and dragged the **AudioStreamPlayer2** node to the right of the = sign in the `Gunshot.gd` script.

When we connected the signal, *line 5* was created. In *line 6*, delete the default pass line and enter `audio.play()`. This will play the gunshot sound every time the button is pushed. We ran the current scene (by pressing *F6*), and you can hear the rain audio playing as the scene is running.

When we clicked on the button, we heard the gunshot at the same time as the rain sounds. We can click the button fast to hear multiple gunshots, along with the background rain sound that the first **AudioStreamPlayer** node is playing, and it still sounds good.

Exploring directional sound in 2D

In this recipe, we will attach **AudioStreamPlayer2D** to a block and create a player. When the player moves toward the block, the sound file will play and get louder as the player gets closer.

Getting ready

For this recipe, open Godot 4 and start a new project called Chapter 7. In the **Scene** tab, click **2D** to add a 2D scene. Click on **Scene** in the main menu next to **Project**, then select **Save Scene As**, and name the scene Audio2D.

How to do it...

We start by creating the background, the box with the **AudioStreamPlayer2D** node, and the player:

1. Left-click on the **Node2D** node and then + in the **Scene** tab. In the **Create New Node** window, type mesh in the **Search** box and then select **MeshInstance2D** to create the node in the **Scene** tab. Left-click the **Create** button.

2. Right-click the **MeshInstance2D** node in the **Scene** tab and rename it Background.

3. In the **Inspector** window, click on **<empty>** to the right of **Mesh** and select **New BoxMesh**.

4. Left-click on the same place to open the properties of the **Background** mesh.

5. In the **Inspector** window, change the **Size** property of **x** to 100 and **y** to 100.

6. In the **Inspector** window, left-click on **Transform** to show the transform properties.

7. To the right of **Position**, change the **x** value to 600px and the **y** value to 340px.

8. To the right of **Scale**, left-click the link icon so that the link is gray and broken.

9. Change the value of **x** to 12 and the value of **y** to 7 in **Scale**.

10. Left-click on the **Node2D** node and then + in the **Scene** tab. In the **Create New Node** window, type spr in the **Search** box and then select **Sprite2D**.

11. Left-click the **Create** button.

12. Drag icon.svg into **<empty>** to the right of **Texture** in the **Inspector** window.

13. Left-click **Transform** in the **Inspector** window.

14. To the right of **Position**, change the **x** value to 85 and the **y** value to 600.

15. To the right of **Scale**, change the **x** value to .5, and the **y** value will also change to .5 because we did not click on the link icon to the right.

16. Left-click on the **Node2D** node and then + in the **Scene** tab. In the **Create New Node** window, type mesh in the **Search** box, and then select **MeshInstance2D** to create the node in the scene.

17. In the **Inspector** window, click on <**empty**> to the right of **Mesh** and select **New BoxMesh**.

18. Left-click on the same place to open the properties of the **MeshInstance2D** mesh.

19. In the **Inspector** window, change the **Size** value of **x** to 50 and the value of **y** to 50.

20. Left-click on **Visibility** under CanvasItem in the **Inspector** window.

21. Left-click on the **white** field to the right of **Modulate**.

22. Enter ff0000 into the **Hex #** field or pick your own color.

23. Left-click on **Transform** in the **Inspector** window.

24. To the right of **Position**, change the **x** value to 1100 and the **y** value to 40.

Figure 7.2 – Audio2D – Transform and CanvasItem in the Inspector window

25. Left-click on the **MeshInstance2D** node and then + in the **Scene** tab. In the **Create New Node** window, type aud in the **Search** box, then select the **AudioStreamPlayer2D** node, and then the **Create** button.

26. Left-click on **AudioStreamPlayer2D** in the **Scene** tab.

27. In the **FileSystem** tab, left-click, hold, and drag soft-rain-ambient-111154.mp3 (or .WAV) to <**empty**> to the right of **Stream** in the **Inspector** window.

28. In the **Inspector** window, check the checkbox to the right of **Autoplay**.

29. In the **Inspector** window to the right of **Max Distance**, left-click **2000** and change it to 1900.

30. Left-click on **Transform** in the **Inspector** window.

31. To the right of **Position**, change the **x** value to 1100 and the **y** value to 40.

32. Left-click on the **Node2D** node and then + in the **Scene** tab. In the **Create New Node** window, type char in the **Search** box and then select **CharacterBody2D**.

33. Left-click on the **Create** button.

34. Left-click on the **CharacterBody2D** node and then + in the **Scene** tab. In the **Create New Node** window, type coll in the **Search** box and then select **CollisionShape2D**.

35. Left-click on the **Create** button.

36. Left-click <**empty**> to the right of **Shape** in the **Inspector** window.

37. Select **New RectangleShape2D** from the drop-down list.

38. In the **Scene** tab, left-click and drag the **Sprite2D** node onto **CharacterBody2D**. **Sprite2D** should be the first child under **CharacterBody2D** and **CollisionShape2D** should be the first child under **Sprite2D**, as shown in *Figure 7.4*.

39. Left-click **CollisionShape2D** in the **Scene** tab, and in the top-left corner, you will see **CollisionShape2D**.

40. Left-click and drag the dots of **CollisionShape2D** to fit the shape of **Sprite2D** in the bottom-left corner.

Figure 7.3 – CollisionShape2D on Sprite2D

41. Left-click on the **CharacterBody2D** node and then **+** in the **Scene** tab. In the **Create New Node** window, type aud in the **Search** box and then select **AudioListener2D**.

42. Left-click the **Create** button.

43. In the **Inspector** window of **AudioListener2D**, check the **On** checkbox to the right of **Current**.

44. Left-click on **CharacterBody2D** in the **Scene** tab.

45. In the **Inspector** window, left-click on **<empty>** to the right of **Script**.

46. Select **New Script** from the drop-down list.

47. In **Template:**, make sure it is empty. If not, click the button to the right of **Template:**.

48. In **Path:**, rename the script Player.gd.

49. Left-click the **Create** button.

50. In the **Script** workspace in the main menu, add the following lines to Player.gd:

```
 1 extends CharacterBody2D
 2
 3 @export var speed = 300
 4
 5 func get_input():
 6     var input_direction = Input.get_vector("ui_left", "ui_right", "ui_up", "ui_down")
 7     velocity = input_direction * speed
 8
 9 func _physics_process(_delta):
10     get_input()
11     move_and_slide()
```

51. In the **Audio2D** scene, click the **Run the current scene** button in the upper-right corner of the editor or hit the *F6* key.

Use the arrow keys to move toward the red box. As you move closer to the red box, you should hear the volume get louder. If you continue going offscreen to the right, the sound will pan to the left speaker.

How it works...

We added a **MeshInstance2D** node as a child of the **Node2D** node and renamed it Background. We added a BoxMesh to the **Mesh** property. We changed the **Size** values of **x** and **y** to 100. We opened the **Transform** properties in the **Inspector** window to change the **Position x** value to 600px and the **y** value to 340px to center the background so that the default camera can see the background.

We left-clicked the link icon so that we could change both the **x** and **y** values independently to the values we want. We changed the scale of the **x** value to 12 and **y** to 7 so that it covered the area that the default camera will show.

We left-clicked on the **Node2D** node and then + in the **Scene** tab to add **Sprite2D** as a child of **Node2D**. We added icon.svg to the texture of **Sprite2D**. We moved the starting location of the player by changing the **Transform Position** values of **x** to 85 and **y** to 600. We scaled the size down by changing the **Transform Scale** values of **x** to .5. Because the link icon was not changed, the **y** value also was changed to .5. We will come back to this later when we add it to **CharacterBody2D**.

We added another **MeshInstance2D** node as a child of the **Node2D** node. We added a BoxMesh to the **Mesh** property. We changed the **Size** values of **x** and **y** to 50. We left-clicked **Visibility** in the **Inspector** window and left-clicked on the white field to the right of **Modulate** to change the color of **MeshInstance2D**. We opened the **Transform** properties in the **Inspector** window to change the **Position x** value to 1100px and the **y** value to 40px.

We left-clicked on **MeshInstance2D** so that when we create a **AudioStreamPlayer2D** node, it will be the child of **MeshInstance2D**. We added the **AudioStreamPlayer2D** node to the **Scene** tab. From the **FileSystem** tab, we dragged the soft-rain-ambient-111154.mp3 file we used in the first recipe into the **Stream** property of the **Inspector** window. We checked the checkbox of the **Autoplay** property in the **Inspector** window.

We changed the value of **Max Distance** to 1900 so that we can only hear it when the player gets close to the **AudioStreamPlayer2D** node that is on **MeshInstance2D**. The **Attenuation** property, under **Max Distance** in the **Inspector** window, is how much the sound will drop off as the player moves away from **MeshInstance2D**. You can experiment with that setting. In the **Transform** properties in the **Inspector** window, we set the **x** value to 1100 and the **y** value to 40 so that the **AudioStreamPlayer2D** node is positioned where **MeshInstance2D** is positioned.

We created a **CharacterBody2D** node as a child of **Node2D**. Left-clicking on the **CharacterBody2D** node, we added a **CollisionShape2D** node as a child of the **CharacterBody2D** node. In the **Inspector** window for **CollisionShape2D**, we selected **New RectangleShape2D** from the drop-down list. We left-clicked and dragged the **Sprite2D** node in the **Scene** tab onto the **CharacterBody2D** node.

The **Sprite2D** node is now a child of the **CharacterBody2D** node. We left-clicked on the **CollisionShape2D** node in the **Scene** tab and saw it highlighted in the top-left corner of the white background. We left-clicked on that, resized it as needed, and then dragged it onto **Sprite2D** at the bottom-left corner of the white background.

We left-clicked **CharacterBody2D** in the **Scene** tab and added **AudioListener2D** as a child node of the **CharacterBody2D** node. In the **Inspector** window, we checked the **On** checkbox to the right of **Current** so that **AudioListener2D** was active.

We added a script to the **CharacterBody2D** node. We left-clicked the **CharacterBody2D** node, and in the **Inspector** window, we left-clicked on <empty> to the right of **Script**. In the dropdown, we selected

New Script. In the popup, we made sure that the template was empty because we are not going to use the default `CharacterBody2D: Basic Movement` script. We named the script `Player.gd`.

We wrote a simple code that moves the player in all directions. In *line 3*, we created a variable called `speed` and assigned it the value of `300`. We used `@export` so that we could change this value in the **Inspector** window. In *line 5*, we created a `get_input()` function, where we look for the input direction and assign the velocity value. In *line 6*, we looked to see whether the arrow key was pressed.

In *line 7*, we assigned the velocity value equal to the direction x speed. In *line 9*, we used the `_physics_process(delta)` function. Since we are not using `delta` in this function, we put an underscore before `delta`. *Line 10* calls the `get_input()` function, and *line 11* calls the `move_and_slide()` function, which moves the player.

When we run the current scene, we move the player up toward the **MeshInstance2D** square, and as we get closer, we hear our sound file. When we move away from the square, the sound fades out.

Figure 7.4 – Moving the player to the red square

Using directional sound in 3D

In this recipe, we will attach an **AudioStreamPlayer3D** node to a cylinder and create a player. When the player moves toward the cylinder, the sound file will play and get louder as the player gets closer.

Getting ready

For this recipe, open Godot 4 and start a new project called Chapter 7. In the **Scene** tab, click on **3D** to add a 3D scene. Click on **Scene** in the main menu next to **Project**, then select **Save Scene As**, and name the scene Audio3D.

How to do it...

Let's first start by making a ground, a post, a player, and a camera. After that, we will add the **AudioStreamPlayer3D** node to the post and **AudioListener** to the player:

1. Left-click the three vertical dots to the left of the **Transform** view on the viewport toolbar.

2. Add **Sun** and **Environment** to the scene by left-clicking the **Add Environment to Scene** button at the bottom while holding down the *Shift* key.

3. Left-click on the **Node3D** node and then + in the **Scene** tab. In the **Create New Node** window, type mesh in the **Search** box and then select **MeshInstance3D** to create the node in the scene. Left-click the **Create** button.

4. Right-click the **MeshInstance3D** node in the **Scene** tab and rename it Ground.

5. In the **Inspector** window, click on <empty> to the right of **Mesh** and select **New PlaneMesh**.

6. Left-click on the same place to open the properties of the **Ground** mesh.

7. In the **Inspector** window, change the **Size** property of **x** to 15 and **y** to 15.

8. Left-click on the **Node3D** node and then + in the **Scene** tab. In the **Create New Node** window, type mesh in the **Search** box and then select **MeshInstance3D** to create the node in the **Scene** tab. Left-click the **Create** button.

9. Right-click the **MeshInstance3D** node in the **Scene** tab and rename it Post.

10. In the **Inspector** window, click on <empty> to the right of **Mesh** and select **New CylinderMesh**.

11. In the **Inspector** window, left-click on **Transform**.

12. Under **Position**, change the values of **x** to 5, **y** to 1, and **z** to −5.

13. Left-click on the **Node3D** node and then + in the **Scene** tab. In the **Create New Node** window, type char in the **Search** box and then select **CharacterBody3D** to create the node in the scene. Left-click the **Create** button.

14. Left-click on the **CharacterBody3D** node and then + in the **Scene** tab. In the **Create New Node** window, type coll in the **Search** box and then select **CollisionShape3D** to create the node in the scene. Left-click the **Create** button.

15. In the **Inspector** window, click on <empty> to the right of **Shape** and select **New CapsuleShape3D**.

16. Left-click on the **CharacterBody3D** node and then + in the **Scene** tab. In the **Create New Node** window, type mesh in the **Search** box and then select **MeshInstance3D** to create the node in the scene. Left-click the **Create** button.

17. Right-click the **MeshInstance3D** node in the **Scene** tab and rename it `Player`.

18. In the **Inspector** window, click on **<empty>** to the right of **Mesh** and select **New CapsuleMesh**.

19. Left-click on the **CharacterBody3D** node.

20. In the **Inspector** window, left-click on **Transform**.

21. Under **Position**, change the values of **x** to -6, **y** to 1, and **z** to 6.

22. In the **Inspector** window, left-click on **<empty>** to the right of **Script**.

23. Select **New Script** from the drop-down list.

24. In **Template:**, make sure it is not empty. If it is, then click on the button to the right of **Template:** to see **CharacterBody3D: Basic Movement**.

25. In **Path:**, rename the script `Player3D.gd`.

26. Left-click on the **Create** button.

27. Change *line 8* to `var gravity = 0`.

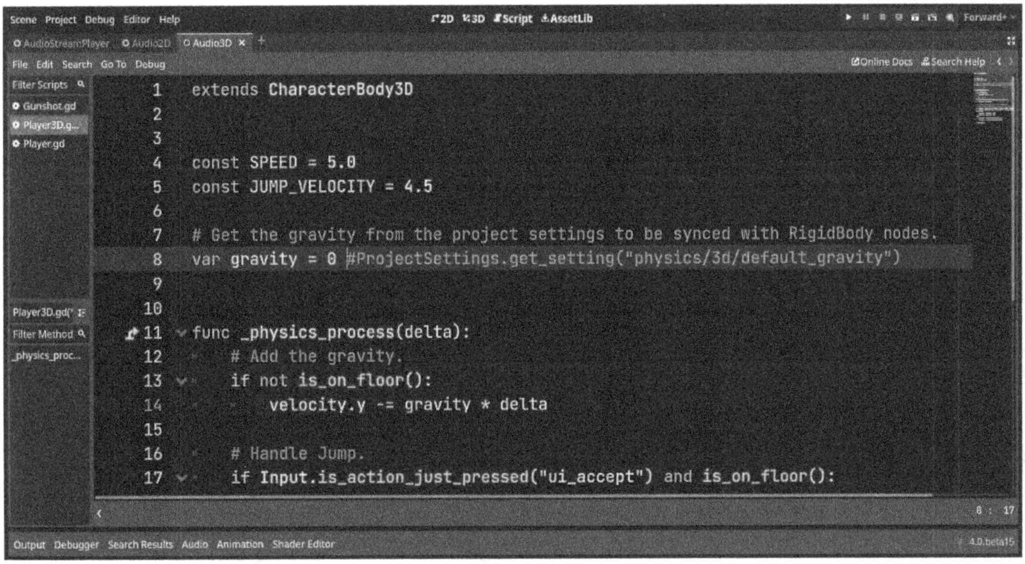

```
1    extends CharacterBody3D
2
3
4    const SPEED = 5.0
5    const JUMP_VELOCITY = 4.5
6
7    # Get the gravity from the project settings to be synced with RigidBody nodes.
8    var gravity = 0 #ProjectSettings.get_setting("physics/3d/default_gravity")
9
10
11   func _physics_process(delta):
12       # Add the gravity.
13       if not is_on_floor():
14           velocity.y -= gravity * delta
15
16       # Handle Jump.
17       if Input.is_action_just_pressed("ui_accept") and is_on_floor():
```

Figure 7.5 – Player3D.gd (the change to line 8)

28. Left-click the 3D workspace above the viewport.

29. Left-click on the **CharacterBody3D** node and then + in the **Scene** tab. In the **Create New Node** window, type `cam` in the **Search** box and then select **Camera3D** to create the node in the **Scene** tab. Left-click the **Create** button.

30. In the **Inspector** window, left-click on **Transform**.

31. Under **Position**, change the values of **x** to 5, **y** to 4, and **z** to 7.

32. Under **Rotation**, change the values of **x** to -8.

33. Left-click on the **CharacterBody3D** node and then + in the **Scene** tab. In the **Create New Node** window, type aud in the **Search** box and then select **AudioListener3D** to create the node in the scene. Left-click the **Create** button.

34. In the **Inspector** window of **AudioListener3D**, check the **On** checkbox to the right of **Current**.

35. Left-click on the **Post** node and then + in the **Scene** tab. In the **Create New Node** window, type aud in the **Search** box and then select **AudioStreamPlayer3D** from the drop-down list to create the node in the **Scene** tab. Left-click the **Create** button.

36. Left-click on the **AudioStreamPlayer3D** node in the **Scene** tab.

37. In the **FileSystem** tab, left-click, hold, and drag soft-rain-ambient-111154.mp3 (or .WAV) to <**empty**> to the right of **Stream** in the **Inspector** window.

38. In the **Inspector** window, check the checkbox to the right of **Autoplay**.

39. In the **Inspector** window to the right of **Unit Size**, left-click on **10** and change it to 1.5.

40. In the **Audio3D** scene, click the **Run the current scene** button in the upper-right corner of the editor or hit the *F6* key.

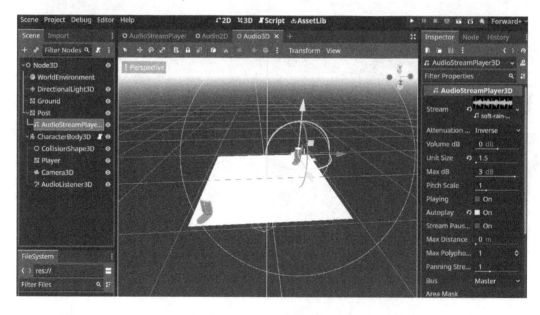

Figure 7.6 – AudioStreamPlayer3D – the Unit Size radius

Use the arrow keys to move the player to the post, and as you get closer, the volume increases. When you get to the post, move from the left of the post, through the post, and then to the right of the post.

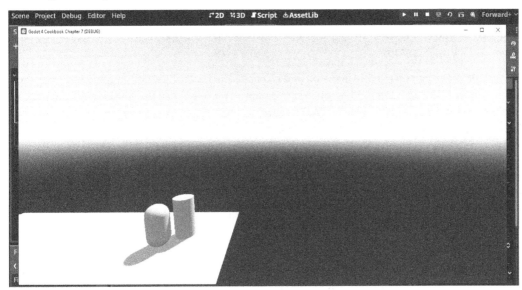

Figure 7.7 – Moving the player to the left of the post

How it works...

We added a **MeshInstance3D** node as a child of the **Node3D** node and renamed it Ground. We added a PlaneMesh to the **Mesh** property. We changed the **Size** values of **x** and **y** to 15.

We added a **MeshInstance3D** node as a child of the **Node3D** node and renamed it Post. We added a CylinderMesh to the **Mesh** property. We left-clicked **Transform** in the **Inspector** window so that we can change the **Position** values to move the post. We changed the **Position** values of **x** to 5, **y** to 1, and **z** to -5. This moved the post to the far-right corner.

We created a **CharacterBody3D** node as a child of the **Node3D** node. We added a **CollisionShape3D** node as a child of the **CharacterBody3D** node. We used **CapsuleShape3D** so that it will fit the player's CapsuleMesh. We added a **MeshInstance3D** node, which we renamed Player. We used a CapsuleMesh for the player.

We left-clicked on the **CharacterBody3D** node and then left-clicked **Transform** in the **Inspector** window to change its position. We changed the **Position** values of **x** to -6, **y** to 1, and **z** to 6. In the **Inspector** window, we created a new script and used the **CharacterBody3D: Basic Movement** template. We renamed the script Player3D.gd. We changed *line 8* to var gravity = 0 so that the player would not fall through the ground.

We went back to the 3D workspace and left-clicked on the **CharacterBody3D** node. We added a **Camera3D** node to the **CharacterBody3D** node. In the **Inspector** properties of **Camera3D**, we changed the **Position** values of **x** to 5, **y** to 4, and **z** to 7. We changed the rotation value of **x** to −8.

The camera will follow the player since we have **Camera3D** as a child of **CharacterBody3D**. It's positioned behind and to the right of the player. The rotation faces slightly down, so we can see the ground while the player moves.

We added **AudioListener3D** to the **CharacterBody3D** node and checked the **On** checkbox located to the right of **Current**. This activates **AudioListener3D** on the player. We added the **AudioStreamPlayer3D** node to the **Post** node in the **Scene** tab. We dragged our `soft-rain-ambient-111154.mp3` file into **<empty>**, located to the right of **Stream**.

If you downloaded another file or have your own MP3, WAV, or OGG file, use that file instead. In the **Inspector** window, we checked the **On** checkbox located to the right of **Autoplay**. We changed the **Unit Size** value to `1.5` in the **Inspector** window. The unit size is how far the sound can be heard. The further out the sound is, the softer it is, and the further in the sound is, the louder it is. The **Max dB** property will adjust how loud the file is at the maximum volume.

Volume dB is the base sound level. Play around with different files and settings. You can move the player off of the ground and not fall because we turned off the gravity in the movement script. When we run the current scene, as we move the player up toward the post, the sound gets louder. Experiment with how loud and soft the sounds are in relation to how near and far the player is to the post.

If you move through the post and in all directions around it, you will see that the sounds come out of the correct speakers relative to where the player is positioned.

Making 2D Games Easier with TileSet and TileMap

In this chapter, we will download a hex tileset and add a TileMap to Godot. We will set up the tileset to paint on the TileMap. We will add two layers to the TileMap: a ground layer for the background and an objects layer to place trees on top of the ground layer. We will use TileMap tools such as **Paint**, **Rect**, **Line**, **Bucket fill**, **Picker**, and **Eraser**, and place random tiles to paint our tiles to the TileMap.

We will edit the color of a tile in the sprite sheet and see what other ways we can use to edit a tile. We will create an alternative tile and add a collision layer to the tile. We will set up a navigation layer on the tiles and use Custom Data Layers to add an Int variable with a value of 10 to a tile.

We will create four terrain tilesets and manually paint them to the TileMap. We will download a new tileset and add a new TileMap. We will set up the tiles as a terrain and paint the terrain to the new TileMap, so they tile automatically (or autotile). We will download an isometric tileset and set up the isometric tiles so we can paint them on the new TileMap.

By the end of the chapter, we will be able to add layers to the TileMap to create a game layout using only one TileMap and edit a tile to create custom tiles and add collision layers to tiles. We will be able to add a navigation layer and add custom data to a tile so that if a player lands on a tile, they can get a coin, for example. We will be able to manually paint terrain and autotile terrain to a TileMap. We will also know how to set up and paint isometric tilesets on a TileMap.

In this chapter, we will cover the following recipes:

- Using the new TileSet editor
- Examining TileMap layers
- Playing with the new TileMap tools
- Playing with Tile Atlas editing
- Exploring the TileSet physics

- Exploring the TileSet navigation
- Creating Custom Data Layers with the TileSet
- Painting terrains in TileMap
- Transitioning TileSet terrains
- Organizing isometric tiles into fixed-sized grids using the TileSet resource

Technical requirements

For this chapter, you need the standard version of Godot 4.0 or later running on any of the following:

- Windows 64-bit or 32-bit
- macOS
- Linux 64-bit or 32-bit
- Android
- Web Editor

You can find the code and the project files for the projects in this chapter at this GitHub link: `https://github.com/PacktPublishing/Godot-4-Game-Development-Cookbook/tree/main/Chapter%208`.

Using the new TileSet editor

In this recipe, we are going to download a hex tileset and bring it into Godot. We will add a TileMap to the **Scene** tab and then add a TileSet to the TileMap in the **Inspector**. In the TileSet editor, we will use the **Setup** tab with the hex file we downloaded to set up the tileset so we can use it to paint with the TileMap.

Getting ready

For this recipe, open Godot 4 and start a new project called `Chapter 8`. In the **Scene** tab, click **2D** to add a 2D scene. Click on the word **Scene** in the main menu next to **Project** and then select **Save Scene As** and name it `TileSet`.

How to do it...

We will start by downloading our hex tileset and then adding a TileMap to the **Scene** tab:

1. Go to `https://opengameart.org/content/hex-tileset-pack` and, at the bottom, click on `HexTilesetv3.png`.

2. From your `Downloads` folder, move or copy/paste the file into the **FileSystem** tab or your `Chapter 8` project folder.

3. Left-click on the **Node2D** node and then the + symbol in the **Scene** tab. In the **Create New Node** window, type `tile` in the search box and then select **TileMap** to create the node in the scene. Left-click on the **Create** button.

4. In the **Inspector**, click on **<empty>** to the right of **Tile Set** and select **New TileSet** from the drop-down list.

5. Left-click on the same place to open the properties of the TileSet.

6. In the **Inspector**, to the right of **Tile Size**, change the **x** value to `32` and the **y** value to `32`.

7. In the **FileSystem** tab, left-click and drag the `HexTilesetv3.png` file to the blank box under the **Tiles** and **Patterns** tabs in the TileSet editor to the right of the **FileSystem** tab.

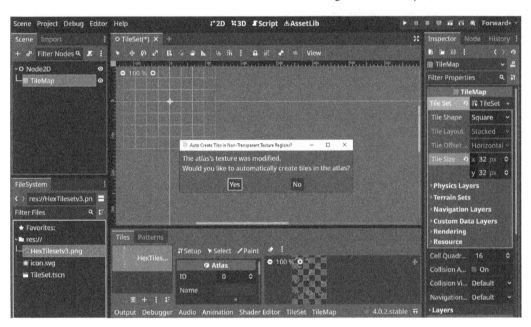

Figure 8.1 – Dragging the HexTilesetv3.png file to the Tiles tab

8. Click **Yes** on the popup asking whether you would like to automatically create tiles in the atlas.

9. In the **Inspector**, left-click on **Square**, which is to the right of **Tile Shape**, and select **Hexagon**.

10. In the **Inspector**, to the right of **Tile Offset**, left-click on **Horizontal Offset** and select **Vertical Offset** from the drop-down list.

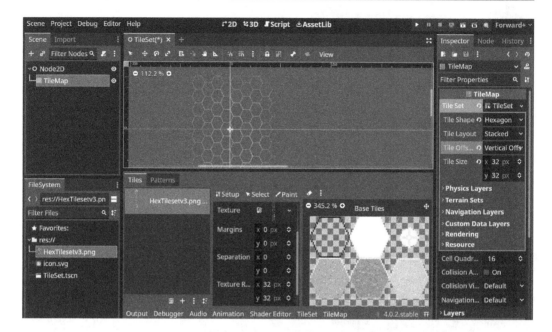

Figure 8.2 – The TileSet and Inspector settings

How it works...

We downloaded `HexTilesetv3.png` at the bottom of the page. Make sure to download this file and not the one above it. From the `Downloads` folder on your computer, drag the `HexTilesetv3.png` file into the **FileSystem** tab of Godot or you can copy the file in the `Downloads` folder and then paste it into your `Chapter 8` project folder, which we created before we started this recipe. If Godot freezes, reboot Godot and notice that the file is in the **FileSystem** tab.

We added a **TileMap** node by left-clicking the + sign in the **Scene** tab and selecting **TileMap** in the **Create New Node** window. Then, in the **Inspector** tab, we left-clicked on **<empty>** (located to the right of **Tile Set**) and selected **New TileSet** from the drop-down list. We left-clicked on the TileSet located to the right of **Tile Set** in the **Inspector** to see the new TileSet properties.

We know that the scale of `HexTilesetv3.png` is 32 x 32 because it was on the preview page where we downloaded the file. In the **Inspector**, we changed the **Tile Size** values of **x** and **y** to `32`. We left-clicked and dragged the `HexTilesetv3.png` file from the **FileSytem** tab in the blank box into the **Tiles** tab in the TileSet editor. When the popup asked whether we would like to automatically create tiles in the atlas, we clicked the **Yes** button.

In the **Inspector**, we select **Tile Shape**, and to the right of that is a field with **Square** selected. We clicked on **Square** and, from the dropdown, we selected **Hexagon** because the tileset we downloaded is hexagonal. In the **Tile Offset Axis** property in the **Inspector**, we selected **Vertical Offset** because the tileset we downloaded is vertically offset.

Examining TileMap layers

In this recipe, we are going to create two layers in the TileMap. One will be for the ground and the other for objects that we can place on top of the ground. We will use this in the next recipe, where we will paint a level using the TileMap tools.

Getting ready

For this recipe, we are going to continue from where we left off in the last recipe.

How to do it...

Let's add the **Ground** and **Objects** layers so we can use the TileMap tools in the recipe:

1. In the **TileMap** section of the **Inspector**, left-click on **Layers**.

2. To the right of **Name**, enter Ground.

3. At the bottom under **Z Index**, left-click on + **Add Element**.

4. In the new layer, to the right of **Name**, enter Objects.

5. To the right of **Z Index** in the new layer, left-click on **0** and enter 1.

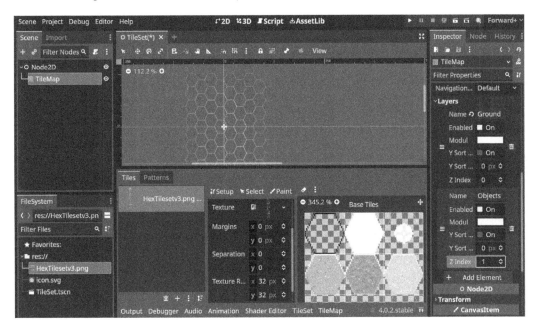

Figure 8.3 – Layers properties in the Inspector

6. At the very bottom of the bottom panel and to the right of **TileSet**, click on the TileMap editor to see the layers we entered.

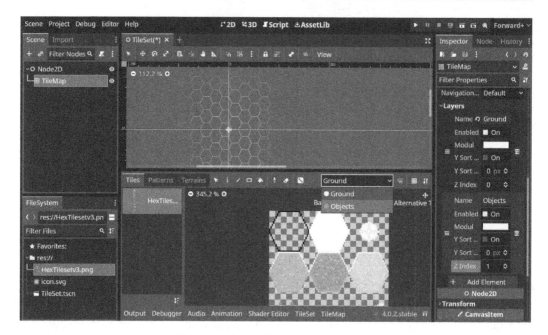

Figure 8.4 – The Ground and Objects layers in the TileMap editor

How it works...

We looked in the **Inspector**, and at the bottom of the **TileMap** section and above the **Node2D** section, we clicked on **Layers** to see the layers' properties. In the **Name** field, we entered Ground to name this layer. We left **Z Index** at 0 because we will always see this layer as this is the background of our level. At the bottom, we clicked on the + **Add Element** button to add another layer.

We entered Objects in the **Name** field to name this layer. We changed the **Z Index** value of this layer to 1 so that when we paint using this layer, we can see the Ground and Objects layers at the same time.

We clicked on **TileMap** at the bottom of the bottom panel to see the TileMap editor. In the upper-right corner of the TileMap editor, we saw the layers that we just created, as shown in *Figure 8.4*.

Playing with the new TileMap tools

In this recipe, we will use the TileMap editor to paint our tiles. We will use **TileMap** tools such as **Paint**, **Rect**, **Line**, **Bucket fill**, **Picker**, and **Eraser**, and place random tiles.

Getting ready

For this recipe, we are going to continue from where we left off in the last recipe.

How to do it...

In the first three steps, we are making sure we are in the TileMap editor and the **Ground** layer is selected. We should be if you just finished the last recipe. Follow these steps now:

1. In the **Scene** tab, left-click on the **TileMap** node.

2. At the very bottom of the bottom panel and to the right of **TileSet**, click on the TileMap editor.

3. Make sure the **Ground** layer is selected. It is to the right of the **TileMap** tools we are going to use in this recipe. See *Figure 8.5* to see the TileMap editor.

4. Select the **Paint (D)** icon located to the right of the **Tile | Patterns | Terrains** tabs, and the **Selection (S)** icon at the top of the bottom panel. It is selected in *Figure 8.5* and is blue with a blue outline around it.

5. Left-click on the green hexagon in the **Base Tiles** sprite sheet and move the mouse to the hexagon grid in the viewport.

6. Left-click on where you want to place the tile.

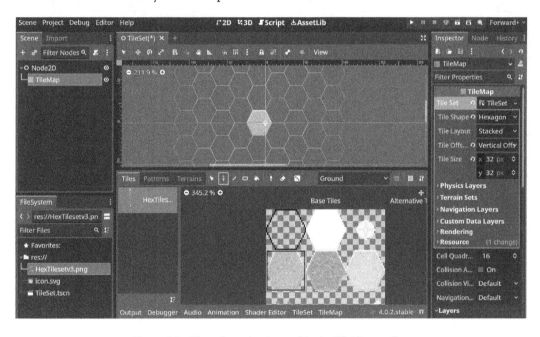

Figure 8.5 – The selected paint tool in the TileMap toolbar

7. Select the **Line (L)** icon located to the right of the **Paint (D)** icon.

8. Left-click on the brown hexagon in the **Base Tiles** sprite sheet and move the mouse to the hexagon grid in the viewport.

9. Left-click and hold, then move the mouse where you want to place the line of tiles.

10. Select the **Rect (R)** icon located to the right of the **Line (L)** icon.

11. Left-click on the blue hexagon in the **Base Tiles** sprite sheet and move the mouse to the hexagon grid in the viewport.

12. Left-click and hold, then move the mouse where you want to place the tiles in a rectangle pattern.

13. Select the **Bucket (B)** icon located to the right of the **Rect (R)** icon.

14. Left-click on the green hexagon in the **Base Tiles** sprite sheet and move the mouse to the hexagon grid in the viewport.

15. Left-click, then move the mouse over the area we put the blue hexagons in and left-click to paint that area green.

16. Let's paint some more using the green, brown, blue, and white hexagons before we start painting on the **Object** layer.

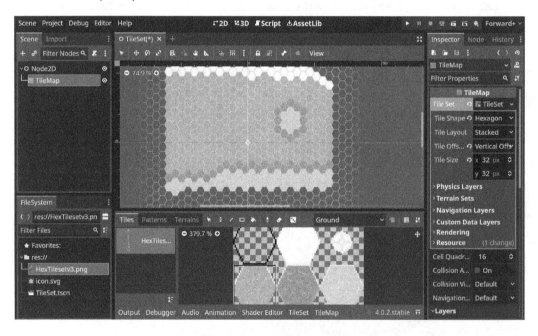

Figure 8.6 – Painting the Ground layer tiles

17. Left-click on **Ground** located to the right of the paint icons and select **Objects** from the drop-down list.

18. Left-click on the **Rect (R)** icon.

19. Left-click on the **Place Random Tile** icon to the left of **Objects**.

20. Change the field to the right of **Scattering** to 5.

21. Left-click on the trees under the green hexagon in the sprite sheet and move the mouse into the viewport. Left-click and hold and drag an area in the hexagons you painted.

22. Left-click on the **Place Random Tile** icon to turn it off.

23. Left-click on the **Eraser (E)** icon to the left of the **Place Random Tile** icon.

24. Click on a tree that was painted and left-click on the **Eraser (E)** icon to turn it off.

25. Left-click on the **Picker (P)** icon to the left of the **Eraser (E)** icon and click on a tree that was painted.

26. Left-click on an empty tile.

How it works...

We made sure that we clicked on the **TileMap** node in the **Scene** tab so we could select the TileMap editor in the bottom panel. We made sure the **Ground** layer was showing so that when we paint, it is on the correct layer.

We found where the TileMap toolbar is located and selected the **Paint** icon. We selected the green hexagon in the **Base Tiles** sprite sheet and moved the mouse to the hexagon grid in the viewport and left-clicked where we wanted to place the tile. While using the **Paint** tool, we can hold *Shift + Ctrl* and drag to draw a rectangle, or *Shift* and drag to draw a line.

We selected the **Line (L)** icon located to the right of the **Paint (D)** icon. We left-clicked on the brown hexagon tile and moved the mouse into the viewport. We left-clicked and held, then moved the mouse to another hexagon in the viewport. We created a line of brown hexagons from the spot we first selected to the last spot at which we stopped dragging.

We selected the **Rect (R)** icon located to the right of the **Line (L)** icon. We left-clicked on the blue hexagon tile and moved the mouse into the viewport. We left-clicked and held, then moved the mouse to another hexagon in the viewport. We created a rectangle of blue hexagons from the spot we first selected to the last spot at which we stopped dragging. Since we are using hexagons, we won't see perfect rectangles, but you can sort of see a rectangle shape.

We selected the **Bucket (B)** icon located to the right of the **Rect (R)** icon. We left-clicked the green hexagon tile and moved the mouse into the viewport. We left-clicked, then moved the mouse over the blue hexagons we just added, and left-clicked to paint them green.

If you paint borders above and below, you can use the **Bucket (B)** tool to fill in the space between them. We used the paint tools we just learned about to paint more tiles, so we have more tiles to use the **Place Random Tile** and the **Picker** icons.

We changed the layer that we are going to work on by left-clicking on **Ground** and selecting **Objects** from the dropdown. We left-clicked on the **Rect (R)** icon so that when we paint the trees onto the layer using the **Place Random Tiles** icon, we can cover a large area. We could also use the **Bucket (B)** icon if we wanted to place the tree over everything we painted on the **Ground** layer.

We left-clicked on the **Place Random Tiles** icon so we can place random tiles over a section that we selected. We changed the value in **Scattering** to 5 to give us a good amount of space and trees. If we left the **Scattering** value at 0, trees would be painted on all of the selected areas. We left-clicked on the tree's hexagon located under the green hexagon in the sprite sheet. Then, we painted the trees on the **Objects** layer over the **Ground** layer.

We left-clicked the **Place Random Tile** icon to select it. We left-clicked on the **Eraser (E)** icon and then left-clicked on a tree that we previously painted to erase that tree. We left-clicked the **Place Random Tile** icon to unselect it. You can right-click a tile to erase the tile as well.

We left-clicked on the **Picker (P)** icon and then left-clicked on a tree tile. We left-clicked on an empty tile to paint a tree. The **Picker (P)** tool is used to select a tile in the TileMap and paint that tile somewhere else.

Playing with Tile Atlas editing

In this recipe, we will edit the color of a tile in the sprite sheet and see the other ways in which we can edit a tile. Then, we will paint the tile on the TileMap with the new color.

Getting ready

For this recipe, we are going to continue from where we left off in the last recipe.

How to do it...

We are going to change the color of the tile in the upper-right corner of the sprite sheet:

1. Make sure the **TileMap** node in the **Scene** tab is selected.
2. In the bottom panel, left-click on **TileSet**.
3. In the section to the left of the sprite sheet, left-click on **Select**, which is between **Setup** and **Paint**.
4. Left-click on the tile in the upper-right corner of the sprite sheet.
5. Left-click on **Rendering** to show the rendering properties we can edit.

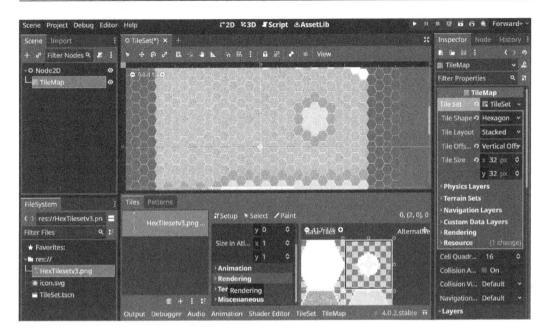

Figure 8.7 – Rendering properties location in Select

6. Left-click on the **White** field to the right of **Modulate**.

7. Change the values of **R** and **G** to 0.

8. Left-click on **Modulate** to exit the popup.

9. Left-click on **TileMap** on the bottom panel to the right of **TileSet**.

10. Make sure we are on the **Objects** layer.

11. Left-click on the tile we just changed and paint it on a tile.

How it works...

We checked to see whether we left-clicked the **TileMap** node in the **Scene** tab so we could see **TileSet** and **TileMap** on the bottom panel. We left-clicked on **TileSet** to see the TileSet editor and then we left-clicked on the tile in the upper-right corner of the sprite sheet so we could edit this tile.

We looked at the section to the left of the sprite sheet located on the right side of the bottom panel. We see **Setup**, **Select**, and **Paint** above a field that shows the properties. The properties of **Setup** are used to edit the Atlas and create or remove base tiles. The **Select** properties are used to edit the tiles. **Paint Properties** are used to paint over the tiles. We left-clicked on **Select** to edit a tile.

We left-clicked on **Rendering** to see its properties. We left-clicked on the white field to the right of **Modulate**. In the color popup, we changed the values of **R** and **G** to 0 so the color of the tile is now blue. We left-clicked **Modulate** to exit the color popup.

We left-clicked on the TileMap in the bottom panel and made sure we were on the **Objects** layer. Then, we painted the tile that we just changed onto the TileMap.

Exploring the TileSet physics

In this recipe, we are going to create an alternative tile and add a collision layer to the tile. We will paint the tiles on our TileMap.

Getting ready

For this recipe, we are going to continue from where we left off in the last recipe.

How to do it...

First, we are going to create an alternative tile to add a collision layer to the tile:

1. In the TileSet editor, go to the section to the left of the sprite sheet. Left-click on **Select**, which is between **Setup** and **Paint**.

2. In the TileSet editor, right-click on the upper-right tile in the sprite sheet. It's the one that we changed the color of.

3. Left-click on **Create an Alternative Tile** from the drop-down list.

4. In the **Inspector**, left-click on **Physics Layers** in the **TileMap** properties located under **Tile Size**.

5. Left-click on + **Add Element**.

6. In the bottom panel, left-click on the tile we just created located under **Alternative Tiles**.

7. In the section to the left of the sprite sheet, left-click on **Select**.

8. Left-click on **Physics** and then **Physics Layer 0**.

9. At the bottom where you see the tile, left-click on the green **Add Polygon** tool.

10. Left-click on the inside of the green area of the tile in a circle and, at the end, click the first place you clicked to close the circle. Adjust as needed by moving the points that you added around the green circle.

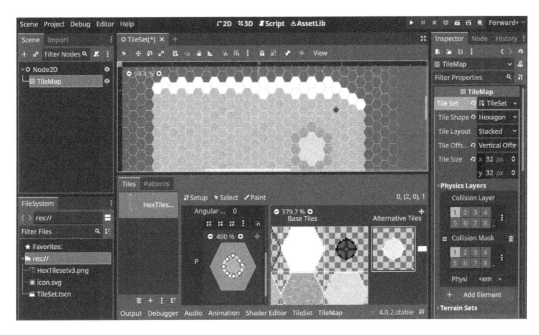

Figure 8.8 – Physics Layers in the Inspector and TileSet

11. Left-click on **Paint**, which is to the right of **Select**.

12. Under **Paint Properties**, left-click on the **Select a property editor** and select **Physics Layer 0** from the drop-down list.

13. Confirm that the title has **Physics Layer** on the tile.

14. Left-click on **TileMap** on the bottom panel to the right of **TileSet**.

15. Make sure we are on the **Objects** layer.

16. Left-click on the tile we just changed and paint it on a tile.

How it works...

We left-clicked **Select** in the TileSet editor so we could edit the tile. We right-clicked on the upper-right tile in the sprite sheet and then left-clicked on **Create an Alternative Tile** from the drop-down list. This created a copy of the tile with its original color. The new tile is located under **Alternative Tiles**, which is to the right of **Base Tiles**.

We left-clicked on **Physics Layers** in the **Inspector**. This adds a **Physics** layer to the TileSet where we can add a collision shape to the tile.

We left-clicked on the alternative tile that we made and left-clicked on **Select** located to the left of the sprite sheet in between **Setup** and **Paint**. We left-clicked on **Physics** and then **Physics Layer 0** to see the tile we were going to add the collision shape to. Under **Angular**, we left-clicked the **Add Polygon** tool and clicked areas inside of the green circle and clicked on the first dot that we placed.

This is the collision shape of the tile. You can left-click on the dots and drag to move the collision shape to exactly where you want it. If you want the whole tile to have a collision shape, then left-click on the three vertical dots to the right of the **Delete Points** tool. Select **Reset to default tile shape** from the drop-down list.

We left-clicked on **Paint**. In **Paint Properties**, we left-clicked on the **Select a property editor** and selected **Physics Layer 0** to check to see whether the hexagon had the **Physics** layer that we edited in the tile. If it does not, then left-click the three vertical dots and left-click the **Add Polygon** tool and click areas inside of the green circle.

We left-clicked on the TileMap in the bottom panel and made sure we were on the **Objects** layer. Then, we painted the tile that we just changed onto the TileMap.

Exploring the TileSet navigation

In this recipe, we will create another alternative tile, and on that tile, we will set up a navigation layer. We paint the tile with the navigation layer on to the TileMap.

Getting ready

For this recipe, we are going to continue from where we left off in the last recipe.

How to do it...

First, we are going to create an alternative tile to add a navigation layer to the tile:

1. In the TileSet editor, go to the section to the left of the sprite sheet. Left-click on **Select**, which is in between **Setup** and **Paint**.
2. In the TileSet editor, right-click on the upper-left tile in the sprite sheet. It's a blank hexagon tile next to the white hexagon tile.
3. Left-click on **Create an Alternative Tile** from the drop-down list.
4. In the **Inspector** left click on **Navigation Layers** in the **TileMap** properties located under **Terrain Sets**.
5. Left click + **Add Element**.
6. In the bottom panel, left-click on the tile we just created located under **Alternative Tiles**.
7. In the section to the left of the sprite sheet, left-click on **Select**.
8. Left-click on **Navigation** and then **Navigation Layer 0**.
9. Below **Navigation Layer 0**, left-click on the three vertical dots.
10. Left-click on **Reset to default tile shape** from the drop-down list.
11. Left-click on **Paint**, which is to the right of **Select**.
12. Under **Paint Properties**, left-click on **Select a property editor** and select **Navigation Layer 0**.

13. Confirm that the tile is blue and has the navigation layer on the tile.

14. Left-click on **TileMap** on the bottom panel to the right of **TileSet**.

15. Make sure we are on the **Objects** layer.

16. Left-click on the tile we just changed and paint it on a tile.

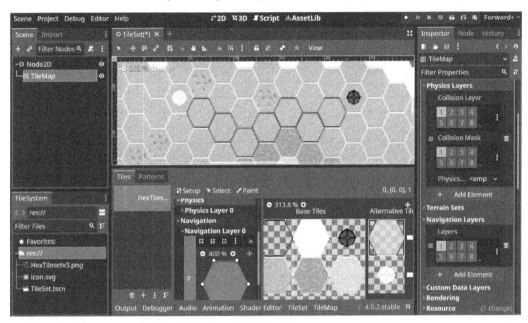

Figure 8.9 – Navigation layers in the Inspector and TileSet

How it works...

We left-clicked **Select** in the TileSet editor so we could edit the tile. We right-clicked on the upper-left tile in the sprite sheet and then left-clicked on **Create an Alternative Tile** from the drop-down list. This created a copy of the blank hexagon tile. The new tile is located under **Alternative Tiles**, which is to the right of **Base Tiles**. We left clicked on the **Navigation Layers** in the **Inspector**. This adds a Navigation Layer to the TileSet.

We left-clicked on the alternative tile that we made and left-clicked on **Select** located to the left of the sprite sheet in between **Setup** and **Paint**. We left-clicked on **Navigation** and then **Navigation Layer 0** to see the tile we were going to add the collision shape to. We left-clicked on the three vertical dots to the right of the **Delete Points** tool and selected **Reset to default tile shape** from the drop-down list. Now, the tile is filled in blue, which is the navigation layer.

We left-clicked on **Paint**. In **Paint Properties**, we left-clicked on the **Select a property editor** and selected **Navigation Layer 0** to check whether the hexagon tile has the navigation layer that we edited in the tile. If it does not, then left-click on the three vertical dots and select **Reset to default tile shape** from the drop-down list.

We left-clicked on the TileMap in the bottom panel and made sure we were on the **Objects** layer. Then, we painted the tile that we just changed onto the TileMap in a path to simulate where the player can walk on the map.

Creating Custom Data Layers with the TileSet

In this recipe, we are going to use a Custom Data Layer. We will name it `Coins` to add an `Int` variable with a value of `10`. In the two previous recipes, we edited the tile and then confirmed the settings in the **Paint** properties. This time, we are going to only set up the **Paint** properties before we paint the tile in the TileMap.

Getting ready

For this recipe, we are going to continue from where we left off in the last recipe.

How to do it...

First, we are going to create an alternative tile to add a navigation layer to the tile:

1. In the TileSet editor, go to the section to the left of the sprite sheet. Left-click on **Select**, which is in between **Setup** and **Paint**.

2. In the **TileSet editor**, right-click on the yellow $ in the sprite sheet. Its atlas coordinates are (2, 14).

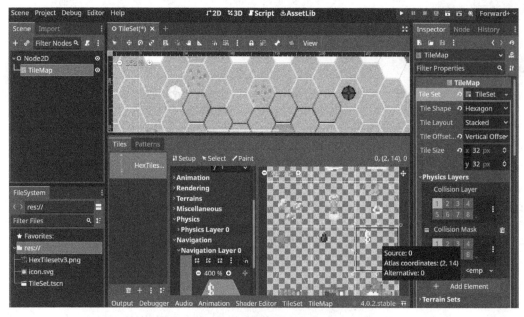

Figure 8.10 – Atlas coordinates (2, 14)

3. Left-click on **Create an Alternative Tile** from the drop-down list.

4. In the **Inspector**, left-click on **Custom Data Layers** in the **TileMap** properties located under **Navigation Layers**.

5. Left click + **Add Element**.

6. To the right of **Name**, type in Coins.

7. To the right of **Type**, left-click on **Any** and select **Int**.

8. In the bottom panel, left-click on the tile we just created located under **Alternative Tiles**.

9. In the middle of the TileSet editor, to the left of the sprite sheet, left-click on **Paint**.

10. Under **Paint Properties**, left-click on **Select a property editor**.

11. Left-click on **Coins** under **Custom Data**.

12. Under **Painting** and to the right of **Coins**, left-click on **0**.

13. Type 10 to replace 0.

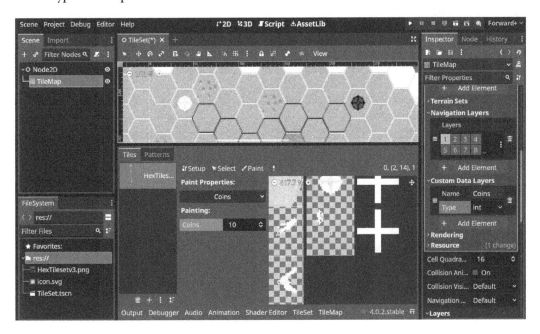

Figure 8.11 – Paint Properties (Custom Data Layers | Inspector and Paint Properties | TileSet)

14. Left-click on **TileMap** on the bottom panel to the right of **TileSet**.

15. Make sure we are on the **Objects** layer.

16. Left-click on the tile we just changed and paint it on a tile.

How it works...

We left-clicked **Select** in the TileSet editor so we could edit the tile. We right-clicked on the yellow $ located at (2, 14) in the atlas. Then, we left-clicked on **Create an Alternative Tile** from the drop-down list. This created a copy of the yellow $ hexagon tile. The new tile is located under **Alternative Tiles**, which is to the right of **Base Tiles**.

We left-clicked on **Custom Data Layers** in the **Inspector**. This added a Custom Data Layer. We entered Coins as the name of this data layer. For the type of this data layer, we selected Int from the drop-down list. In the bottom panel, we left-clicked on the tile we just created located under **Alternative Tiles** just to make sure we were still on that tile.

We left-clicked on **Paint**. In **Paint Properties**, we left-clicked on **Select a property editor**. We left-clicked **Coins** under **Custom Data**. Under **Painting** and to the right of **Custom Data 0**, we left-clicked on **0** and typed 10 into the field.

We left-clicked on the TileMap in the bottom panel and made sure we were on the **Objects** layer. Then, we painted the tile that we just changed onto the TileMap. In a real game, you would get the value returned when the player walks on the tile by the game code.

Painting terrains in TileMap

In this recipe, we are going to create four terrain sets in the **Inspector** and TileSet. Then, in the TileMap, we are going to paint the terrains.

Getting ready

For this recipe, we are going to continue from where we left off in the last recipe.

How to do it...

First, we will set up the terrain sets in the **Inspector** and then in the TileSet:

1. In the **Inspector**, left-click on **Terrain Sets** located in between **Physics Layers** and **Navigation Layers**.
2. Left-click on the + **Add Element** button below **Terrain Sets** and left-click on **Terrains**.
3. Under **Terrains**, left-click on the + **Add Element** button.
4. To the right of **Name**, change it to Dirt.
5. Left-click on the + **Add Element** button at the bottom of the **Terrain Sets** section in the **Inspector**.
6. To the right of **Name**, change it to Grass.
7. Left-click the field that shows the color to the right of **Color**. Change the color to **Green** (hex 80d840).

8. Left-click on the + **Add Element** button at the bottom of the **Terrain Sets** section in the **Inspector**.

9. To the right of **Name**, change it to `Water`.

10. Left-click on the field to the right of **Color**. Change the color to **Blue** (hex `2c53f0`).

11. Left-click on the + **Add Element** button at the bottom of the **Terrain Sets** section in the Inspector.

12. To the right of **Name**, change it to `Snow`.

13. Left-click the field to the right of **Color**. Change the color to **White** (hex `ffffff`).

14. In the bottom panel, left-click on **Paint**.

15. In **Paint Properties**, left-click on **Select a property editor** and select **Terrains**.

16. Under **Painting** and to the right of **Terrain Set**, left-click on **No terrains**.

17. Left-click on **Terrain Set 0**.

18. To the right of **Terrain**, left-click on **No terrain**.

19. In the dropdown, select **Dirt**.

20. On the sprite sheet, left-click on the brown hexagon in the atlas coordinate `(1, 1)`.

21. Left-click and drag all over the hexagon until it's filled.

22. To the right of **Terrain**, left-click **Dirt**.

23. In the dropdown, select **Grass**.

24. On the sprite sheet, left-click on the green hexagon in the atlas coordinate `(0, 1)`.

25. Left-click and drag all over the hexagon until it's filled.

26. To the right of **Terrain**, left-click **Grass**.

27. In the dropdown, select **Water**.

28. On the sprite sheet, left-click on the blue hexagon in the atlas coordinate `(2, 1)`.

29. Left-click and drag all over the hexagon until it's filled.

30. To the right of **Terrain**, left-click **Water**.

31. In the dropdown, select **Snow**.

32. On the sprite sheet, left-click on the white hexagon in the atlas coordinate `(1, 0)`.

33. Left-click and drag all over the hexagon until it's filled.

34. In the bottom panel at the bottom right, left-click on **TileMap**.

35. At the top left of the bottom panel, there are **Tiles**, **Patterns**, and **Terrains** tabs. Left-click on the **Terrains** tab.

36. Off to the side of the painted tiles that we did previously, pick a terrain tile and paint a terrain. You will see the **Terrains** tab with a list of terrain tiles, as shown in the following figure:

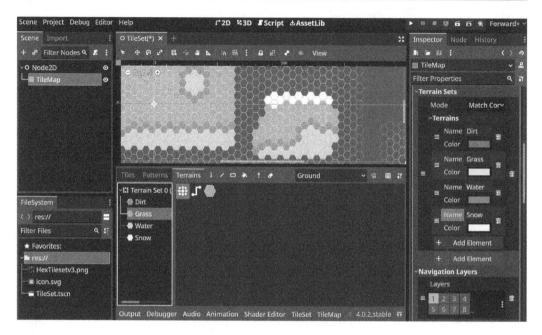

Figure 8.12 – The Terrains tab with a list of terrain tiles

How it works...

We left-clicked on **Terrain Sets** located in between **Physics Layers** and **Navigation Layers** in the **Inspector**. We left-clicked on the + **Add Element** button below **Terrain Sets**. Under **Terrain Sets**, in the **Inspector**, we saw **Mode with Match Corners** and **Sides**. We ignored that and left-clicked on the + **Add Element** button below it. We will learn about the **Mode** options in the next recipe. We left-clicked **Terrains** in the **Inspector**.

Then, under **Terrains**, we left-clicked on the + **Add Element** button. We changed the name of the terrain that appeared to `Dirt`. The color was brown by default, so we didn't change anything. If the color is not brown, then left-click on the field to the right of **Color** and change the color to brown (hex `805840`). We left-clicked on + **Add Element** at the bottom of the **Terrain Sets** section in the Inspector and changed the name of the next terrain to `Grass`. We changed the color to green. We repeated that two more times to add a blue **Water** and white **Snow** terrain.

We go to the bottom panel and select **Paint** to see **Paint Properties** for **Terrains**. Under **Painting**, we change the **Terrain Set** field to **Terrain Set 0**. This shows **Terrain** with a field to the right that says **No terrain**. We left-clicked on **No terrain** and the terrains that we created in the Inspector were listed below **No terrain** in the drop-down list.

At the top of the sprite sheet, we saw the tiles that we were going to use for these terrains. We selected **Dirt** in the drop-down list and left-clicked on the brown hexagon that we used in a previous recipe.

We left-clicked and dragged all over the hexagon until it was filled. We did the same for **Grass**, **Water**, and **Snow** in the drop-down list.

We went to the TileMap on the bottom panel and selected the **Terrains** tab to see all of the terrain tiles that we just finished setting up. In the viewport, we went to a clear spot and selected the terrain tiles and painted a terrain.

Transitioning TileSet terrains

In this recipe, we will use a new TileSet, which we are going to download. We will add a new TileMap and set up the tiles so they will autotile when we paint the terrain to the new TileMap.

Getting ready

For this recipe, we are going to continue from where we left off in the last recipe.

How to do it...

First, let's download a new TileSet to use with a square tile shape. We are going to use it in the new TileMap that we will add in the **Scene** tab. You can create a new scene and add the new TileMap if you want to keep the TileMaps separate:

1. Go to `https://opengameart.org/content/happyland-tileset` and download `tileset.png`.

2. From your `Downloads` folder, move or copy/paste the file into the **FileSystem** tab or your `Chapter 8` project folder.

3. Left-click on the **Node2D** node and then + in the **Scene** tab. In the **Create New Node** window, type `tile` in the search box and then select **TileMap** to create the node in the **Scene**. Left-click the **Create** button.

4. In the **Inspector**, click on <empty> to the right of **TileSet** and select **New TileSet** from the drop-down list.

5. Left-click on the same place to open the properties of the TileSet.

6. Left-click and drag `tileset.png` into the **Tiles** tab in the TileSet editor on the bottom panel and select **No** in the pop-up window.

7. In the **TileSet** on the bottom panel, left-click **Setup** located to the right of the **Tiles** tab.

8. Left-click and drag over the tiles in the upper-left corner with the water and grass, as shown in *Figure 8.13*.

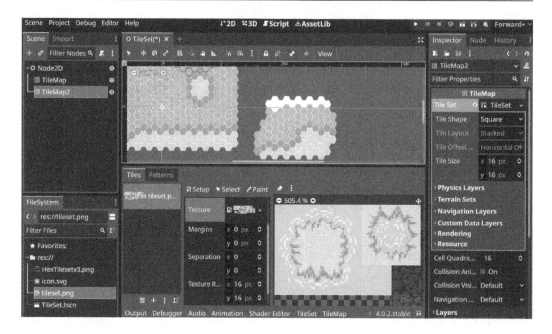

Figure 8.13 – Manually selecting tiles

9. In the **Inspector,** left-click on **Terrain Sets** located in between **Physics Layers** and **Navigation Layers**.

10. Left-click on the + **Add Element** button below **Terrain Sets**.

11. Left-click on the field to the right of **Mode**.

12. Select **Match Sides**.

13. Left-click **Terrains**.

14. Under **Terrains,** left-click on the + **Add Element** button.

15. To the right of **Name**, change it to Water.

16. Left-click on the field to the right of **Color**.

17. Change the color to **Blue** (hex 0000ff).

18. Left-click on the + **Add Element** button below **Color** and **Water**.

19. To the right of **Name**, change it to **Grass**.

20. Left-click on the field to the right of **Color**.

21. Change the color to **Green** (hex 002e00).

22. Left-click on **Paint** located to the left of the sprite sheet on the right side of the bottom panel.

23. Under **Paint Properties**, left-click on **Select a property editor**.

24. Select **Terrains** in the drop-down list.

25. Left-click on **No terrains**, located to the right of **Terrain Set** under **Painting**.

26. Select **Terrain Set 0** in the drop-down list.

27. Left-click on **No terrain**, located to the right of **Terrain** under **Terrain Set**.

28. Select **Water** from the drop-down list.

29. Left-click in the center of the nine water squares so a blue dot appears in the middle.

30. Left-click on each side that faces away from the grass tile in the center. Be sure to fill the blue square on the bottom right, as shown in *Figure 8.14*.

31. To the right of **Terrain**, left-click on **Water**.

32. Select **Grass** in the drop-down list.

33. Left-click on the center of the five grass squares so a green dot appears in the middle.

34. Left-click on each side that faces in toward the grass tile on the edges. Be sure to fill the green square in the center of the water tiles, as shown in *Figure 8.14*.

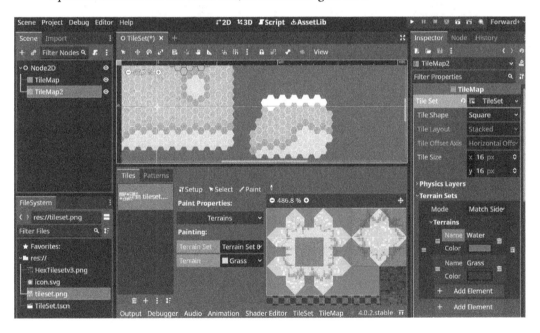

Figure 8.14 – Painting the Water and Grass terrain tiles

35. Left-click on **TileMap** in the bottom panel to the right of **TileSet**.

36. In the top left of the bottom panel, there are **Tiles**, **Patterns**, and **Terrains** tabs. Left-click on the **Terrains** tab.

37. Left-click on **Grass** and, in a space off to the side of the other TileMap, paint some grass. Then, left-click on **Water** to add some water, as shown in the following figure:

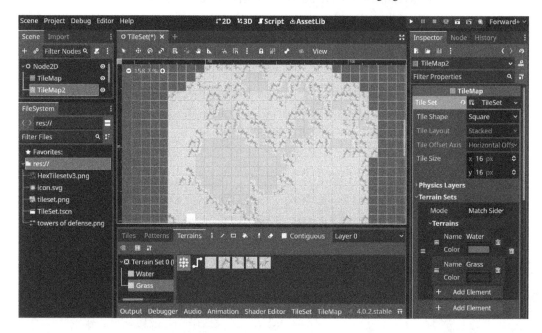

Figure 8.15 – Painting grass and water on TileMap2

How it works...

We downloaded `tileset.png` at the bottom of the page. From the `Downloads` folder on your computer, drag the `tileset.png` file into the **FileSystem** tab of Godot or you can copy the file in the `Downloads` folder and paste it into your `Chapter 8` project folder, which we created before we started this recipe. If Godot freezes, reboot it and notice that the file is in the **FileSystem** tab.

We added a **TileMap** node by left-clicking the + sign in the **Scene** tab and selecting **TileMap** in the **Create New Node** window. Then, in the **Inspector** tab, we left-clicked on **<empty>** located to the right of **Tile Set** and selected **New TileSet** from the drop-down list. We left-clicked on the TileSet located to the right of **Tile Set** in the **Inspector** to see the new **TileSet** properties of **TileMap2**.

We left-clicked and dragged the `tileset.png` file into the **Tiles** tab of the TileSet in the bottom panel. This time, we manually selected the tiles by selecting **No** when the pop-up window asked whether we wanted to automatically create the tiles. We left-clicked the **Setup** tab in the bottom panel to select the tiles we wanted to use in this TileSet. We left-clicked and dragged on the tiles in the upper-left corner with the water and grass to select these tiles and use only these tiles in the tile sheet.

We left-clicked on **Terrain Sets** located in between **Physics Layers** and **Navigation Layers** to see the properties. We left-clicked on the field to the right of **Mode** and selected **Match Sides**. The **Match**

Sides, **Match Corners**, and **Match Corners and Sides** options are used for terrains to match each other in the terrain set.

We left-clicked **Terrains** in the **Inspector**. Then, under **Terrains**, we left-clicked on the + **Add Element** button. We changed the name of the terrain that appeared to `Water`. We changed the color to blue. We left-clicked on the + **Add Element** button at the bottom of the **Terrain Sets** section in the Inspector and changed the name of the next terrain to `Grass`. We changed that color to green.

We left-clicked **Paint** located to the left of the sprite sheet on the right side of the bottom panel and left-clicked on **Select a property editor**. We selected **Terrains** in the drop-down list and left-clicked **No terrains**, located to the right of **Terrain Set**. We selected **Terrain Set 0** in the drop-down list. We left-clicked **No terrain** located to the right of **Terrain**. We saw **Water** and **Grass** in the drop-down list and left-clicked on **Water**. We left-clicked in the middle of all of the water squares.

We left-clicked on each side that faces away from the grass tile in the center, and we made sure to fill the blue square with no grass in the tile. For the **Grass** tiles, we left-clicked on each side that faces toward the grass tile in the center, and we made sure to fill the green square in the center of the water tiles. By left-clicking in the center of a tile, you have selected the tile to be used when we paint the TileMap. When we left-clicked on the sides of a tile, we set it up so that a tile would spawn in the direction we selected.

We went to the TileMap in the bottom panel and selected the **Terrains** tab to see the **Water** and **Grass** terrain tiles that we just finished setting up. In the viewport, we went to a clear spot and selected the terrain tiles and painted a terrain. For this tileset, autotiles work most of the time. You can select a specific tile and paint that as well as using autotiles.

Organizing isometric tiles into fixed-sized grids using the TileSet resource

In this recipe, we are going to download an isometric tileset. We will add a new TileMap, set up the tiles, and paint the tiles onto the new TileMap.

Getting ready

For this recipe, we are going to continue from where we left off in the last recipe.

How to do it...

We are going to download an isometric tileset and add a new TileMap to the **Scene** tab. You can create a new scene and add the new TileMap if you want to keep the TileMaps separate:

1. Go to `https://opengameart.org/content/towers-of-defense` and download `towers of defense.png`.

2. From your `Downloads` folder, move or copy/paste the file into the **FileSystem** tab or your `Chapter 8` project folder and left-click on **No** in the pop-up window.

3. Left-click on the **Node2D** node and then + in the **Scene** tab. In the **Create New Node** window, type `tile` in the search box and then select **TileMap** to create the node in the scene. Left-click on the **Create** button.

4. In the **Inspector**, click on **<empty>** to the right of **Tile Set** and select **New TileSet** from the drop-down list.

5. Left-click on the same place to open the properties of the TileSet.

6. In the **Inspector**, change the **Tile Size** values of **x** and **y** to 32.

7. Left-click and drag `towers of defense.png` into the **Tiles** tab in the TileSet editor in the bottom panel and select **No** in the pop-up window.

8. In the TileSet on the bottom panel, left-click **Setup** located to the right of the **Tiles** tab, and then left-click on the top two tiles.

9. In the **Inspector**, to the right of **Tile Shape**, left-click on **Square** and select **isometric** from the drop-down list.

10. To the right of **Tile Offset Axis**, left-click on **Horizontal Offset** and select **Vertical Offset** from the drop-down list.

11. In the **Inspector** under **CanvasItem**, left-click on **Ordering**.

12. To the right of **Y Sort Enabled**, check the **On** checkbox.

13. In the **Inspector** above **Node2D**, left-click on **Layers**.

14. To the right of **Y Sort Enabled**, check the **On** checkbox.

15. In the TileMap, make sure the **Tiles** tab is selected.

16. Left-click on the grass tile and place two or four tiles on an empty part of the grid in the viewport.

17. In the **Inspector**, left-click and hold on the number 32 of the **y** value in the **Tile Size** property; then move the mouse to the left to adjust the tiles so they fit together.

18. The value of **y** should be 16. Place more grass and concrete tiles down, as shown in the following figure:

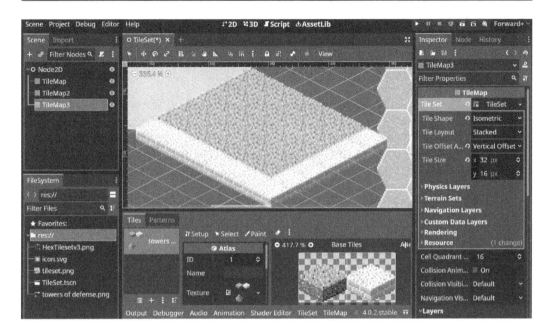

Figure 8.16 – Isometric tiles Inspector and TileSet settings

How it works...

We downloaded `towers of defense.png` at the bottom of the page. From the `Downloads` folder on your computer, drag the `towers of defense.png` file into the **FileSystem** tab of Godot or you can copy the file in the `Downloads` folder and then paste the file into your `Chapter 8` project folder, which we created before we started this recipe. If Godot freezes, reboot it and notice that the file is in the **FileSystem** tab.

We added a **TileMap** node by left-clicking on + in the **Scene** tab and selecting **TileMap** in the **Create New Node** window. Then, in the **Inspector** tab, we left-clicked on <**empty**> located to the right of **Tile Set** and selected **New TileSet** from the drop-down list. We left-clicked on the TileSet located to the right of **Tile Set** in the **Inspector** to see the new **TileSet** properties of **TileMap3**. We changed the **TileSize** values of **x** and **y** to `32`. We are going to change the value of **y** later, but by changing these now, we will have the correct **x** and **y** values of the tiles when we drag the `tower of defence.png` file into the **TIleSet**.

We left-clicked and dragged the `tower of defence.png` file into the **Tiles** tab of the TileSet on the bottom panel. We manually selected the tiles by selecting **No** when the pop-up window asked whether we wanted to automatically create the tiles. We left-clicked the **Setup** tab in the bottom panel to select the tiles we wanted to use in this TileSet. We left-clicked on the top two tiles to use only these tiles in the tilesheet.

We looked for **Tile Shape** in the **Inspector** and left-clicked **Square** to open the drop-down list, and then we selected **Isometric**. We looked to the right of **Tile Offset Axis** and left-clicked on **Horizontal Offset** and selected **Vertical Offset** from the drop-down list. This set up the TileMap to work with the tiles we downloaded.

We saw that on **TileMap3**, we have a warning about Y sort not being enabled on all of its layers. To fix this, we looked for **Ordering** in the **Inspector** under **CanvasItem**. We left-clicked on it and then, to the right of **Y Sort Enabled**, we checked the **On** checkbox. We left-clicked on **Layers** located above **Node2D** in the **Inspector** to see its properties. We looked to the right of **Y Sort Enabled** and checked the **On** checkbox.

We left-clicked on the TileMap on the bottom panel and made sure that we were on the **Tile** tab. Since we are going to just paint the tiles and did not set up these tiles to use as terrain, we need to stay on the **Tile** tab. We left-clicked on the grass tile and added two to four tiles in an empty space in the viewport on the TileMap. The tiles are spread apart because the **Tile Size** value of **y** is too big set at 32.

We left-clicked and held on to the number 32, then moved the mouse to the left to lower the size to see how the tiles fit as we slid the mouse. We saw that 16 is a good number for **y** and now the tiles look good. We can add more tiles if we want.

9

Achieving Better Animations Using the New Animation Editor

In this chapter, we are going to create a 3D cube, and in the animation player, we will use the new 3D Position, 3D Rotation, and 3D Scale tracks on the cube. We will create an animation with the improved Bezier curve to spin a cube one way and then the other way at the end of the animation. In Godot 4, we can use Euler, Quaternion, and Basis on rotation in animations. We are going to create an animation that has a rotation animation on the *x*, *y*, and *z* axes.

We will change the rotation order of the Euler rotations to see the effect of the **MeshInstance3D** node we rotated. With animations, Godot 4 removed the dependency on bone rests. Now, skeletons only have a final pose for each bone. One of the results of this change is that we can use animations across different models with similar skeletons.

We will download a model with a walking animation and use that animation on a model without animations that we downloaded as well. We look at the **Transition** node in the **AnimationTree** node. First, we will create two very basic 2D animations. Then, in the **AnimationTree** node, we add these two animations to the **Transition** node and connect the **Transition** node to the **Output** node to run the animation.

We could do this in Godot 3.x, but it is a little easier in Godot 4. We look at the new **Movie Maker** mode, where we will create and animate a scene and record it.

In this chapter, we will cover the following recipes:

- Exploring changes with transform tracks
- Investigating the new Bezier curve workflow
- Playing with 3D rotation animations
- Working with bone poses

- Triggering a transition
- Playing with the new **Movie Maker** mode

Technical requirements

For this chapter, you need the standard version of Godot 4.0 or later running on one of the following platforms:

- Windows 64-bit or 32-bit
- macOS
- Linux 64-bit or 32-bit
- Android
- Web Editor

You can find the code and the project files for the projects in this chapter on GitHub at `https://github.com/PacktPublishing/Godot-4-Game-Development-Cookbook/tree/main/Chapter%209`.

Exploring changes with transform tracks

In this recipe, we are going to create a **MeshInstance3D** node. In the Animation Player, we will animate the 3D mesh using the new 3D Position, Rotation, and Scale tracks.

Getting ready

For this recipe, open Godot 4 and start a new project called `Chapter 9`. In the **Scene** tab, click **3D** to add a 3D scene. Click on the word **Scene** in the main menu next to **Project**, then select **Save Scene As**, and name it `Animation`.

How to do it...

First, we will add a **MeshInstance3D** node and the **AnimationPlayer** node to our scene:

1. Left-click on the **Node3D** node and then left-click the + button in the **Scene** tab. In the **Create New Node** window, type `mesh` in the search box and then select **MeshInstance3D** to create the node in the scene. Left-click the **Create** button.
2. In the **Inspector** tab, click on **<empty>** to the right of **Mesh** and select **New BoxMesh**.
3. Left-click on the **Node3D** node and then left-click the + button in the **Scene** tab. In the **Create New Node** window, type `anim` in the search box and then select **AnimationPlayer** to create the node in the scene. Left-click the **Create** button.

4. Left-click on **Animation** in the top part of the bottom panel:

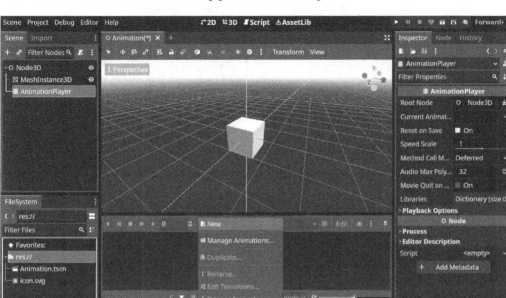

Figure 9.1 – Animation Editor

5. Left-click **New** from the drop-down list.

6. When the **Create New Animation** window appears, left-click the **OK** button.

7. Left-click **MeshInstance3D** in the **Scene** tab.

8. Left-click on + **Add Track**, located in the top-left corner of the Animation Editor.

9. Left-click **3D Position Track**.

10. In the **Pick a node to animate** window, left-click on **MeshInstance3D** and then left-click the **OK** button.

11. Left-click on + **Add Track**, located in the top-left corner of the Animation Editor.

12. Left-click **3D Rotation Track**.

13. In the **Pick a node to animate** window, left-click on **MeshInstance3D** then left-click the **OK** button.

14. Left-click on + **Add Track**, located in the top-left corner of the Animation Editor.

15. Left-click **3D Scale Track**.

16. In the **Pick a node to animate** window, left-click on **MeshInstance3D** then left-click the **OK** button.

17. Left-click on the field to the left of the **Animation Looping** button just below the top-right corner of the Animation Editor and change the 1 value to 5. See the highlighted section in *Figure 9.2*:

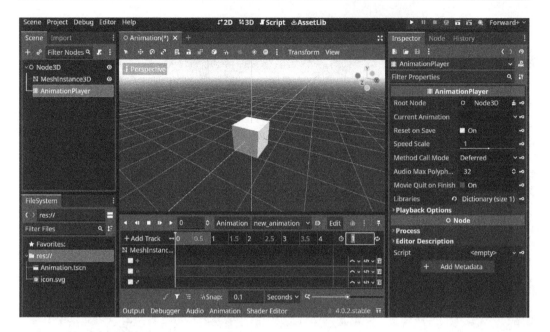

Figure 9.2 – Changing the animation length

18. Left-click in the seconds bar to the right of + **Add Track**, and a vertical blue line appears. Move the line to 0.

19. Left-click on **MeshInstance3D** in the **Scene** tab.

20. In the animation player editor, on the 0 value in **3D Position Track**, right-click, and then left-click on the **Insert Key** button that appears.

21. In the animation player editor, on the 0 value in **3D Rotation Track**, right-click, and then left-click on the **Insert Key** button.

22. In the animation player editor, on the 0 value in **3D Scale Track**, right-click, and then left-click on the **Insert Key** button.

23. Move the blue line to 2.5 seconds.

24. Move the cube to the right.

25. In the animation player editor, on the blue line in **3D Position Track**, right-click, and then left-click on the **Insert Key** button.

26. Rotate the cube.

27. In the animation player editor, on the blue line in **3D Rotation Track**, right-click, and then left-click on the **Insert Key** button.

28. In the animation player editor, on the blue line in **3D Scale Track**, right-click, and then left-click on the **Insert Key** button.

29. Move the blue line to 5 seconds.

30. Move the cube back to where it started.

31. In the animation player editor, on the blue line in **3D Position Track**, right-click, and then left-click on the **Insert Key** button.

32. Rotate the cube so that it is now in its original position.

33. In the animation player editor, on the blue line in **3D Rotation Track**, right-click, and then left-click on the **Insert Key** button.

34. In the animation player editor, on the blue line in **3D Scale Track**, right-click, and then left-click on the **Insert Key** button.

35. Left-click the key we just inserted for **Scale** and, in the **Inspector** tab, change the **x** and **y** values to 1.5.

36. In the top-left corner of the Animation Editor, left-click on the **Play selected animation from start** button by pressing *Shift + D*.

How it works...

We created a **MeshInstance3D** node with a **BoxMesh**. We added an **AnimationPlayer** node to the scene.

We looked in the Animation Editor. At the top, we left-clicked on **Animation** and then **New** in the drop-down list to create a new animation. We used the default name new_animation when we clicked the **OK** button instead of changing the name.

We left-clicked the **MeshInstance3D** node in the **Scene** tab so that when we add an animation track, the track will be used with the **MeshInstance3D** node. We left-clicked on + **Add Track** to add the new **3D Position Track**, **3D Rotation Track**, and **3D Scale Track**. When the **Pick a node to animate** window appeared, we selected **MeshInstance3D** because the position, rotation, and scale tracks we are using are not using the **Transform** property's location but the **MeshInstance3D** properties itself.

We changed the length of the animation (seconds) from 1 to 5. We left-clicked in the seconds area between 0 and 5 to bring up the vertical blue line that indicated where the animation is in the timeline. We moved the blue line to 0. We left-clicked on **MeshInstance3D** in the **Scene** tab so that when we add the keys to the animation, it tracks **MeshInstance3D**.

With the blue line at 0 in the timeline, we right-clicked on the line of **3D Position Track** and then left-clicked on the **Insert Key** button that appeared. We did the same for **3D Rotation Track** and **3D Scale Track**. This created a starting point for each track.

We moved the blue line to 2.5 seconds and moved the cube to the right. We right-clicked on the line of **3D Position Track** and then left-clicked on the **Insert Key** button. We rotated the cube, then right-clicked on the line of **3D Rotation Track**, and then left-clicked on the **Insert Key** button. On the blue line in **3D Scale Track**, we right-clicked and then left-clicked on the **Insert Key** button. Halfway through the animation, the cube moves to the right and rotates.

We moved the blue line to 5 seconds and moved the cube back to its starting position. We right-clicked on the line of **3D Position Track** and then left-clicked on the **Insert Key** button. We rotated the cube back to its original position, then right-clicked on the line of **3D Rotation Track**, and then left-clicked **Insert Key**.

We right-clicked on the blue line in **3D Scale Track**, and then left-clicked on the **Insert Key** button. We left-clicked the key we had just inserted and, in the **Inspector** tab, changed the **x** and **y** values to 1.5. At the end of the animation, the cube rotates and moves back to where it started while it gets bigger.

We left-clicked on the **Play selected animation from start** button by pressing *Shift + D* to see the animation.

Investigating the new Bezier curve workflow

Bezier curves create smooth curves between points set in an animation track or vector graphics. In this recipe, we will create a cube, and using the Bezier curve track, we will rotate the *x* axis to spin one way for half of the animation and the opposite way for the last half.

Getting ready

For this recipe, click the + button to the right of the **Animation** scene we just completed to add a new scene. In the **Scene** tab, click **3D Scene**. Click on the word **Scene** in the main menu next to **Project**, then select **Save Scene As**, and name it Bezier.

How to do it...

First, we add a **MeshInstance3D** node and **AnimationPlayer** to the **Scene** tab;

1. Left-click on the **Node3D** node and then left-click the + button in the **Scene** tab. In the **Create New Node** window, type mesh in the search box and then select **MeshInstance3D** to create the node in the scene. Left-click the **Create** button.

2. In the **Inspector** tab, click on **<empty>** to the right of **Mesh** and select **New BoxMesh**.

3. Left-click on the **Node3D** node and then left-click the + button in the **Scene** tab. In the **Create New Node** window, type anim in the search box and then select **AnimationPlayer** to create the node in the scene. Left-click the **Create** button.

4. Left-click on **Animation** in the top part of the bottom panel.

5. Left-click **New** from the drop-down list.

6. When the **Create New Animation** window appears, left-click the **OK** button.

7. Left-click on the field to the left of the **Animation Looping** button just below the top-right corner of the Animation Editor and change the 1 value to 5:

Figure 9.3 – Animation looping button

8. Left-click **MeshInstance3D** in the **Scene** tab.

9. Left-click on + **Add Track**, located in the top-left corner of the Animation Editor.

10. Left-click **Bezier Curve Track**.

11. In the **Pick a node to animate** window, left-click on **MeshInstance3D**, then left-click the **OK** button.

12. In the window that appears, under **Node3D**, left-click on **Rotation** and then left-click **Open**.

13. Right-click to the right of **rotation:x** and **Insert Key**.

14. Move the key to 0.

15. Right-click to the right of **rotation:x** and **Insert Key**.

16. Move the key to 5.

17. Left-click the **Toggle between the bezier curve editor and track editor**, button located on the bottom—it's the first icon on the left, as shown in *Figure 9.4*:

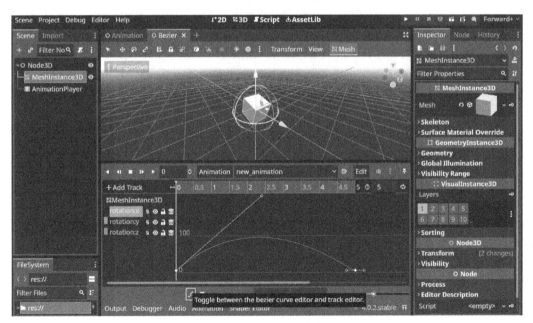

Figure 9.4 – Bezier curve Editor

18. Move the Bezier curve so that it arches to 100 in the middle. You may need to zoom in on the timeline.

19. In the top-left corner of the Animation Editor, left-click on the **Play selected animation from start** button by pressing *Shift + D*.

How it works...

We created a **MeshInstance3D** node with a **BoxMesh**. We added an **AnimationPlayer** node to the scene.

We looked in the Animation Editor. At the top, we left-clicked on **Animation** and then **New** in the drop-down list to create a new animation. We used the default name new_animation when we clicked the **OK** button instead of changing the name.

We changed the seconds of the animation from 1 to 5. We left-clicked the **MeshInstance3D** node in the **Scene** tab so that when we add an animation track, the track will be used with the **MeshInstance3D** node.

We left-clicked on + **Add Track**, located in the top-left corner of the Animation Editor, and selected **Bezier Curve Track**. When the pop-up window appeared, we left-clicked on **MeshInstance3D** and then left-clicked the **OK** button to animate the **MeshInstance3D** cube. In a window that appeared, we looked under **Node3D** in the list. We left-clicked on **Rotation** and then left-clicked **Open**. This gave us the animation tracks of **rotation:x**, **rotation:y**, and **rotation:z**.

We right-clicked to the right of **rotation:x** and **Insert Key** twice. The first key we moved to 0, and the second key we moved to 5. We have a starting and ending animation point, so now we can show the Bezier curve.

We left-clicked the **Toggle between the bezier curve editor and track editor**, button to switch to the **Bezier Curve Editor**. We moved the Bezier curve so that it arches to 100 in the middle, as shown in *Figure 9.4*. This will rotate the cube in one direction for 2 seconds, then slow down, and rotate the cube in the opposite direction. We left-clicked on the **Play selected animation from start** button by pressing *Shift + D* to play the animation.

Playing with 3D rotation animations

In this recipe, we create an animation that has a rotation animation on the x, y, and z axes. We are going to use the Euler in the **Rotation Edit** mode and also look at the other options you can use in the **Rotation Edit** mode. We change the rotation order in the **Euler Rotation Order** properties.

Getting ready

For this recipe, click the + button to the right of the **Bezier** scene we just completed to add a new scene. In the **Scene** tab, click **3D Scene**. Click on the word **Scene** in the main menu next to **Project**, then select **Save Scene As**, and name it Euler.

How to do it...

Let's add a **MeshInstance3D** node and the **AnimationPlayer** node to the **Scene** tab:

1. Left-click on the **Node3D** node and then left-click the + button in the **Scene** tab. In the **Create New Node** window, type mesh in the search box and then select **MeshInstance3D** to create the node in the scene. Left-click the **Create** button.

2. In the **Inspector** tab, click on <**empty**> to the right of **Mesh** and select **New BoxMesh**.

3. Left-click on the **Node3D** node and then left-click the + button in the **Scene** tab. In the **Create New Node** window, type anim in the search box and then select **AnimationPlayer** to create the node in the scene. Left-click the **Create** button.

4. Left-click on **Animation** in the top part of the bottom panel.

5. Left-click **New** from the drop-down list.

6. When the **Create New Animation** window appears, left-click the **OK** button.

7. Left-click on the field to the left of the **Animation Looping** button just below the top-right corner of the Animation Editor and change the 1 value to 5.

8. Left-click **MeshInstance3D** in the **Scene** tab.

9. Left-click on 5 seconds in the animation timeline.

10. Left-click on **Transform** in the **Inspector** tab.

11. In the **Inspector** tab, under **Scale**, left-click the white chain link icon to the far right of **z 1**.

12. In the **Inspector** tab, under **Scale**, change the value of **x** to 5.

13. In the **Inspector** tab, change the **Rotation** values of **x** to 500, **y** to 1000, and **z** to 250.

14. In the **Inspector** tab, to the far right of **Rotation**, left-click on the key icon ( ) to insert the key.

15. In the pop-up window, left-click on **Create**.

16. Left-click on 0 seconds in the animation timeline.

17. In the Animation Editor, right-click to the right of the rotation track under **MeshInstance3D** and left-click **Insert Key** in the popup.

18. Left-click on the key you placed at 0, and in the **Inspector** tab, change the **x**, **y**, and **z** values to 0.

19. In the **Inspector** tab, to the far right of **Rotation Order**, left-click on the key icon.

20. In the pop-up window, left-click on **Create**.

21. Left-click on the rotation_order key to see the properties in the **Inspector** tab.

22. In the top-left corner of the Animation Editor, left-click on the **Play selected animation from start** button by pressing *Shift* + *D*.

23. Left-click **YXZ** to the right of **Value** in the **Inspector** tab and select another value.

24. In the top-left corner of the Animation Editor, left-click on the **Play selected animation from start** button by pressing *Shift + D*:

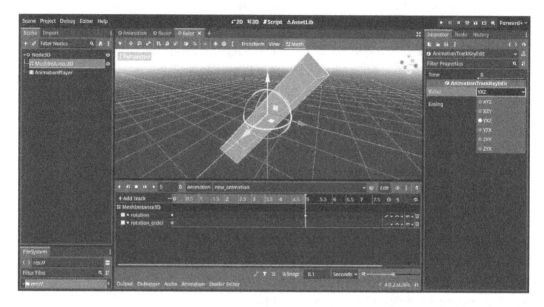

Figure 9.5 – Euler rotation animation

How it works...

We created a **MeshInstance3D** node with a **BoxMesh**. We added an **AnimationPlayer** to the scene.

We looked in the Animation Editor. At the top, we left-clicked on **Animation** and then **New** in the drop-down list to create a new animation. We used the default name new_animation when we clicked the **OK** button instead of changing the name.

We changed the seconds of the animation from 1 to 5. We left-clicked the **MeshInstance3D** node in the **Scene** tab so that when we add an animation track, the track will be used with the **MeshInstance3D** node. We also did this to add the animation keys from the properties in the **Inspector** tab.

We left-clicked on **Transform** in the **Inspector** tab to see its properties. We left-clicked on the chain link icon located to the right of **Scale** so that we can change the **x** value in **Scale** and not change all of the values. We changed the value to 5 so that we can tell where the cube is rotating.

We changed the **x**, **y**, and **z** values of **Rotation** to 500, 1000, and 250 so that we can change the rotation order later. In **Rotation properties** in the **Inspector** tab, we left-clicked on the key icon to add **Rotation** to the animation. In the Animation Editor, a key was created with the values we set in the **Inspector** tab at the 5-second mark.

In the animation timeline, we clicked on the 0-second mark. We left-clicked on the key to show the **x**, **y**, and **z** values in the **Inspector** tab. We changed all of the values to 0. We started the rotation animation at 0, 0, and 0 values and ended at the 500, 1000, and 250 values.

In the animation timeline, we clicked on the 0-second mark so that when we add the key for **Rotation Order**, it will start at 0 seconds. In the **Inspector** tab, we left-clicked the key icon located to the far right of **Rotation Order**. The key was automatically placed at the 0-second mark, so when we start the animation it will rotate the **x**, **y**, and **z** values in the order we set in this key. We left-clicked the rotation_order key to see the properties in the **Inspector** tab when we play the animation.

We played the animation using the default order; then we changed the rotation_order value and played the animation again to see that the animation changed. If you change the **Rotation Order** values in the **Inspector** tab, it will not work as expected. You must change the values in the animation by clicking on the animation key.

Working with bone poses

In this recipe, we will download a model with animations and a model without any animations. We will extract the animations from the model with animations and put them into the model without animations.

Getting ready

For this recipe, click the + button to the right of the **Euler** scene we just completed to add a new scene. In the **Scene** tab, click **3D Scene**. Click on the word **Scene** in the main menu next to **Project**, then select **Save Scene As**, and name it Bones.

How to do it...

First, we are going to download our two models from https://free3d.com/:

1. Go to https://free3d.com/user/renderpeople and download the FBX files of **Nathan Animated 003 Walking** and **Eric Rigged 001** to your computer and unzip the files into folders named Nathan and Eric.

2. Click and drag the two folders into the **FileSystem** tab in Godot.

3. Left-click on the arrow to the left of the Nathan folder to open the folder.

4. Double left-click on rp_nathan_animated_003_walking.fbx.

5. In the **Scene** tab of the **Advanced Import Settings** window, left-click on **Skeleton3D**.

6. Left-click on **<empty>**, located to the right of **Bone Map** under **Retarget**.

7. Left-click on **New BoneMap** from the drop-down list:

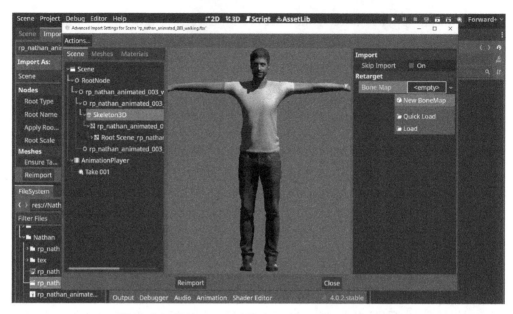

Figure 9.6 – Nathan model Skeleton3D and New BoneMap

8. Left-click on **BoneMap**, located to the right of **Bone Map** under **Retarget**.

9. Left-click on **<empty>**, located to the right of **Profile** under **Bone Map**.

10. Left-click on **New SkeletonProfileHumanoid** from the drop-down list:

Figure 9.7 – Nathan model Skeleton3D and New SkeletonProfileHumanoid

11. To the right of **Group** is **Body**. Notice the picture of the body has all green dots.

12. Left-click on **Body** to the right of **Group** and click **Face**. All of the dots should be green.

13. Left-click on **Face** to the right of **Group** and click **LeftHand**. All of the dots should be green.

14. Left-click on **LeftHand** to the left of **Group** and click **RightHand**. All of the dots should be green.

15. Left-click the **Reimport** button at the bottom of the **Advanced Import Settings** window.

16. Double left-click on `rp_nathan_animated_003_walking.fbx`.

17. In the **Scene** tab of the **Advanced Import Settings** window, left-click on **Skeleton3D**.

18. Left-click on the down arrow, located to the right of **Bone Map | BoneMap** under **Retarget**.

19. Select **Save** from the drop-down list.

20. Name the file `Nathan_bonemap.tres`.

21. Left-click the **Close** button at the bottom of the **Advanced Import Settings** window.

22. Left-click `rp_nathan_animated_003_walking.fbx` in the **FileSystem** tab.

23. Left-click the **Import** tab located next to the **Scene** tab above the **FileSystem** tab.

24. Left-click on **Scene** located under **Import As:**.

25. Select **Animation Library**:

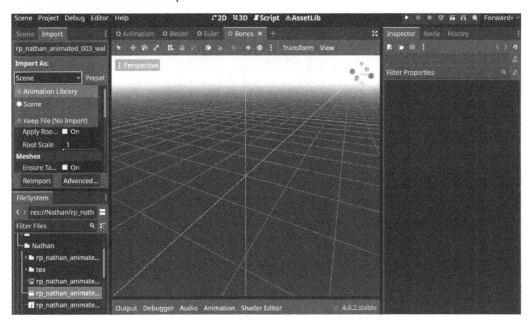

Figure 9.8 – Changing the file of an animation library

26. Left-click on the **Reimport** button on the bottom left.

27. Left-click on the **Save Scenes, Re-Import, and Restart** button.

28. Left-click on the arrow to the left of the `Eric` folder to open the folder.

29. Double left-click on `rp_eric_rigged_001_zup_t.fbx` at the bottom.

30. In the **Scene** tab of the **Advanced Import Settings** window, left-click on **Skeleton3D**.

31. Left-click on the down arrow to the right of **<empty>**, which is located to the right of **Bone Map** under **Retarget**.

32. Left-click on **Load** from the drop-down list.

33. In the **Open a File** window, select `Nathan_bonemap.tres` and left-click the **Open** button.

34. Left-click on `Nathan_bonemap`, located to the right of **Bone Map** under **Retarget**.

35. Notice that all dots on the body are red. Left-click on the red dot that is on the top, which is the head part of the skeleton.

36. Below the body, it should now say **Head** with the name `Nathan bonemap` to the right of it. Left-click the button to the right of that to attach the bonemap we loaded to this model's bonemap.

37. Left-click on all of the down arrows by **hip**, **spine_01**, **upperleg_l**, and **upperleg_r** to attach the skeleton to the body:

Figure 9.9 – Mapping the skeleton to the bonemap file we loaded

38. Left-click and match each dot to the corresponding skeleton in the **Bone Picker** window. Do this for **Body**, **Face**, **LeftHand**, and **RightHand**. They should be all green when you are finished.

39. Left-click on the **Reimport** button on the bottom left.

40. Right-click on the `rp_eric_rigged_001_zup_t.fbx` file, at the bottom of the `Eric` folder, and select **New Inherited Scene**.

41. Left-click on **AnimationPlayer** in the **Scene** tab.

42. In the Animation Editor in the bottom panel, left-click **Animation** and select **Manage Animations** in the drop-down list:

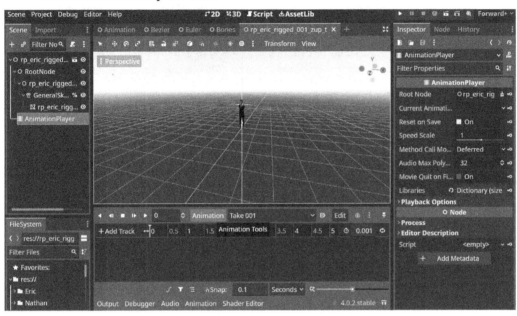

Figure 9.10 – Animation Tools button in the Animation Editor

43. In the **Edit Animation Libraries** window that popped up, left-click **Load Library**.

44. Double-click on the `Nathan` folder and left-click on the `rp_nathan_animated_003_walking.fbx` file.

45. Left-click on the **Open** button at the bottom of the window.

46. Left-click on the **OK** button at the bottom of the **Edit Animation Libraries** window.

47. Left-click on **Take 001** to the right of **Animation** and select `rp_nathan_animated_003_walking/Take 001` from the drop-down list.

48. In the top-left corner of the Animation Editor, left-click on the **Play selected animation from start** button by pressing *Shift + D*.

How it works...

We downloaded two models. We unzipped them into a new folder for each that we named `Nathan` and `Eric`. We dragged the two folders into the **FileSystem** tab in Godot.

We opened the `Nathan` folder and double left-clicked on `rp_nathan_animated_003_walking.fbx` to bring up the **Advanced Import Settings** window. We left-clicked on **Skeleton3D** in the **Scene** tab of the **Advanced Import Settings** window. Then, we left-clicked on **<empty>**, located to the right of **Bone Map** under **Retarget**, and selected **New BoneMap** from the drop-down list.

We left-clicked on **BoneMap** located to the right of **Bone Map** under **Retarget** to see the **BoneMap** properties. We left-clicked on **<empty>** located to the right of **Profile** under **Bone Map** and selected **New SkeletonProfileHumanoid** from the drop-down list.

To the right of **Group** is **Body**, which you can left-click on and change to see **Face**, **LeftHand**, and **RightHand**. We looked at all of these to make sure all of the dots were green. This is taking the model's animation points and mapping them to Godot's internal skeleton. We clicked the **Reimport** button so that the model is now mapped to Godot's internal skeleton.

We double left-clicked on `rp_nathan_animated_003_walking.fbx` to bring up the **Advanced Import Settings** window. We left-clicked on **Skeleton3D** in the **Scene** tab of the **Advanced Import Settings** window. We left-clicked on the down arrow located to the right of **Bone Map | BoneMap** under **Retarget** to bring up the drop-down list.

We selected **Save** from that list and named the file `Nathan_bonemap.tres`. We left-clicked on the **Close** button of the **Advanced Import Settings** window. This file is the bonemap of our model, which has the animation that we will add to our other model that does not have an animation.

We left-clicked the `rp_nathan_animated_003_walking.fbx` file in the **FileSystem** tab to make sure the file that we were working on was selected. We left-clicked on the **Import** tab next to the **Scene** tab. We left-clicked on **Scene**, located under **Import As:**, to change this file to an animation library instead of a scene. This will take out the mesh and keep the bones so that it can run the animation on a new model.

We clicked on the **Reimport** button to apply the changes. A **Save Scenes, Re-Import, and Restart** button appeared, and we clicked it. Godot will save, re-import, and then reboot. If you look at the `rp_nathan_animated_003_walking.fbx` file, you should see that the scene icon has been replaced with a new icon indicating that it is now an animation library file.

We opened the `Eric` folder and double left-clicked on `rp_eric_rigged_001_zup_t.fbx` at the bottom. In the **Advanced Import Settings** window, we left-clicked on **Skeleton3D**. We left-clicked on the down arrow to the right of **<empty>**, which was located to the right of **Bone Map** under **Retarget**.

This opened a drop-down list, and we selected **Load** from that list. In the **Open a File** window, we selected `Nathan_bonemap.tres` and left-clicked the **Open** button. The **Nathan** bonemap and animation that we saved are now on our `Eric` model, which previously didn't have animation.

We left-clicked on **BoneMap** located to the right of **Bone Map** under **Retarget**. This brought up a picture of the body with black and red or blue dots all over. When we did this with the `Nathan` model, they were all green dots. Since we loaded the `Nathan` library to the `Eric` model, the two skeletons don't match. We left-clicked on the red dot where the head is, and under the picture of the body, we saw **Head**, and to the right of that, we saw the skeleton name of the `Nathan` model that we loaded to the `Eric` model.

We left-clicked on the icon to the right of that to bring up the **Bone Picker** window with a listing of all of the `Eric` model's skeleton parts. We left-clicked the **Head** node in the **Bone Picker** window, and after that, it should have turned green. If the dot was red after you connected a bone, that means you connected the wrong bone.

Look at the filename when you click on a dot, and that should tell you exactly which bone to select in the **Bone Picker** window. We connected all of the red dots so that they are now green in the **Body**, **Face**, **LeftHand**, and **RightHand** sections. We left-clicked on the **Reimport** button on the bottom left to import the changes we made to the model.

We right-clicked on the `rp_eric_rigged_001_zup_t.fbx` file, at the bottom of the `Eric` folder, and selected **New Inherited Scene**. We clicked on the **AnimationPlayer** node in the **Scene** tab to see the Animation Editor in the bottom panel. We left-clicked on the **Animation Tools** button so that we can select **Manage Animations** from the drop-down list.

In the **Edit Animation Libraries** window that appeared, we left-clicked **Load Library** to load the `rp_nathan_animated_003_walking.fbx` file. We left-clicked on **Take 001** to the right of **Animation** and selected **rp_nathan_animated_003_walking/Take 001** from the drop-down list to add the `Nathan` model animation to the `Eric` model. We ran the animation and saw the `Eric` model walk.

A great resource to get free character and animation models is the following website: `https://www.mixamo.com/#/`. You do need to sign up for a free Adobe account, though. Putting Mixamo animations into a Mixamo character is generally easier because the animation recognizes the bones, so you don't have to bone map as much or at all as we did in this recipe.

Triggering a transition

In this recipe, we will create two animations. The first will shrink and spin the background. The second will expand and spin the background like a scene transition. We added these animations to the **AnimationTree** node. We add a **Transition** node to use as a bridge to run the animations when we hook them up to the **Transition** node and out to the **Output** node.

Getting ready

For this recipe, click the + button to the right of the **Bones** scene we just completed to add a new scene. In the **Scene** tab, click **2D Scene**. Click on the word **Scene** in the main menu next to **Project**, then select **Save Scene As**, and name it `Transition`.

How to do it...

Let's create our **MeshInstance2D** background. Then, we'll create **Shrink** and **Expand** animations in **AnimationPlayer**:

1. Left-click on the **Node2D** node and then left-click the + button in the **Scene** tab. In the **Create New Node** window, type mesh in the search box and then select **MeshInstance2D** to create the node in the scene. Left-click the **Create** button.

2. Right-click on the **MeshInstance2D** node in the **Scene** tab and select **Rename** from the drop-down list.

3. Enter Background as the new name of the **MeshInstance2D** node.

4. In the **Inspector** tab, click on <empty> to the right of **Mesh** and select **New BoxMesh**.

5. Left-click on **Transform** in the **Inspector** tab.

6. To the right of **Position**, change the **x** value to 580 and the **y** value to 322.

7. To the far right of **Scale**, click on the white link icon.

8. To the right of **Scale**, change the **x** value to 1175 and the **y** value to 670.

9. Left-click on the **Node2D** node and then left-click the + button in the **Scene** tab. In the **Create New Node** window, type anim in the search box and then select **AnimationPlayer** to create the node in the scene. Left-click the **Create** button.

10. Left-click on **Animation** in the top part of the bottom panel.

11. Left-click **New** from the drop-down list.

12. When the **Create New Animation** window appears, enter Shrink as the name of the animation and then click the **OK** button.

13. Left-click on + **Add Track** located in the top-left corner of the Animation Editor.

14. Left-click **Property Track**.

15. In the **Pick a node to animate:** window, select **Background** and left-click the **OK** button.

16. In the **Select Property** window, under **Node2D**, select **Scale**, and left-click on the **Open** button.

17. Left-click on + **Add Track**, located in the top-left corner of the Animation Editor.

18. Left-click **Property Track**.

19. In the **Pick a node to animate:** window, select **Background** and left-click the **OK** button.

20. In the **Select Property** window, under **Node2D**, select **Rotation**, and left-click on the **Open** button.

21. Left-click on **Background** in the **Scene** tab.

22. Make sure the blue line is on 0 in the **Timeline** section of the **AnimationPlayer** editor.

23. In the **Inspector** tab, left-click on the **Key** icon to the far right of **Scale**.

24. In the **Inspector** tab, left-click on the **Key** icon to the far right of **Rotation**.

25. Make sure the blue line is on 1 in the **Timeline** section of the **AnimationPlayer** editor.

26. Change the **Scale x** and **y** values to 0 in the **Inspector** tab.

27. In the **Inspector** tab, left-click on the **Key** icon to the far right of **Scale**.

28. Change the **Rotation** value to 360 in the **Inspector** tab.

29. In the **Inspector** tab, left-click on the **Key** icon to the far right of **Rotation**:

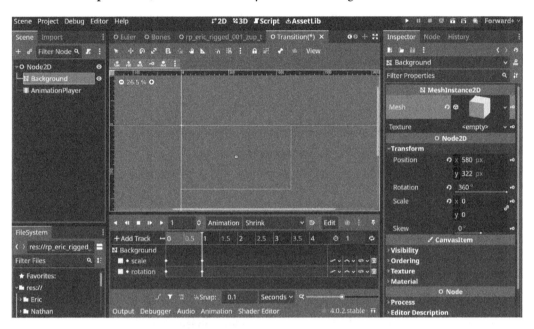

Figure 9.11 – Adding the animation keys to the Timeline

30. Left-click on **Animation** in the top part of the bottom panel.

31. Left-click **New** from the drop-down list.

32. When the **Create New Animation** window appears, enter Expand as the name of the animation and then click the **OK** button.

33. Left-click on the field to the left of the **Animation Looping** button just below the top-right corner of the Animation Editor and change the 1 value to 3.

34. Left-click on + **Add Track**, located in the top-left corner of the Animation Editor.

35. Left-click **Property Track**.

36. In the **Pick a node to animate:** window, select **Background** and left-click the **OK** button.

37. In the **Select Property** window, under **Node2D** select **Scale**, and left-click on the **Open** button.

38. Left-click on + **Add Track**, located in the top-left corner of the Animation Editor.

39. Left-click **Property Track**.

40. In the **Pick a node to animate:** window, select **Background** and left-click the **OK** button.

41. In the **Select Property** window, under **Node2D** select **Rotation**, and left-click on the **Open** button.

42. Left-click on **Background** in the **Scene** tab.

43. Make sure the blue line is on 0 in the **Timeline** section of the **AnimationPlayer**.

44. In the **Inspector** tab, left-click on the **Key** icon to the far right of **Scale**.

45. In the **Inspector** tab, left-click on the **Key** icon to the far right of **Rotation**.

46. Make sure the blue line is on 1 in the **Timeline** section of the **AnimationPlayer**.

47. To the far right of **Scale**, click on the white link icon.

48. Change the **Scale x** value to 1175 and the **y** value to 670 in the **Inspector**.

49. In the **Inspector** tab, left-click on the **Key** icon to the far right of **Scale**.

50. Change the **Rotation** value to 0 in the **Inspector**.

51. In the **Inspector** tab, left-click on the **Key** icon to the far right of **Rotation**.

52. Left-click on the **Node2D** node and then left-click the + button in the **Scene** tab. In the **Create New Node** window, type anim in the search box and then select **AnimationTree** to create the node in the scene. Left-click the **Create** button.

53. In the **Inspector** tab, to the right of **Tree Root**, left-click on <empty>.

54. In the drop-down list, left-click **New AnimationNodeBlendTree**.

55. In the **Inspector** tab, to the right of **Anim Player**, left-click on **Assign**.

56. Select **AnimationPlayer** in the **Select a Node** window and left-click the **OK** button.

57. In the **Inspector** tab, to the right of **Active**, check the **On** checkbox.

58. In the bottom panel, right-click to the left of the **Output** node.

59. In the drop-down list, select **Transition**.

60. In the **Inspector** tab, left-click on **Inputs**.

61. Left-click the + **Add Element** button.

62. To the right of **Name**, enter Shrink.

63. To the right of **Auto Advance**, under **Name**, check the **On** checkbox.

64. Left-click the + **Add Element** button.

65. To the right of **Name**, enter Expand.

66. To the right of **Auto Advance**, under **Name**, check the **On** checkbox.

67. In the bottom panel, right-click to the left of the **Transition** node.

68. In the drop-down list, select **Animation**.

69. Highlight Animation in the box under **Animation** and change the name to Shrink:

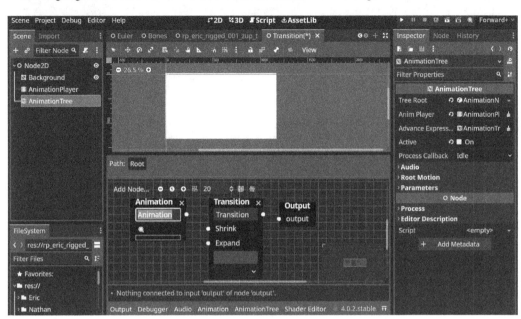

Figure 9.12 – Animation node in AnimationTree panel

70. Left-click to the right of the **Film Reel** icon and select **Shrink** from the drop-down list.

71. In the bottom panel, right-click to the right of the **Transition** node and under the **Shrink Animation** node.

72. In the drop-down list, select **Animation**.

73. Highlight Animation in the box under **Animation** and change the name to Expand.

74. Left-click to the right of **Film Reel** and select **Expand** from the drop-down list.

75. Left-click and drag the white dot on the right side of the **Shrink** animation node to the white dot to the left of **Shrink** in the **Transition** node.

76. Left-click and drag the white dot on the right side of the **Expand** animation node to the white dot to the left of **Expand** in the **Transition** node.

77. Left-click and drag the white dot on the right side of the **Transition** node to the white dot to the left of the **Output** node:

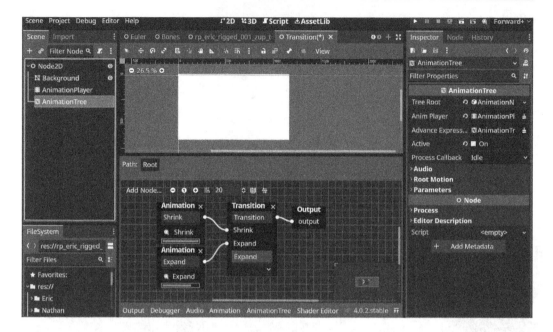

Figure 9.13 – AnimationTree bottom panel

How it works...

We created a **MeshInstance2D** node with a **BoxMesh**. We renamed the **MeshInstance2D** node **Background**.

We left-clicked on **Transform** in the **Inspector** to see the properties. We changed the **Position** values of **x** and **y** to center the background in the middle of the viewable default camera. We clicked on the white link icon located to the far right of **Scale** so that we could change the **x** and **y** values to different values. We changed the **Scale** values of **x** and **y** to cover the viewable default camera.

We added the **AnimationPlayer** node to the **Scene** tab. At the top of the **AnimationPlayer** node, we left-clicked on **Animation** to create a new animation that we named Shrink. We left-clicked on + **Add Track**, located in the top-left corner of the Animation Editor, and selected **Background** from the drop-down list to animate the **Background** node. We selected **Property Track** from the next drop-down list so that we could add the **Scale** and **Rotation** properties to animate the background.

We made sure the blue line in the **Timeline** section of the **AnimationPlayer** node was at 0. We left-clicked on the **Key** icons located to the right of **Scale** and **Rotation**, so we start the animation with the default values. We moved the blue line to the 1-second mark and changed the **x** and **y** values of **Scale** to 0 and the **Rotation** value to 360. This will spin and fade out the background when the animation is run. You can press the **Play selected animation from start** button by pressing *Shift + D*.

We added the **AnimationPlayer** node to the **Scene** tab. At the top of the **AnimationPlayer** node, we left-clicked on **Animation** to create a new animation, which we named Expand. We left-clicked on the field to the left of the **Animation Looping** button just below the top-right corner of the Animation Editor and changed the 1 value to 3 so that for the last 2 seconds of the animation, we could see the full background.

We left-clicked on + **Add Track**, located in the top-left corner of the Animation Editor, and selected **Background** from the drop-down list to animate the **Background** node. We selected **Property Track** from the next drop-down list so that we could add the **Scale** and **Rotation** properties to animate the background. We made sure the blue line in the **Timeline** section of the **AnimationPlayer** node was at 0.

We left-clicked on the **Key** icons located to the right of **Scale** and **Rotation** so that we start the animation with the now default values from the end of Shrink. The values of **Scale x** and **y** are 0 and **Rotation** is 360. We left-clicked on the white link icon located to the far right of **Scale** so that we could change the **x** and **y Scale** values to a different number for each.

We moved the blue line to the 1-second mark and changed the **Scale** value of **x** to 1170, the **y** value to 670, and the **Rotation** value to 0. This will spin and fade in the background when the animation is running. You can press the **Play selected animation from start** button by pressing *Shift* + *D* to run the animation.

We added an **AnimationTree** node to the **Scene** tab. In the **Inspector**, we selected **New AnimationNodeBlendTree** for the **Tree Root** property. We added the **AnimationPlayer** node in the **Scene** tab to the **Anim Player** property in the **Inspector** tab. We checked the **On** checkbox located to the right of **Active**. This will run anything in the **AnimationTree** node. In our case, anything hooked up to **Output** in the grid on the bottom panel will run. Other uses for the **AnimationTree** node are **BlendSpace 2D** or **BlendSpace3D** and **StateMachine**.

We right-clicked to the right of the **Output** node in the bottom panel and selected **Transition** from the drop-down list. With the **Transition** node selected in the bottom panel, we left-clicked **Inputs** in the **Inspector** tab. We left-clicked the + **Add Element** button and changed the name to Shrink.

We checked the **On** checkbox to the right of **Auto Advance** so that the **Shrink** animation we will add later will advance to the **Expand** animation we will also add later. We left-clicked the + **Add Element** button and changed the name to Expand. We checked the **On** checkbox to the right of **Auto Advance** so that the Expand animation we will add later will advance to the Shrink animation to loop the animation.

We right-clicked to the right of the **Transition** node in the bottom panel and selected **Animation** from the drop-down list. We changed the name of the **Animation** node to **Shrink**. We left-clicked to the right of the **Film Reel** icon and selected the Shrink animation we created earlier.

We added another **Animation** node to the left of **Transition** and under the Shrink animation. We named this node **Expand**. We left-clicked to the right of the **Film Reel** icon and selected the Expand animation we created earlier.

We connected the white dots of the `Shrink` and `Expand` animation nodes to **Shrink** and **Expand** in the **Transition** node. We connected the white dots of the **Transition** node and the **Output** node. We can see that both animations are playing.

Playing with the new Movie Maker mode

In this recipe, we will create a scene with a ground and a pillar in the center. We will animate the light to go from one side to the other while rotating so that we can see the shadow. We will set up and use the new **Movie Maker** mode to record the animation. The **Movie Maker** mode is a great tool to use to make promotional videos.

Getting ready

For this recipe, click the + button to the right of the **Transition** scene we just completed to add a new scene. In the **Scene** tab, click **3D Scene**. Click on the word **Scene** in the main menu next to **Project**, then select **Save Scene As**, and name it `Movie`.

How to do it...

First, we are going to make the scene and add the lighting:

1. Left-click on the three vertical dots to the left of **Transform View** on the viewport toolbar to edit the **Sun** and **Environment** settings.

2. Add the **Sun** and **Environment** nodes to the scene by left-clicking the **Add Sun to Scene** button at the bottom while holding down the *Shift* key.

3. Click on **DirectionalLight3D** in the **Scene** tab.

4. In the **Inspector**, left-click **Transform**.

5. Change the values in **Position** to **x** `0`, **y** `7`, and **z** `11`.

6. Change the values in **Rotation** to **x** `-60`, **y** `-20`, and **z** `0`.

7. Left-click on the **Node3D** node and then left-click the + button in the **Scene** tab. In the **Create New Node** window, type `mesh` in the search box and then select **MeshInstance3D** to create the node in the scene. Left-click the **Create** button.

8. Right-click on the **MeshInstance3D** node in the **Scene** tab and select **Rename** from the drop-down list.

9. Enter `Ground` as the new name of the **MeshInstance2D** node.

10. In the **Inspector** tab, click on **<empty>** to the right of **Mesh** and select **New PlaneMesh**.

11. Left-click on **Transform** in the **Inspector** tab.

12. Change the **Scale** value of **x** to 10. All of the **Scale** values should have changed to 10 because the white link icon was not clicked.

13. At the top of the **Inspector** tab, left-click on the **PlaneMesh** node to the right of **Mesh**.

14. Left-click on <**empty**> to the right of **Material**.

15. From the drop-down list, select **New StandardMaterial3D**.

16. Left-click on **StandardMaterial3D** to the right of **Material**.

17. Left-click on **Albedo** and left-click on the white box to the right of **Color**.

18. Change the values of **R** to 0, **G** to 255, and **B** to 0.

19. Left-click on the **Node3D** node and then left-click the + button in the **Scene** tab. In the **Create New Node** window, type mesh in the search box and then select **MeshInstance3D** to create the node in the scene. Left-click the **Create** button.

20. In the **Inspector** tab, click on <**empty**> to the right of **Mesh** and select **New BoxMesh**.

21. Left-click on **Transform** in the **Inspector** tab.

22. Change the **Position** value of **y** to 2.

23. Left-click on the white **Link** icon to the far right of **Scale**.

24. Change the **Scale** value of **y** to 5.

25. Left-click on the **Node3D** node and then left-click the + button in the **Scene** tab. In the **Create New Node** window, type cam in the search box and then select **Camera3D** to create the node in the scene. Left-click the **Create** button.

26. Left-click on **Transform** in the **Inspector** tab.

27. Change the **Position** values of **x** to -11 and **y** to 3.

28. Change the **Rotation** value of **y** to -90.

29. Left-click on the **Node3D** node and then left-click the + button in the **Scene** tab. In the **Create New Node** window, type anim in the search box and then select **AnimationPlayer** to create the node in the scene. Left-click the **Create** button.

30. Left-click on **Animation** in the top part of the bottom panel.

31. Left-click **New** from the drop-down list.

32. When the **Create New Animation** window appears, enter Sun as the name of the animation and then click the **OK** button.

33. Left-click on the field to the left of the **Animation Looping** button just below the top-right corner of the Animation Editor and change the 1 value to 15.

34. Left-click on + **Add Track** located in the top-left corner of the Animation Editor.

35. Left-click **3D Position Track**.

36. In the **Pick a node to animate:** window, select **DirectionalLight3D** and left-click the **OK** button.

37. Left-click in the animation timeline and move the blue line to 0.

38. Left-click on the **DirectionalLight3D** node in the **Scene** tab.

39. In the **Inspector** tab, under **Transform**, left-click on the **Key** icon to the far right of **Position**.

40. In the **Please Confirm** window, left-click on the **Create** button.

41. In the **Inspector** tab, under **Transform**, left-click on the **Key** icon to the far right of **Rotation**.

42. In the **Please Confirm** window, left-click on the **Create** button.

43. In the bottom animation panel, left-click at the 15-second mark. The blue line should now be at the 15-second mark.

44. Make sure we are still clicked on the **DirectionalLight3D** node in the **Scene** tab.

45. In the **Inspector** tab, left-click **Transform**.

46. In the **Inspector** tab, under **Transform**, change the values in **Position** to **x** 0, **y** 7, and **z** -11.

47. In the **Inspector** tab, under **Transform**, change the values in **Rotation** to **x** -60, **y** 160, and **z** 0.

48. In the **Inspector** tab, under **Transform**, left-click on the **Key** icon to the far right of **Position**.

49. In the **Please Confirm** window, left-click on the **Create** button.

50. In the **Inspector** tab, under **Transform**, left-click on the **Key** icon to the far right of **Rotation**.

51. In the **Please Confirm** window, left-click on the **Create** button.

52. Left-click on **Camera3D** in the **Scene** tab.

53. Left-click <**empty**>, located to the right of **Script** at the bottom of the **Inspector**.

54. Select **New Script** from the drop-down list.

55. To the right of **Path:**, name the file runanimation.

56. Copy this code into runanimation:

```
1 extends Camera3d
2
3 @onready var anim = $"../AnimationPlayer"
4
5 func _ready():
6     anim.play("Sun")
```

57. Create a folder outside of the project folder where you want to save your movie AVI files.

58. Left-click on **Projects** in the top left-hand corner of Godot and select **Project Settings** in the drop-down list.

59. On the left side under **Editor**, left-click on **Movie Writer:**

Figure 9.14 – Movie Writer in Project Settings

60. Left-click on the folder icon to the far right of **Movie File**.

61. Change the path to the folder you created.

62. In the **File** field, type Sun_Demo for the name of the movie you are going to record:

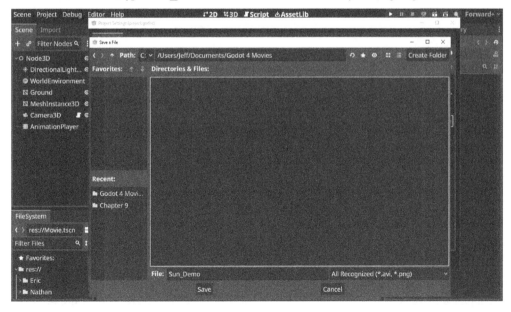

Figure 9.15 – Path to the folder and name of the file

63. Left-click on the **Save** button.

64. Left-click on the **Close** button in the **Project Settings** window.

65. In the upper right-hand corner, to the left of **Forward**, left-click the **Enable Movie Maker** mode button. It will highlight in blue when clicked on:

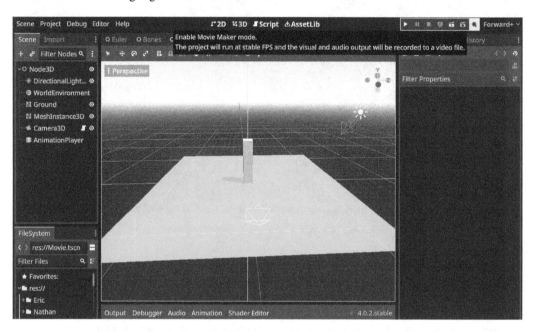

Figure 9.16 – Enable Movie Maker mode button

66. In the **Movie** scene, click the **Run the current scene** button in the upper-right corner of the editor or hit the *F6* key.

67. When the animation is done, then exit the scene and left-click the **Enable Movie Maker mode** button. It will no longer be highlighted in blue.

68. Go to the folder where you saved the movie and play the movie.

How it works...

We added the **DirectionalLight3D** node and the **World** environment to the **Scene** tab. We changed the **Position** and **Rotation** values of the **DirectionalLight3D** node to position the light on the left side of the ground. We changed the rotation of the light to face toward the center of the ground mesh that we are going to place in the next steps.

We created a **PlaneMesh** node that we named Ground. We changed the **Scale** value to 10x10x10 by only changing the **x** value because the white link icon was not clicked. We added a **StandardMaterial3D** node to the **Material** property in the **Inspector** tab so that we could change the color of the ground. This will make it easier to see the shadow and the pillar we are going to add to the scene next.

We created a **BoxMesh** node that changed the y **Position** to 2 so that it would stand on the ground plane. We changed the **y Scale** value to 5 to create a shadow. This time, we left-clicked on the white link icon so that it turned gray and we could change only one value.

We added a **Camera3D** node to the **Scene** tab. We moved the camera by left-clicking on **Transform** in the **Inspector** tab and changing the **Position** values of **x** to 11 and **y** to 3. We changed the **Rotation** value of **y** to 90 so that the camera would face the pillar.

We added an **AnimationPlayer** node to the **Scene** tab. In the **AnimationPlayer** editor, we created a new animation, which we named **Sun**. We changed the length of the animation to 15 seconds. We left-clicked on + **Add Track** and selected **3D Position Track** from the drop-down list. In the **Pick a node to animate:** window, we selected **DirectionalLight3D**.

The blue line that shows where the animation should be at 0 seconds. We left-clicked on the **DirectionalLight3D** node in the **Scene** tab so that we can change the **Position** and **Rotation** values of the node. We left-clicked on the **Key** icons to the right of **Position** and **Rotation** to set the starting point of the animation. In the timeline section of the **AnimationPlayer** node, we left-clicked at 15 seconds, which is the end of the animation.

We make sure we were still clicked on the **DirectionalLight3D** node in the **Scene** tab, and then we change the **Position** and **Rotation** values to where the **DirectionalLight3D** node should be at the end of the animation. We made sure the blue line was on the 15 second mark and left-clicked the **Key** icon to the far right of **Property** and **Rotation**.

We left-clicked on the **Camera3D** node in the **Scene** tab. In the **Inspector** tab, we left-clicked on **<empty>** to the right of **Script** and created a new script. We named the script runanimation. On *line 3* of the code, we used @onready to load the **AnimationPlayer** node into the anim variable. You should drag the **AnimationPlayer** node to the right of = if it doesn't work just by typing it out. In the ready function, we told the **AnimationPlayer** node to run our **Sun** animation.

We created a new folder outside of the project folder that we were working on. This is where we will save the movie files that we create. We opened **Project Settings**, and under **Editor**, we left-clicked on **Movie Writer**. We left-clicked on the folder on the far right of **Movie File**, and at the top of **Path**, we changed the path to point to the folder we created to store our movie files.

In the field to the right of **File**, we typed Sun_Demo as the name of the file we were going to record. You can change the audio mix rate. If we had audio playing in the scene, when we recorded the scene, the audio would not play but it would be on the movie. We can change the speaker layout to **Stereo**, **3.1**, **5.1**, or **7.1**.

We can change the MJPEG quality. Higher values will look better but the movie file size will be bigger. We can disable **V-Sync**, which can speed up the video writing, but your hardware should be fast enough to render, encode, and save the video at a higher frame rate than your monitor's refresh rate. We can also change the **frames per second (FPS)** of the movie.

We left-clicked the **Enable Movie Maker mode** button. It was highlighted in blue after we clicked on it. We left-clicked on the **Run the current scene** button to play the scene. After the animation finished, we exited the scene we just ran and left-clicked on the **Enable Movie Maker mode** button.

If we didn't, every time we ran the scene, it would save a movie. If you wanted to make another movie of something else, you would have to go back to **Project Settings** and change the filename so that it wouldn't overwrite the old file. We went to the folder in which we saved the movie file and ran the movie file.

10

Exploring New Multiplayer Features in Godot 4

In this chapter, we will set up a **CharacterBody3D** scene for the player with the default movement script attached and a scene where the players will spawn a character into a multiplayer game. We will create a menu with **Host** and **Join** buttons so that we can run two debug scenes.

The first button is to simulate a game as the host server and the other one joins a game as a client. We will use the new **MultiplayerSpawner** node to spawn an instance of the player to the hosted scene. We will synchronize players with the **MultiplayerSynchronizer** node. We will also make the player unique when they spawn into a multiplayer game. We export the **Spawner** project and use Windows **Command Prompt** (**CMD**) to create a headless server. We will write a GDScript script to use the **Universal Plug and Play** (**UPnP**) class to port-forward on a **peer-to-peer** (**P2P**) network.

In this chapter, we will cover the following recipes:

- Using the new **MultiplayerSpawner** node
- Using the new **MultiplayerSynchronizer** node
- How to use the **Headless** mode
- How to use UPnP with P2P networking

Technical requirements

For this chapter, you need the standard version of Godot 4.0 or later running on one of the following platforms:

- Windows 64-bit or 32-bit
- macOS
- Linux 64-bit or 32-bit

- Android
- Web Editor

You can find the code and the project files for the projects in this chapter on GitHub at `https://github.com/PacktPublishing/Godot-4-Game-Development-Cookbook/tree/main/Chapter%2010`.

Using the new MultiplayerSpawner node

In this recipe, we need to set up a **CharacterBody3D** scene to use as the player. We will also create a scene to simulate the game. We will create buttons where we can host or join and hook them up in a script. After that, we use the new **MultiplayerSpawner** node to spawn a player to the scene on the server. We can move the player we spawned into the scene independent of the player we will load into the server scene as a default.

Getting ready

For this recipe, open Godot 4 and start a new project called `Chapter 10`. In the **Scene** tab, click **3D** to add a 3D scene. Click on the word **Scene** in the main menu next to **Project**, then select **Save Scene As**, and name it `Spawner`.

How to do it...

We will start by creating the player scene. After that, we will work on the **Spawner** scene to hook up the server and client to simulate a multiplayer game:

1. Click the + button to the right of the **Spawner** scene we just completed to add a new scene. In the **Scene** tab, click **Other Node**. In the **Create New Node** window, type `char` in the **Search** box and then select **CharacterBody3D** to create the node in the scene. Left-click the **Create** button. Click on the word **Scene** in the top-left corner next to **Project**, then select **Save Scene As**, and name it `Character`.

2. Left-click on the **CharacterBody3D** node and then left-click the + button in the **Scene** tab. In the **Create New Node** window, type `mesh` in the **Search** box and then select **MeshInstance3D** to create the node in the scene. Left-click the **Create** button.

3. In the **Inspector** tab, click on <empty> to the right of **Mesh** and select **New CapsuleMesh**.

4. Left-click on the **CharacterBody3D** node and then left-click the + button in the **Scene** tab. In the **Create New Node** window, type `coll` in the **Search** box and then select **CollisionShape3D** to create the node in the scene. Left-click the **Create** button.

5. In the **Inspector** tab, click on <empty> to the right of **Shape** and select **New CapsuleShape3D**.

6. Left-click on the **CharacterBody3D** node and then left-click the + button in the **Scene** tab.

7. Left-click on **Transform** in the **Inspector** tab.

8. Under **Position**, change the value of **y** to 1.

9. In the **Inspector** tab, click on **<empty>** to the right of **Script** and select **New Script**.

10. In the **Attach Node Script** window, to the right of **Template**, make sure the **CharacterBody3D: Basic Movement** checkbox is checked.

11. You can keep the default filename as **Character** and left-click on the **Create** button.

12. Left-click on the **Spawner** scene.

13. Left-click on the three vertical dots to the left of **Transform View** on the viewport toolbar to edit the **Sun and Environment** settings.

14. Add the **Sun** and **Environment** nodes to the scene by left-clicking the **Add Sun to Scene** button at the bottom while holding down the *Shift* key.

15. Left-click on the **Node3D** node and then left-click the + button in the **Scene** tab. In the **Create New Node** window, type panel in the **Search** box and then select **Panel** to create the node in the scene. Left-click the **Create** button.

16. Right-click on the **Panel** node and select **Rename** from the drop-down list. Rename the node Menu.

17. Left-click on the **Menu** node and then left-click the + button in the **Scene** tab. In the **Create New Node** window, type vbox in the **Search** box and then select **VBoxContainer** to create the node in the scene. Left-click the **Create** button.

18. Left-click on the **VBoxContainer** node and then left-click the + button in the **Scene** tab. In the **Create New Node** window, type button in the **Search** box and then select **Button** to create the node in the scene. Left-click the **Create** button.

19. Right-click on the **Button** node and select **Rename** from the drop-down list. Rename it HostButton.

20. In the **Inspector** tab, under **Text**, enter Host in the box.

21. Left-click on the **VBoxContainer** node and then left-click the + button in the **Scene** tab. In the **Create New Node** window, type button in the **Search** box and then select **Button** to create the node in the scene. Left-click the **Create** button.

22. Right-click on the **Button** node and select **Rename** from the drop-down list. Rename it JoinButton.

23. In the **Inspector** tab, under **Text**, enter Join in the box.

24. Left-click on the **Node3D** node and then left-click the + button in the **Scene** tab. In the **Create New Node** window, type mesh in the **Search** box and then select **MeshInstance3D** to create the node in the scene. Left-click the **Create** button.

25. In the **Inspector** tab, click on **<empty>** to the right of **Mesh** and select **New PlaneMesh**.

26. Right-click on the **MeshInstance3D** node and select **Rename** from the drop-down list. Rename it Ground.

27. In the **Inspector** tab, click on **PlaneMesh** to the right of **Mesh**.

28. Change the **x** and **y** values to the right of **Size** to 10 and 10.

29. To the right of **Transform View**, left-click on **Mesh** and select **Create Trimesh Static Body** in the drop-down list.

30. Left-click on the **Node3D** node and then left-click the + button in the **Scene** tab. In the **Create New Node** window, type cam in the **Search** box and then select **Camera3D** to create the node in the scene. Left-click the **Create** button.

31. In the **Inspector** tab, click on **Transform**.

32. Under **Position**, change the **y** value to 1 and the **z** value to 5.

33. Left-click on the **Node3D** node and then in the **Inspector**, click on **<empty>** to the right of **Script**. Select **New Script**.

34. To the right of **Path**, change the name of the script to Server.gd.

35. Left-click on **HostButton** in the **Scene** tab.

36. Left-click on the **Node** tab to the right of the **Inspector** tab.

37. Left-click on pressed() under **BaseButton** and left-click the **Connect...** button on the bottom right of the screen:

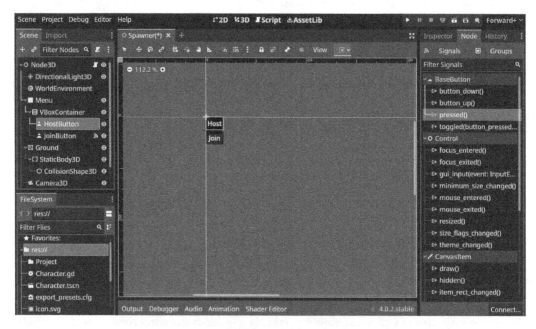

Figure 10.1 – Adding signals to the buttons

38. Left-click on the **Node3D** node in the **Connect to Script** section in the **Connect a Signal to a Method** window.

39. Left-click on the **Connect** button in the **Connect a Signal to a Method** window.

40. Left-click on **JoinButton** in the **Scene** tab.

41. Left-click on `pressed()` under **BaseButton** and left-click the **Connect…** button on the bottom right of the screen.

42. Left-click on the **Node3D** node in the **Connect to Script** section in the **Connect a Signal to a Method** window.

43. Left-click on the **Connect** button in the **Connect a Signal to a Method** window. Add the following code to `Server.gd`:

```
1 Extends Node3D
2
3 var character = preload("res://Character.tsc")
4 var Port = 5555
5 var multi_peerer = ENetMultiplayerPeer.nav()
6
7 func _on_host_button_pressed():
8      multi_peer.create_server(Port)
9      multiplayer.multiplayer_peer = multi_peer
10     multiplayer.peer_connected.connect(add_player)
11     add_player(multiplayer.get_unique_id())
12
13 func _on_join_button_pressed():
14     multi_peer.create_client("localhost", Port)
15     multiplayer.multiplayer_peer = multi_peer
16
17 func add_player(peer_id):
18     var player = character.instantiate()
19     player.name = str(peer_id)
20     add_child(player)
```

44. Click on the word **Scene** in the top-left corner next to **Project** and then select **Save All Scenes**:

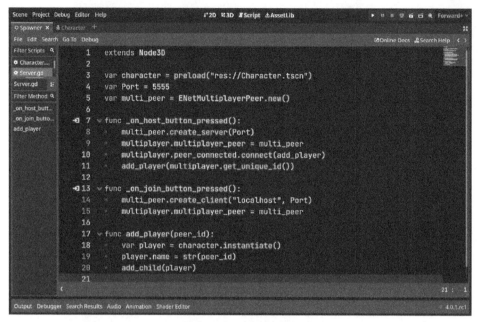

Figure 10.2 – Server.gd

45. Left-click on **Debug** in the main menu between **Project** and **Editor**.

46. At the bottom of the drop-down list, mouse over **Run Multiple Instances** and select **Run 2 Instances**:

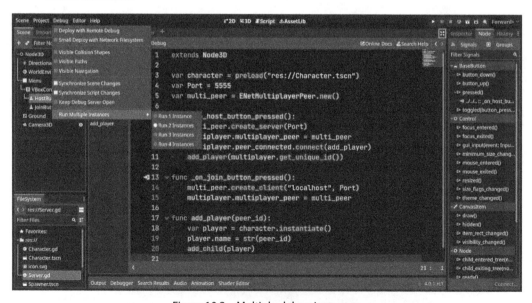

Figure 10.3 – Multiple debug instances

47. Left-click on the **Node3D** node and then left-click the + button in the **Scene** tab. In the **Create New Node** window, type mul in the **Search** box and then select **Multiplayer Spawner** to create the node in the scene. Left-click the **Create** button.

48. In the **Inspector** tab, to the right of **Spawn Path**, left-click on **Assign**.

49. Left-click on **Node3D** and then the **OK** button.

50. In the **Inspector** tab, left-click on **Auto Spawn List**.

51. Left-click on the + **Add Element** button.

52. Left-click on the folder icon to the right of **Element 0**.

53. In the **Open a File** window, select Character.tscn.

54. In the **Spawner** scene, click the **Run the current scene** button in the upper-right corner of the editor or hit the *F6* key.

55. A pop-up window asks whether we want to grant public and or private access. Check **private** and uncheck **public**.

56. Separate the windows. In the first window, left-click **Host** and move the player with the arrow keys.

57. In the second window, left-click **Join**. Click back to the first window and move the players.

How it works...

We created a new scene for our player. In the **Scene** tab, we used **Other Node** so that our base node would be **CharacterBody3D**. We added a **MeshInstance3D** node as a child of the **CharacterBody3D** node. We used a **CapsuleMesh** node on the **MeshInstance3D** node and also added a **CapsuleShape3D** node. We moved the **CharacterBody3D** node's **y Position** value to 1 so that it is on the ground level. We added the **CharacterBody3D: Basic Movement** script so that we could move the player around.

We added the **DirectionalLight3D** and the **WorldEnvironment** nodes so that we could see the scene when we ran the scene at the end of the recipe.

We added a **Panel** node and renamed it Menu. We added a **VBoxContainer** node as a child of the **Menu** node. We added two buttons as child nodes to the **VBoxContainer** node. We renamed the first button **HostButton**, and in the **Text** field, we entered Host. We renamed the second button **JoinButton**, and in the **Text** field, we entered Join.

We created a **MeshInstance3D** node, and for the mesh, we used a **PlaneMesh**. We renamed it Ground. We changed the **Size** value of **x** to 10 and **y** to 10. This gave us more room to spawn players later. We left-clicked on **Mesh** in the toolbar above the viewport to the right of **Transform View** and selected **Create Trimesh Static Body** from the drop-down list. This is so that our **CharacterBody3D** node won't fall through the ground. We created a **Camera3D** node, and in the **Inspector** tab, we left-clicked on **Transform**. We changed the **Position** values of **y** to 1 to raise up the camera and **z** to 5 to move the camera back.

We left-clicked on **Node3D** and added a new script to the node. We named the script `Server.gd`. We left-clicked on the **HostButton** node in the **Scene** tab so that we can add a signal to the button. We left-clicked on the **Node** tab to the right of the **Inspector** tab and selected `pressed()`. We connected the `pressed()` method to the `Server.gd` script on the **Node3D** node. We did the same thing with the **JoinButton** node in the **Scene** tab.

We wrote code to set up a server where we can host or join. In *line 3*, we preloaded the **Character** scene into the `character` variable. In *line 4*, we set the `Port` variable to `5555`. We used `5555` because it's well over `1024`. Port numbers `0 -1024` are reserved for privileged services and are well-known port numbers.

In *line 5*, we assigned a new instance of `ENetMultiplayerPeer` to the `multi_peer` variable. In the `_on_host_button_pressed()` function, we created a server in *lines 8* and *9*. In *lines 10* and *11*, we added the **Character** scene to the **Spawner** scene on the server. In the `_on_join_button_pressed()` function, we created a client. In *lines 14* and *15*, we joined the local server on port `5555`.

In the `add_player(peer_id)` function, we added the **Character** scene with a network ID. In *line 18*, we instantiated a new instance of the character that we preloaded and assigned it to the `player` variable. In *line 19*, we created a unique ID for the player. In *line 20*, we added the player as a child to the scene where it is called.

We left-clicked on **Debug** in the main menu in the top-left section of the Godot editor. When the drop-down list appeared, we went to **Run Multiple Instances** and selected **Run 2 Instances**. We did this so that after we add the **MultiplayerSpawner** node and run it, two windows will appear. In one window, we can run it as the host, and in the other window, we can run it to join the server.

We added a **MultiplayerSpawner** node to the **Spawner** scene. In the **Inspector**, to the right of **Spawn Path**, we left-clicked **Assign** and selected **Node3D** from the drop-down list. We left-clicked on **Auto Spawn List** to see its properties in the **Inspector** tab. We left-clicked on the + **Add Element** button. We left-clicked on the folder icon to the right of **Element 0** and selected our `Character.tscn` file in the **Open a File** window. This will spawn our player.

We ran the current scene and we separated the two debug windows from the start on top of each other. If this is the first time we run this server, a pop-up window will ask whether we want to grant public and/or private access. We checked the **private** checkbox and unchecked the **public** checkbox.

We left-clicked on **Host** and the player spawned in the scene. We moved the player around with the arrow keys. We left-clicked on the second window and selected **Join**. The player bounced out of the window, but if you go back to the first window, you will see both players and notice that both players use the same movement as the host player. In the next recipe, we will fix this by adding a **MultiplayerSynchronizer** node to the **CharacterBody3D** scene.

Using the new MultiplayerSynchronizer node

In this recipe, we are going to add the **MultiplayerSynchronizer** node to the **CharacterBody3D** scene. We will also add some code to the `Character.gd` script so that each player that spawns into a game is unique.

Getting ready

For this recipe, we are going to continue where we left off in the last recipe.

How to do it...

We are going to start in the **Character** scene and add the **MultiplayerSynchronizer** node:

1. Left-click on the **CharacterBody3D** node and then left-click the + button in the **Scene** tab. In the **Create New Node** window, type `mult` in the **Search** box and then select **MultiplayerSynchronizer** to create the node in the scene. Left-click the **Create** button.

2. In the bottom **Replication** panel, left-click on the + **Add property to sync...** button:

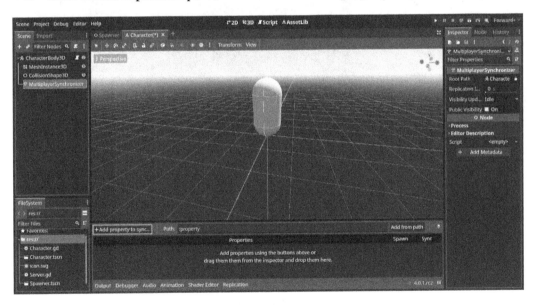

Figure 10.4 – The bottom Replication panel of the MultiplayerSynchronizer node

3. In the **Pick a node to synchronize** window, select **CharacterBody3D** and left-click the **OK** button.

4. In the **Select Property** window, under **Node3D**, left-click on **Position** and then left-click on the **Open** button.

5. In the top middle of the editor, left-click on **Script**.

6. Select the `Character.gd` script to edit this script.

7. On *line 10*, enter `func _enter_tree():`.

8. On *line 11*, enter `set_multiplayer_authority(str(name).to_int())`.

9. Create an empty line so that *line 12* is blank and *line 13* is the `_physics_process(delta)` function.

10. On *line 14*, enter `if not is_multiplayer_authority(): return:`

```
1    extends CharacterBody3D
2
3
4    const SPEED = 5.0
5    const JUMP_VELOCITY = 4.5
6
7    # Get the gravity from the project settings to be synced with RigidBody nodes.
8    var gravity = ProjectSettings.get_setting("physics/3d/default_gravity")
9
10 ∨ func _enter_tree():
11       set_multiplayer_authority(str(name).to_int())
12
13 ∨ func _physics_process(delta):
14       if not is_multiplayer_authority(): return
15       # Add the gravity.
16 ∨     if not is_on_floor():
17           velocity.y -= gravity * delta
```

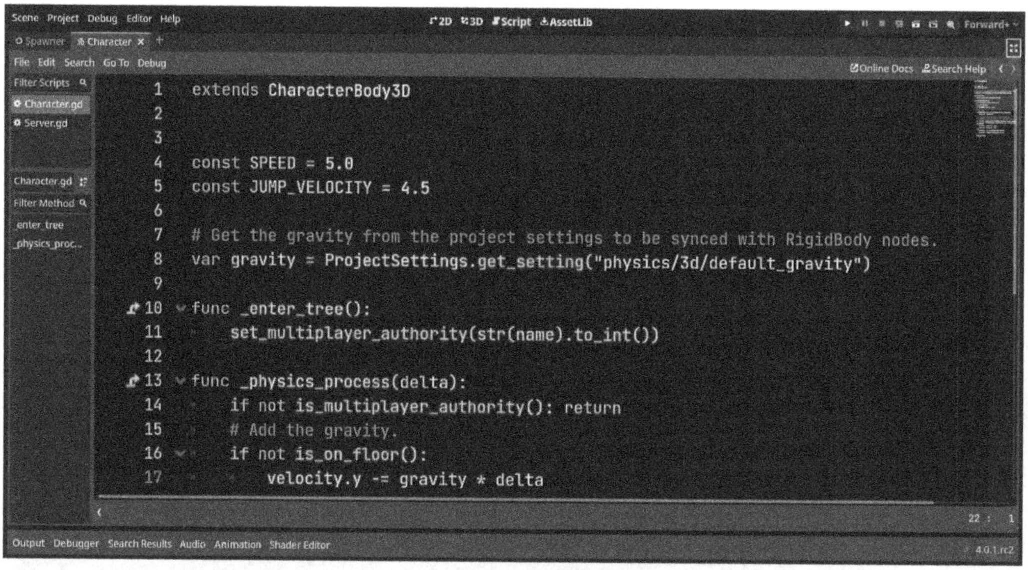

Figure 10.5 – Setting up the multiplayer authority

11. In the **Spawner** scene, click the **Run the current scene** button in the upper-right corner of the editor or hit the *F6* key.

12. A pop-up window asks whether we want to grant public and/or private access. Check **private** and uncheck **public**.

13. Separate the windows. In the first window, left-click **Host** and move the player with the arrow keys.

14. In the second window, left-click **Join**. Click back to the first window and move the players.

How it works...

We started in the **Character** scene. We left-clicked on the **CharacterBody3D** node in the **Scene** tab and then added a **MultiplayerSynchronizer** node. In the bottom **Replication** panel, we left-clicked on the **+ Add property to sync...** button. We selected the **CharacterBody3D** node in the pop-up window. We selected **Position** located toward the bottom of the **Select Property** window. We only used one property, but in a real game project, you would probably use more.

We edited the `Character.gd` script so that we could set the authority for each player that spawned in the game. This will let each player control only themselves. At the end of the last recipe, when we moved the host or the client player, the other moved as well. In *line 10*, we created an `_enter_tree()` function because the players can spawn in and out at any time. In *line 11*, we set the multiplayer authority string, `name`, to an integer. In *line 14*, we checked at the beginning of the `_physics_process(delta)` function to see whether the local system is the multiplayer authority. If not, then exit the code.

We selected the **Spawner** scene. We ran the current scene and we separated the two debug windows since they start on top of each other. If this is the first time we run this server, a pop-up window will ask whether we want to grant public and/or private access. We checked **private** and unchecked **public**. We left-clicked on **Host**, and the player spawned in the scene.

We moved the player around with the arrow keys. We left-clicked on the second window and selected **Join**. The player spawned on top of the host player. We moved the player and noticed that the host player stays where they are while the joined player moves around the scene. You can see in the host window that the movement is happening in real time.

How to use the Headless mode

In this recipe, we will export the **Spawner** project that we have worked on so far in this chapter. We use **Command Prompt (CMD)** to create a headless server for our **Spawner** project. A headless server is used in multiplayer games where you only need processing done because graphics and sound are not included in a headless server.

Getting ready

For this recipe, we are going to use the **Spawner** project that we built in the last two recipes to export as a Windows headless server. In the **FileSystem** tab, right-click on **res//** and mouse over **New**. In the drop-down list that appears, left-click on **Folder**. Name the folder `Project`.

Click on the **Spawner** tab and then left-click the **Run Project** (*F5*) button located above and to the left of the **Inspector** tab. In the **Please Confirm** window, left-click on the **Select Current** button.

How to do it...

We will start by exporting the **Spawner** project that we made in the last two recipes:

1. In the main menu, left-click on **Project**, to the right of **Scene**, in the top-left corner of the Godot editor.
2. Left-click on **Export** in the drop-down list.

3.   Select **Windows Desktop (Runnable)**.

4.   If you have not installed **Windows Desktop (Runnable)**, left-click on **Add** at the top of the window and select **Windows Desktop (Runnable)**. Left-click on **Manage Export Template** at the bottom of the window and left-click on the **Download and Install** button. After it has been installed, left-click on the **Close** button to close the window. Repeat steps *1-3* after you have installed **Windows Desktop (Runnable)**.

5.   At the bottom of the **Export** window, left-click on the **Export Project...** button.

6.   Double-click on the `Project` folder in the **Save a File** window and left-click on the **Save** button.

7.   Left-click on the **OK** button in the **Project Export** window.

8.   Click on the **Close** button in the **Export** window.

9.   Right-click on the `Project` folder.

10.   At the bottom of the drop-down list, left-click on **Open in File Manager**.

11.   In the **File Manager** window, left-click in the address field and enter `cmd`, then press the *Enter* key:

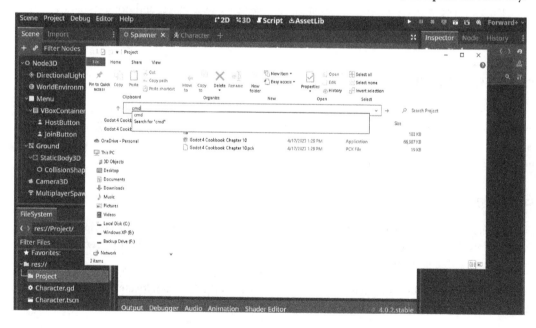

Figure 10.6 – Searching for CMD in the folder address field

12.   In the **Command Prompt (CMD)** window, type the first three letters of the first filename in the list and hit the *Tab* key.

13.   Use the left arrow key to move the cursor in **Command Prompt (CMD)** and *Backspace* to delete `console`. An example is `filename.console.exe`.

14. Move the cursor back to the right of the last quotation mark. It should now look like `filename.exe` with the cursor on the right-hand side of the last quotation mark.

15. Press the spacebar, then type `--headless`, and press *Enter*:

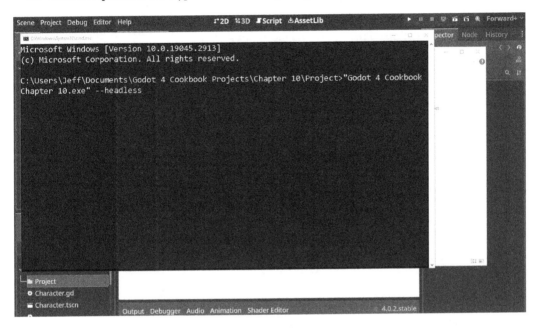

Figure 10.7 – The .exe file with the --headless command

16. In the **File Manager** window, double-click on the `Chapter 10.exe` file.

How it works...

We looked in the main menu section of the Godot editor and left-clicked on **Project**. In the drop-down list, we left-clicked on **Export** and selected **Window Desktop (Runnable)**.

If we didn't see it listed, then we left-clicked on **Add** located at the top toward the middle of the window. We selected **Windows Desktop (Runnable)** and left-clicked on **Manage Export Template** located near the bottom of the window. We left-clicked on the **Download and Install** button in the pop-up window. After we installed **Windows Desktop (Runnable)**, we selected **Windows Desktop (Runnable)**.

We left-clicked on the **Export Project...** button at the bottom of the **Export** window. We double-clicked on the `Project` folder we created in the *Getting ready* section and left-clicked the **Save** button to save the export of the `Chapter 10` project to the `Project` folder. We didn't worry about the yellow warnings we got.

We right-clicked on the Project folder and selected **Open in File Manager** at the bottom of the drop-down list. We left-clicked in the **Address** field and typed cmd. When we pressed *Enter*, the **Command Prompt (CMD)** window opened. We used the left arrow to move the cursor to the period in front of .exe and backspaced to delete console. It should end in Chapter 10.exe". We pressed the spacebar and then typed –headless. We pressed the *Enter* key to run the headless file. We double-clicked on the Chapter 10.exe file to run the program.

How to use UPnP with P2P networking

In this recipe, we will use the UPnP class to port-forward, which is used in P2P networking. We will create a new scene, then add a script to the **Node2D** node, which searches for ports that can be forwarded, and then forward the port. The script can be used in your multiplayer game to look for internal and external ports and gateways (routers).

Getting ready

For this recipe, click the + button to the right of the **Character** scene we just completed to add a new scene. In the **Scene** tab, click **3D Scene**. Click on the word **Scene** in the main menu next to **Project**, then select **Save Scene As**, and name it UPNP.

How to do it...

First, we will add an empty script to the **Node2D** node in the **Scene** tab:

1. Left-click on the **Node2D** node in the **Scene** tab.

2. In the **Inspector** tab, click on **<empty>** to the right of **Script**.

3. Left-click on **New Script** from the drop-down list.

4. In the **Attach Node Script** window, uncheck the checkbox to the right of **Template**.

5. To the right of **Path**, name the script UPNP.gd and left-click on the **Create** button.

6. Starting on *line 3*, type the following code:

```
3 func _ready():
4     var upnp = UPNP.new()
5     var find_result = upnp.discover()
6
7     if find_result == UPNP.UPNP_RESULT_SUCCESS:
8         if upnp.get_gateway() and upnp.get_gateway().is_valid_
gateway():
9             var map_result_udp = upnp.add_port_mapping(5555,
0, "game_udp:", "UDP, 0)
10             var map_result_tcp = upnp.add_port_mapping(5555,
0, "game_tcp", "TCP", 0)
11
```

```
12                    if not map_result_udp == UPNP.UPNP_RESULT_SUCCESS:
13                        upnp.add_port_mapping(5555, 0, "", "UDP")
14                    if not map_result_tcp == UPNP.UPNP_RESULT_SUCCESS:
15                        upnp.add_port_mapping(5555, 0, "", "TCP")
16
17            var external_ip = upnp.query_external_address()
18            upnp.delete_port_mapping(5555, "UDP")
19            upnp.delete_port_mapping(5555, "TCP")
```

7. Save the UPNP.gd script:

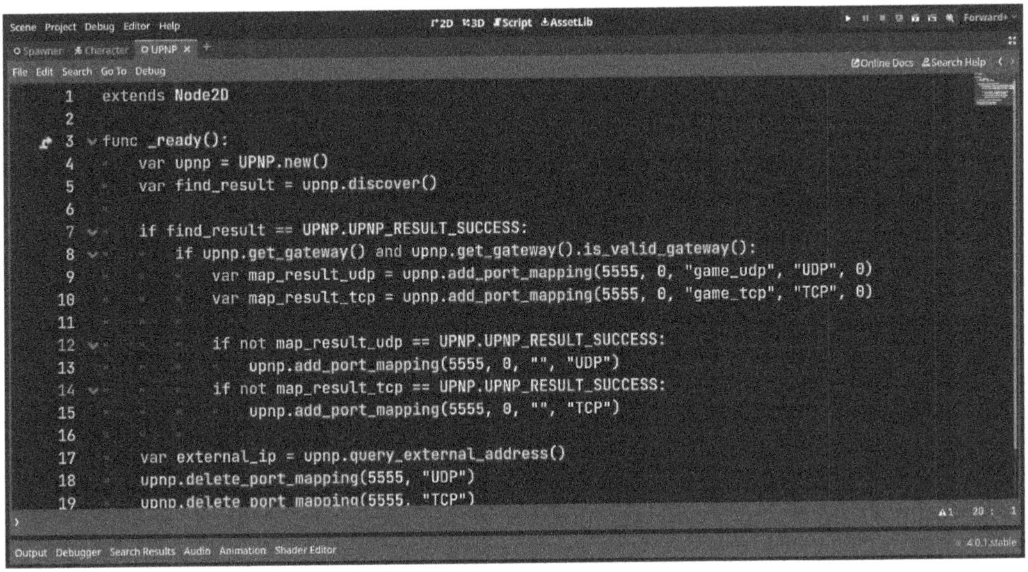

Figure 10.8 – UPNP.gd

How it works...

We left-clicked on the **Node2D** node in the **Scene** tab and left-clicked on **<empty>** to the right of **Script** in the **Inspector** tab to add a new script. We unchecked the checkbox to the right of **Template** in the **Attach Node Script** window so that our new script would be empty except for the first line. We named the script UPNP.gd.

We entered the code in the script. In *line 3*, we created the _ready() function. In *line 4*, we created a upnp object. In *line 5*, we assigned the find_result variable to the discover method of upnp. In *line 7*, we checked to see whether it had found a port. In *line 8*, we looked for a gateway and made sure that it was a valid gateway.

In *line 9*, we created a variable called `map_result_udp` to call `add_port_mapping`. The first argument is the external port, and the second is the internal port. The default on the second argument is 0, which is the same as the first argument. The third argument is a description shown in some routers. The fourth argument determines the protocol to use, either UDP or TCP, to transmit the data.

The fifth argument is the duration in seconds, and the default 0 that we used means that there is no duration. In *line 10*, we did the same as in *line 9*, except we used TCP. In *lines 12-15*, we did the same as in *line 9* and *line 10*, but we used no description. We did this because some routers want a description while others don't. In *line 17*, we created a variable called `external_ip`, which returns an external IP address of the default gateway as a string.

This variable is not used in this code and would be used to hook it up in your game. In *lines 18-19*, we called `delete_port_mapping` to shut down the server. The first argument is the port number and the second is the protocol. We shut down both UDP and TCP protocols. Finally, we saved the script.

Index

www.packtpub.com

Subscribe to our online digital library for full access to over 7,000 books and videos, as well as industry leading tools to help you plan your personal development and advance your career. For more information, please visit our website.

Why subscribe?

- Spend less time learning and more time coding with practical eBooks and Videos from over 4,000 industry professionals

- Improve your learning with Skill Plans built especially for you

- Get a free eBook or video every month

- Fully searchable for easy access to vital information

- Copy and paste, print, and bookmark content

Did you know that Packt offers eBook versions of every book published, with PDF and ePub files available? You can upgrade to the eBook version at packtpub.com and as a print book customer, you are entitled to a discount on the eBook copy. Get in touch with us at customercare@packtpub.com for more details.

At www.packtpub.com, you can also read a collection of free technical articles, sign up for a range of free newsletters, and receive exclusive discounts and offers on Packt books and eBooks.

Other Books You May Enjoy

If you enjoyed this book, you may be interested in these other books by Packt:

Game Development with Blender and Godot

Kumsal Obuz

ISBN: 978-1-80181-602-1

- Discover what low-poly modeling is and why it matters
- Understand how to use materials, shaders, and textures in your models
- Explore how to render and animate a scene in Blender
- Focus on how to export Blender assets and import them into Godot
- Use 3D low-poly models in Godot to create fun games
- Design a dynamic and easy-to-navigate game world
- Explore how to interact with the game via interfaces
- Understand how to export your game for Windows

Godot Engine Game Development Projects

Chris Bradfield

ISBN: 978-1-78883-150-5

- Get started with the Godot game engine and editor
- Organize a game project
- Import graphical and audio assets
- Use Godot's node and scene system to design robust, reusable game objects
- Write code in GDScript to capture input and build complex behaviors
- Implement user interfaces to display information
- Create visual effects to spice up your game
- Learn techniques that you can apply to your own game projects

Packt is searching for authors like you

If you're interested in becoming an author for Packt, please visit authors.packtpub.com and apply today. We have worked with thousands of developers and tech professionals, just like you, to help them share their insight with the global tech community. You can make a general application, apply for a specific hot topic that we are recruiting an author for, or submit your own idea..

Share Your Thoughts

Now you've finished *Godot 4 Game Development Cookbook*, we'd love to hear your thoughts! Scan the QR code below to go straight to the Amazon review page for this book and share your feedback or leave a review on the site that you purchased it from.

https://www.amazon.in/review/create-review/error?asin=1838826076

Your review is important to us and the tech community and will help us make sure we're delivering excellent quality content

Download a free PDF copy of this book

Thanks for purchasing this book!

Do you like to read on the go but are unable to carry your print books everywhere?

Is your eBook purchase not compatible with the device of your choice?

Don't worry, now with every Packt book you get a DRM-free PDF version of that book at no cost.

Read anywhere, any place, on any device. Search, copy, and paste code from your favorite technical books directly into your application.

The perks don't stop there, you can get exclusive access to discounts, newsletters, and great free content in your inbox daily

Follow these simple steps to get the benefits:

1. Scan the QR code or visit the link below

https://packt.link/free-ebook/9781838826079

2. Submit your proof of purchase
3. That's it! We'll send your free PDF and other benefits to your email directly

Printed in the USA
CPSIA information can be obtained
at www.ICGtesting.com
JSHW062248280723
45521JS00002B/154